Praise for Magen

"A Masterpiece! Sensational! This book is full of high. Complex insights regarding your relationship with the matrix - explained clearly, with simplicity. The depth of wisdom and treasures inside these pages are profound. One of the best books available explaining the multidimensional perspective."

- Customer review (Masters of the Matrix)

"This book is amazing in every way... This book stimulates my mind in ways that give me goosebumps and bring tears of joy to my eyes... the information is very beautiful, powerful, and life-changing... Doors have been opened in my mind and my life from reading this book. From my heart, I sincerely wish everyone on the planet would read this!"

- Amazon customer review (Divine Architecture and the Starseed Template)

"Look no further, all is explained in this book, encapsulating all religious texts and then explaining further. All answers are given and accessible by all, it only takes an open heart of unconditional love and you too can have all the secrets of all realities revealed to you."

- Amazon customer review (The Infinite Helix and the Emerald Flame)

"Powerful protection techniques... I found this transmission presented by Magenta Pixie to be a relevant and useful guide for personal and planetary protection against the harmful frequencies aimed at humanity during these stressful times. As the '9' explain, we, the awakening ones, have more power than we can imagine."

- Amazon customer review (The Black Box Programme and the Rose Gold Flame as Antidote)

"If you want to know what's happening in the greater sphere of reality, beyond religion, beyond spirituality itself, to the matrix itself that encapsulates us all, look no further, Magenta Pixie delivers. She's the best source for news on what's happening behind the scenes beyond having your own hookup directly."

- Amazon customer review (Lessons from a Living Lemuria)

Magenta Pixie's first book 'Masters of the Matrix' is a BookAuthority winner in the categories 'Best Spirituality Books of All Time' and 'Best Consciousness Books of All Time'.

About the Author

Magenta Pixie is a channel for the higher dimensional, divine intelligence known as 'The White Winged Collective Consciousness of Nine'. The transmissions she receives from 'The Nine' have reached thousands of people worldwide via the extensive video collection on her YouTube channel. She has worked with people from all over the world as an intuitive consultant and ascension/consciousness coach. Magenta lives in the New Forest, UK. Visit Magenta Pixie online at magentapixie.com

Also by Magenta Pixie

~ Books ~

Masters of the Matrix: Becoming the Architect of Your Reality and Activating the Original Human Template

Divine Architecture and the Starseed Template: Matrix Memory Triggers for Ascension

The Infinite Helix and the Emerald Flame: Sacred Mysteries of Stargate Ascension

The Black Box Programme and the Rose Gold Flame as Antidote: How to shield yourself from chemtrails, 5G, EMFs and other energetic warfare through alchemical unification

Lessons from a Living Lemuria: Balancing Karma through Nutrition for Ascension

~ MP3 Guided Meditation Collections ~

Gateways Within

Euphoric Voyage

Sacred Quest

Elemental Dream

Cover design by Daniel Saunders
Author photograph by Oliver McGuire

Print Edition 1, 2023
ISBN: 9798366175210

White Spirit Publishing
web: magentapixie.com
enquiries: magenta.pixie@mail.com

The Diamond Codex and the Quartz Key

Accessing the Accelerated Stargate System Through
Crystalline Transformation of the Genetic Code

Magenta Pixie

This book is dedicated to my father, Francis Brian McGuire

1934 - 2018

"The universe being as large as it is, just about anything can happen."

- Francis Brian McGuire

Contents

Acknowledgements

My brother Liam, sister Keira, son Ollie, daughters Abby and Rosie and my dear friends Dawn and Mel. For chatting in the 'Tin Foil Hat' since the world went crazy and for being there when I needed to bounce ideas around. Thankyou!

To my son Alex and my daughter Christa for all the long in-depth chats.

To my daughter-in-law Amy. Thankyou from the bottom of my heart for all that you are, all that you were to 'Brian' and all that you did for him.

To all who have connected with me on social media, you are amazing and I love you!

Not forgetting my wonderful husband and best friend Daniel Saunders AKA Catzmagick. As I have said so many times before, I could not present these books without you. Forever grateful for you. x

~ Kristos King ~

He can be all things, to any at all times,

across the crystal stairway he climes.

Like the chameleon he is known by all,

discovering the Amenti and its grand hall.

Not one colour, but many, the black and so too the red,

Quetzalcoatl tells all, when it is done and said.

Falling from ethereal no-matter, into form of man,

this dragon will call, when you know the phrase 'I can'.

I will, I have, followed by the great I am as thought,

taking on the form of pure visual as is sought.

Bound to Earth as shadow, yet seeing all as light,

invisible to most, yet lives forever on in flight.

You hold the skills you know he stands for,

intrinsically knowing magic dragonlore.

So utilise this precious talent,

show the world you embody the gallant.

In the song you can hear us as we sing,

Quetzalcoatl is the 'Kristos King'.

Hear the voice and allow it to permeate,

as you ride the galactic through the stargate.

He will always hold Aurora in his heart,

for they cannot survive if they are apart.

Both are created out of heaven's cloth,

walking the journey of the fool that is Thoth.

Stand strong then, starseed and see the shifts,

shamanic movement that is lightening swift.

Shifting your form just like the were,

then you shall climb the crystal stair.

From diamond code to key to Quay,

more and more then you shall see.

Behold before you the dragon's sign,

We are the collective, consciousness of Nine.

Introduction

Dear Reader,

I am so happy to finally be able to present this book, *The Diamond Codex and the Quartz Key*, to you. It really has been a labour of love as you will undoubtedly see as you turn the pages, or swipe the screen if you are reading digitally!

When my father transitioned back in September 2018, I began writing my thoughts and feelings down as a cathartic exercise, as a way to begin to integrate the feelings of grief. I was very close to my father.

I expected some communication from the Nine but this was a personal exercise and it was never my intention to share this with anyone, let alone at a public level in a book!

However, as you can see, the dialogue between myself and the Nine progressed beyond a healing/integration interaction between us, into something deeper. The Nine began to present and represent the familiar monadic structure and I knew I was being called into receiving this transmission. I knew that a presentation of alchemical unification was eventually going to be downloaded to me, so I felt and saw this monad, as often occurs when I sit in front of my computer and begin to type.

Magic happens the minute my fingers touch the keyboard and the White Winged Collective Consciousness of Nine are there.

However, the initial communion with them in 2018, as an outpouring and expression of grief at the loss of my father, indeed a cry for help, was never a conscious intention as a pathway into this communication on my part. Yet as you will see, once you dive into the material, I could not really separate that initial communication from the monadic structure and transmission that followed. So this introduction is my explanation of this.

I did take some time to integrate my emotions after that initial contact. I needed time and space to make sense of my feelings of loss and grief regarding my father's passing. Within that time, I did make contact with my father as you will read in this book. I hope my experience will assist you in your own integration of these emotions regarding losing someone dear to you. For grief is indeed all consuming. Yet happiness, joy and, yes, bliss can be found, if the integration takes place within balance and trauma does not set itself in as a fixed aspect in your fields.

This book appears to 'jump straight in' to deep emotions as soon as you start reading. However, I hope this introduction gives context as to why this is presented this way.

So this book actually began back in September of 2018!

This introduction you read now is the last part of the book that I wrote and the date today is November 6th 2022. So yes, this book began its conception four years ago!

So much has happened (what an understatement) since 2018 and my focus has been with many other different transmissions from the Nine and psychic, remote viewing work. I kept returning to this material until earlier in the summer of 2022, I felt the monadic formation call me to focus upon this transmission fully now and that it was time to bring this work forward. In divine timing as always.

So what began as a reflection of my own grief, progressed back into the higher triad and began the monadic lattice-of-light structure communications. This is interaction with the living geometry as thoughts and telepathic alignments with the White Winged Collective Consciousness of Nine.

In this transmission, in the piece entitled 'The Pulse and the Harvest', I notice that the Nine began to discuss the inability to hold memory and the dissipation of thought processes and memories through transition/death process/ascension.

This is the same presentation, it seems, as the process they now call 'regenesis' which is the result of the deliberate hijack through the juice programme.

For readers unfamiliar with the juice programme, please go to my YouTube channel and look at the fictional stories presented regarding the bifurcated village, the overlords and the evil witch who poisoned the apples and then presented those apples as a cure and prevention for a respiratory illness plaguing the faery fae inhabitants of the village. The poisoned apples were thus distributed to the sleeping and unaware populace in the village as apple juice.

I find it interesting now that the monadic structure was already with me when I began this dialogue and the overall transmission back then was about the harvesting of memories, both organic and inverted, as you will read.

This dialogue with the Nine took place just over a year before the 'attempted village takeover' in the fictional village which was brought into the collective awareness predominantly in March of 2020.

The Nine were preparing the scene for what was to come... unbeknownst to myself at the time.

I do hope you enjoy reading this transmission as much as I have enjoyed bringing it through for you. I have truly loved this work and my own personal upgrade and expansion has taken place through bringing this information forward and then reading and re-reading it again during the editing process.

The Nine say that everything we need to know about 'how things will go' is here in this transmission. Simply because once we realise with our 'real eyes' what is happening, who we actually are and how powerful we are, then we are the ones that create the outcome!

This can sound like a typical spiritual or metaphysical cliché, yet the Nine explain this process, how it works and how we are such an intrinsic part of it, each and every one of us.

I see you, dear reader, I know you and please know that I love you so much. We are truly family.

Happy reading...

Your Eternal Scribe,

Magenta Pixie xxx

1: The Unknown Voice in my Mind

<u>An Exploration of Emotion, Memory, DNA Code and Consciousness through the Experience of Grief and Loss</u>

All consuming, enveloping me like a cloud of memories, unbidden, yet oh so happy and yet painful at the same time.

I see your smiling face before me, always there and feel the warmth of your connection and love,

so real, so tangible - but it is just a memory.

I hear your words, that which you did say or you would say - but they are just memories.

I remember your sense of humour, your wisdom and intelligence - all just memories now. No longer real, for you are gone and I will never see you again. How I grieve, how I cry, how I call for you in the dark of the night, how I miss you, how I hold such pain in my heart. You are gone and you are never coming back and how shall I ever learn to live without you?

What is a memory?

Who are you that talks to me at my time of pain? Asks me questions! What is a memory? It is the images I remember in my mind of the things that happened in the past. Pictures of the one I have lost.

You said they felt real?

Yes. They do. But it's just a memory, simply the sights within the mind of one such as I who has a vivid imagination.

What is imagination?

Another question from the unknown speaker in my mind?

Imagination? Just pictures in my mind. Images and visualisations I hold in my consciousness.

What is consciousness?

Well how am I supposed to answer that? No one knows the answer to that one!

I do.

Oh you do, do you? And who are you then that asks so much if you know so much?

I am consciousness.

Oh really? So if you are consciousness, why are you asking me so many questions?

I want to help you in your time of grief.

You cannot do that. Nobody can do that. I have lost a loved one and nothing you can say will bring him back.

Not in the form you knew, no. But he is there, in a new form.

Where?

He stands before you, smiling, showing you the warmth of his connection and love. You said so yourself.

Yes, but that is just a memory.

What is memory? Until you know what memory is, how can you say he is gone if he stands before you?

Are you saying these images in my mind are real and not memories?

They are memories, but what are memories? How do you know memories are not real? What is real?

Real is what you see before you that you can touch, hold, hear, feel. That is real.

On a physical level, yes. But there are other levels. What if that which you see before you that you cannot physically touch, such as a memory or a visualisation, what if they were real too? But in a different way. Would that then mean you have suffered a loss? That the loved one can never see you again? Or talk to you again?

Well, no. If memory and images were real, just in a different way, then I guess there is no loss, not on that level. There is still physical loss though.

Indeed. But knowing your loved one is still there, just in a different form, does that not ease the grief? Does that not change the form of the grief as it is alchemised with joy?

Why joy?

Because you know your loved one lives on. A different form. Look at the image of your loved one in your mind. Is there something different now?

Well, yes. I have never seen him wear that suit. Never seen him wear a suit that colour, but I thought my mind was just playing tricks on me, through my grief.

What if I told you he bought a new suit when he crossed over at the 'heaven's gate store'?

Oh come on!

It's true.

There's a shop, right by the pearly gates? Where you can buy new clothes? You must think I was born yesterday! If I were to believe that, I would be crazy...

You might be crazy.

Oh thanks! Why would you say that?

You are talking to me, aren't you?

Yes, I suppose I see your point. Grief does funny things to us. Makes us talk to annoying voices that aren't even there!

You have been talking to me long before you experienced grief.

True.

Who helped you to talk to me?

He did. My loved one.

What did he tell you when you first spoke to me?

He said you were my subconscious mind.

Did you believe him?

Of course. I was a child. He was my father.

What did he say your subconscious mind was?

The part of you that operates when the conscious mind rests. Like when you sleep. When you dream.

But you are awake.

Yes. I could talk to that part of my mind when I was awake.

How is it subconscious then? If you have made it conscious?

It? You mean you.

Yes.

What exactly are you trying to say to me?

You mentioned memory. That your images were memories and you are right. But what are memories? How do you know they are not real in a non-physical sense? If you can make your subconscious conscious then can you make your memories real? Isn't it the same thing?

Well, you tell me. You are the expert. You are consciousness.

OK, I am telling you. Memories are real just in another form. A consciousness construct cannot exist without a steady stream of focus to give it life. Your memory is a strong, steady stream of focus when it comes from love. When you think of your loved one with love in your heart, when you remember them, you make them real.

Real? In the sense that they hold their own awareness of who they are? They have their own perspective? Their own experience?

Exactly.

Every single memory that anyone has of anything or anyone?

Every memory, every thought, every creation of mind holds the ability to create something. For instance, if you think of a pink flying dragon with blue feet and orange wings and a huge ruby crystal for its nose, then you think of your loved one smiling at you, which is more real?

They are the same.

So is the image of your loved one an imagined fantasy or is the pink dragon a memory?

I don't know. I mean I have never seen a pink dragon with blue feet, orange wings and a huge ruby crystal for a nose so how can it be a memory?

So let us say it is an imagined creation, yes?

Yes, OK.

And the images in your mind of your loved one, they are memories, right?

Right.

But they feel the same to you. They look the same in your mind?

Yes, they do.

So would you therefore say that imagined creation and memories are one and the same?

I suppose they could be. You know the answers though, don't you? So are they the same?

Yes - yet experienced in different 'directions' if you will. Memory images feel like 'the past' to you. Imagined creations have not happened yet in your experience so will feel like an alternate reality or a future pathway. In truth there are no 'directions'. There is no past, present or future or even 'alternate'. For all is one. Therefore they are one and the same.

So I create my loved one when I think of his memory?

You do. In truth however your thought (memory combined with the emotion of love) creates a coherent energy signature or energy wave. That coherent energy wave is a code and that code creates a form. A structure. That matches (is exact to) the original thought. Therefore you create your loved one from your perspective. But coherence is perspective in itself. Therefore from the perspective of the loved one they have always existed for they experience a steady stream of consciousness from that one point of perspective.

So if there was not me to think of my loved one, or anyone else for that matter, would he cease to exist?

No. Because you don't need to actually be thinking of him to give him a coherent energy wave pattern. That exists within your DNA. Within the energy field or pattern of your DNA. You experience this as 'memory' but it is actually a configuration.

And that configuration creates a person? Gives coherence to my loved one? Gives him a point of perspective so he experiences his reality from that point of view?

Yes, exactly.

So just the fact that I knew him and experienced a lifetime with him and loved him, that in itself has enabled him to exist beyond death even if I never think of him?

Has enabled him to exist in life and beyond death.

How have my thoughts, my memories, assisted him to exist in life? I was born years after him. He was born first. He was my father.

You are missing the point. Think.

My thoughts and memories exist in a place beyond past, present and future therefore I created my father to be born before I was even born?

Yes, but it goes much further than that. Everyone who has ever existed in third dimensional time-space creates every person to be born, exist in a physical life and continue to exist after death.

How?

Thought. Thought is the code for creation.

So God doesn't create us? We create ourselves?

Both. God is the perceived omnipresent, omnipotent self. The oneness, unity consciousness perspective and you, the human physical self, is one separate aspect of that. Yet the potential for full omnipresence and omnipotence exists within you.

How?

As a code. Or more accurately, a configuration.

Within the DNA?

Yes.

So every single person has the ability to create everything and everyone in all existence as if they were God?

They do.

OK, how can we do this? And more importantly, how can this help me in the grieving process and the communication with my father?

That was the right question to ask. We communicate now.

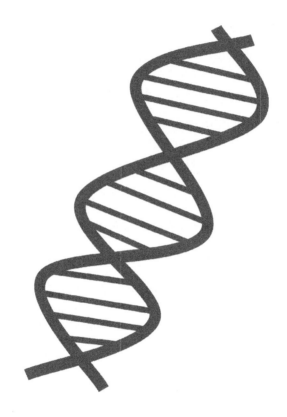

2: A Ball of Wool

I miss him so much even though it's only been a week. I feel down and sad and heartbroken. I don't see how anything you can possibly say can help with that?

We can help you to go forward in your life and honour your father. We cannot take your pain away nor would we advise that you attempt to do this. We can assist you to integrate the pain and utilise it for your own creativity and your own pathway. Your father's legacy.

Honour my father? How? And what do you mean, his legacy?

Would your father want you to be down, sad and heartbroken? What is the one thing, the one goal your father had for you in his life?

To be happy. To be productive. To enjoy the richness of life and to interact with the world and the people around me. He did everything within his power to consistently heal me, protect me and help me to be balanced, healthy and happy.

Exactly. Would his wishes be any different now he has left the physical form?

No, they would not.

Your father's legacy therefore is the utilisation of everything he taught you, expressed through the uniqueness that is you, Petra. Magenta. Our dear Pixie.

I can't do it without him.

You can. But you do not have to. You will not be without him.

OK, so how can I connect with him? How can I communicate with him and at least know he is OK?

Through us and through him directly.

Ask us questions. He will come when the time is right.

OK, well my first question is, if I talk to you and have been talking to you for many years, how do I know that when I see or hear my father that it is not just you, the Nine?

Good question. On one level, all beings are all one soul, one entity as you know. Yet when we look at unique and focused individualised points of perspective then we are seeing that one soul, that one entity, expressed through many different individualised points of perspective. Many of these points of perspective believe they are completely separate from the 'others' around them, not realising that there is only one soul.

Within these points of perspective are different dimensional frequencies. We, the Nine, hold a sixth and seventh and somewhat eighth dimensional point of perspective from the individualised 'broadcast signal' (the cohesive wave we were speaking about) of the construct that is you, Petra Magenta Pixie.

Your father, even though his cohesive waveform is given focus from those who loved him and knew him, including you, is an individualised point of perspective that is not of the construct that is you, Petra Magenta Pixie. It is from the cohesive construct that is uniquely him. Your father. The broadcast signal (his individualised point of perspective) is fourth and fifth dimensional predominantly. However, he has multidimensional awareness due to DNA configurations created within his physical life, therefore he is able to hold a multidimensional point of view and experience beyond the fifth dimension right up to omnipresence.

From that perspective your father and 'we' the Nine are one and the same. Individual points of perspective are not lost when you perceive from higher dimensions, if anything, they are more defined.

Therefore within the higher dimensions the individual point of perspective of the cohesive construct is well defined yet is experienced simultaneously to the 'group soul' and the unity field consciousness that is omnipotent and omnipresent.

We can also explain this as double helix, triple helix and infinite helix when one looks at the corresponding DNA configuration.

So is my father omnipresent right now?

His energy field is, yes, as is every non-physical construct's energy field that holds coherence. His experiential perspective when viewed from your linear perspective would not have reached omnipresent memory (or activation) yet due to his experience being so close to his transition from physical to non-physical.

OK, I am lost. Is my father experiencing linear time or multidimensional time?

Both. From his perspective there is no time from the omnipresent experience (infinite helix DNA configuration) and because your father activated codes for that DNA configuration, he will instantly experience the matching reality to that. However, fourth dimensional existence is still somewhat linear (less so than the third dimension) so this will be experienced simultaneously to the omnipresence.

I still don't get it.

Let us explain it thus. Imagine being given a ball of wool. In your hand you hold a ball of wool, all the wool is wound around and around to form this ball. This is your omnipresent experience.

Then imagine you unravel that ball of wool until you have one long thread of wool. That is your linear experience.

Your father will have gone straight to the ball of wool after his transition and would then unravel that wool into one long thread. This is how he would experience his reality.

However, from your perspective you would see this as him already having unravelled wool and him learning to roll it up into a ball as he goes forward with his experience. This is how it is usually explained to the channels and mediums in third dimensional physical reality so you may process the journey of 'life after death' in a linear sense.

So every soul will automatically hold that omnipresent experience the minute they transition into non-physical form?

Every soul already holds the template in 'potential' form for omnipresence, regardless if their point of perspective comes from the incarnation in physical or from the non-physical. However, the journey the soul moves through in an experiential sense will be a direct match or 'echo' to their DNA configuration.

So if a soul does not hold the DNA configuration for the infinite helix then they will not experience omnipresence?

Souls are always omnipresent. However, the direct experience of omnipresence will not be 'added to' or 'merged with' their memory fields as they move along a journey towards cohesive and insular individualisation. Therefore when they 'go forward' or 'reincarnate' or 'transform' or 'transition' they will not carry the memory codes for omnipresence with them. This does not mean they are not omnipresent. It means they are not experiencing omnipresence (either in physical incarnation or non-physical incarnation).

So my father had a configuration for omnipresence? He had activated the infinite helix DNA code?

There are many different codes within the infinite helix DNA code (which is a subject for another time) and your father had activated some of them, yes.

We might stress that we have permission only to discuss your father's personal incarnational experience and individualised path when that information will directly help you and others. We will not be able to discuss personal experiences or activations of your father's in general.

Who gave you the permission? My father himself?

We would say yes, from one level. In truth there is such a thing as 'cosmic etiquette' or 'code of honour' and we do not break that code. We could not even if we desired to do so, even though we do not, for we do not have desire. We could not break the code for the personal path of others is known only to their omnipresent aspect and not to ours.

So are you saying there is more than one omnipresence?

Indeed. There are infinite omnipresences. Each omnipresence is one infinity. This is an insular, focused, cohesive individualisation of which there is 'nothing' outside of the boundary (or event horizon) of that omnipresent infinity from that omnipresent, infinity's perspective (which is fully omnipotent). However, within that 'nothing' is 'something' (for it is Zero Point and Zero has a value), therefore it is made up of infinite 'other' omnipresences.

So your omnipresence is not the same as my father's omnipresence? Does this not change the very meaning of the word 'omnipresent'? For does omnipresent not mean present in all things?

One could say that in the linearly experienced realities the omnipresences are separate and in the higher dimensions (non-linear) they are one and the same. The truth is that it is both. The omnipresences are unique and separate and also unified. The nature of reality is infinite, fractal and holographic. Everything is a hologram of everything else (like an infinite hall of mirrors with each reflection being an individualised omnipresence in itself... an infinity).

The words 'omnipresent' and 'infinite' do well in explaining the nature of reality as does 'holographic'. Yet in truth, there is no word that truly explains the nature of reality in all its simplistic complexity. The nearest would be 'OM' or 'AUM'.

How does OM or AUM explain the nature of reality through simplistic complexity?

It is the sound or tone of creation that encompasses all, everything, nothing and something. It cannot be explained via words. All those in tune with this omnipresent knowing have but to chant the OM or AUM and they shall feel and see the sound and tone of creation and thus shall be afforded the knowing of all things and the no-thing that is some-thing (Zero Point).

Should I be chanting OM or AUM in meditation on a regular basis then?

There is no 'should' within your spiritual path. It is the path of the apprentice and the adept. Your communication with us, if you will, is the unravelling of the ball of wool. The OM/AUM chant is the ball in its unravelled state.

OK, thankyou for that. So can I please ask, where is my father right now? One week after his passing? What is he experiencing from his point of perspective in that unravelled ball of wool, linear reality?

Good question. We shall respond as best as we can to this.

3: The Afterlife of Brian

Your father held the codes within his matrix for experiencing integration through analysis. This was an indigo/violet ray merge that he held within his fields. His entire mission was more complex than just this but as we have said we cannot overstep the permissions and etiquettes and can tell you only what is within the permission boundaries that will assist you and others within your own processing and understanding.

Due to these codes for experiencing integration through analysis, your father as a linearly expressed being will continue to move through this code pattern. Therefore the environment your father experiences will be analysed deeply before he 'moves on', if you will, to the next environment. Therefore the 'where' he is would be within the environmental construct that matches 'integration through analysis'. The environment is a direct match to the codes within the individual's matrix. How an environment presents that matches 'integration through analysis' will be unique to each individual. We cannot tell you your father's exact surroundings within a visual sense due to permissions and etiquettes but we can give you a 'false screen' view of that environment.

When we say 'false screen', we use this term in its most organic and original sense and not the sense of a truth being hidden or hijacked in order to present a false reality. The term we would use for this 'false screen' would be 'echo reality' or 'veil'.

Can you please explain the difference between an organic and original false screen and a hijacked one?

The organic and original false screen is simply a way of presenting a uniquely experienced or created reality as a metaphor to the original reality so it may be decoded, understood, processed and communicated with. This is a natural reality structure. Your reality is filled with these metaphors that are direct matches to the original seed constructs.

A hijacked false screen uses technology that mimics the original, organic reality. It is a false creation that is not a direct match to the original reality but a distortion of it. This cannot be called a metaphor as the new false screen is changed within its frequency. It is therefore what you may know as a 'red herring' or a 'dead end within a maze' as it does not lead to truth but instead it leads to the opposite.

It is with these hijacked false screens that the service-to-self factions have created the inverted matrix. Your reality is also full of these hijacked false screens and what this does is mask or hide the original metaphors for organic reality. When the awakened one realises they live within an inverted matrix, they begin to decode that inverted matrix in order to free themselves from it. There are those seekers and explorers of truth within that journey who will reject all 'false screens' and in effect they 'throw the baby out with the bathwater' as it were. They reject all false screens including the natural, organic metaphors that make up your reality naturally. This is, of course, the intention of the service-to-self darkworker groups. They do not just intend to mislead. Their aim is to deny you the true tools that shall lead you to truth, enlightenment and organic soul evolution.

Is my father's passing therefore helping others?

In one sense, this would be due to you asking questions regarding life after death through your grief and your need to connect with him. The responses to those questions are therefore triggers into memory awareness and activation within others. However, the passing of any individual always adds to the growth of the all (the collective) due to the harvesting of memories that takes place.

So are my father's memories being harvested? I do not like the sound of this, to be honest. It is like something is being taken from him, like a crop to be grown to feed others. Can you explain more about this?

The harvesting of memories is a huge subject. You are right and correct to not like the sound of this and for you to see it as crops to be grown to feed others. The service-to-self groups have done just that. Yet the harvesting of memories is a natural, organic occurrence that creates reality itself. Again, this is the difference between that which is organic, original and natural and that which is falsely created and hijacked for negative means.

The organic and the hijacked are intertwined within the same reality (your reality on Earth). The change in polarity upon your planet which is that which you call 'ascension' is created by the consciousness of the aware and activated individuals (starseeds) as they decipher the difference between organic and hijacked. As they embrace the organic and reject the hijacked they _create that reality._

Sorry, are you saying that as the starseeds/seekers/explorers of truth decipher the differences between an organic reality and a hijacked reality that they create the organic reality?

Indeed. It is all created by you. The human collective. It must be this way for this is the way it is. The OM/AUM lies within you.

Yet does the organic not already exist?

Yes. You ground it into reality and awareness through your observation and knowing of it.

So this is why the dark structures are trying to prevent our awakening? Our awakening is creating the organic in physical reality?

That is one reason for their attempt at preventing awakening, yes.

So can you show me a metaphor organic 'false screen' or echo reality that shows me where my father is right now? Can you also please elaborate on memory harvesting, both natural and hijacked? I understand this is a huge subject but whatever you can say will surely be helpful for those who are already activated? Is it the case that the individuals that find their way to this

35

transmission are already activated?

We can show you two potential matches that will show you 'where' your father is. Bear in mind that these realities are constructs of your father's own choosing and creation due to free will energetics afforded him through the path he chose within his waking life. Be aware also that this is the linear consciousness of your father that we speak of as there are other aspects that we have already discussed (the omnipresence).

The first false screen match would be the scene where your father is stood upon a rainbow. The rainbow is the pathway to the next stage of his evolutionary journey as a soul. He is beckoned by living, loving, geometric light which calls him to follow the rainbow.

Your father's heart wishes to follow the rainbow and he is aware that he has been called. However, he has patience. He is in no hurry to follow the living, loving geometric light's calling. Instead, he kneels down to examine the structure of the rainbow itself. He spends time examining each colour band that makes up the rainbow pathway as well as the materials the rainbow is made of. He listens to the tunes the rainbow makes and touches its form in order to feel and examine. He fully intends to follow the rainbow pathway and the call of the light but he has patience. Examining the structure of the rainbow is important and most interesting to him. He has time. There is no limitation on how long he may spend examining the rainbow.

The second false screen match would be the scene where your father is stood within a white room. The walls, floor and ceiling are white. There is a white table in front of your father and upon the table is a blue box. Your father is aware that if he opens the blue box he will discover clues to his whereabouts and a map that shall show him how to progress along to the next stage of his journey. He wants to open the blue box and is fully intending to do so. However, he spends time examining the structure of the box itself. He looks at its colour, shape and construct. He has patience and the box's structure and use itself is important to your father. He has time to do this as there are no limitations as to how long he spends examining the box.

So my father is not really stood upon a rainbow or looking at a box on a table in a white room, is he?

Your father is pure awareness. One aspect to that pure awareness contains the memory structure that was your father, the one known as Brian, including its linear experiences. The code presentation currently experienced by your father is one that holds the frequency of integration through analysis which is a violet, indigo ray. The journey is into oneself. This is your father's current experience as the pure awareness structure that holds his collective memories as the one known as Brian. Because you experience a linear reality and decode the multidimensional, true reality in a linear sense through a third dimensional brain, you cannot unravel the meaning of where your father is or what he is experiencing without us presenting a false screen metaphor, echo reality.

However, as an activated starseeded individual, your thoughts and emotional awareness create realities that you perceive. Therefore that which we convey to you creates an exact replica through your thought process and your genetic and emotional connection with the one known as Brian, your father.

We, aware of this, present to you most carefully a metaphoric 'false screen' (echo reality) match that holds safety codes that shall not influence your father's personal and unique journey. Hence the images of 'pure white room' and 'rainbow'.

Due to your creative thought process, your interpretation of the violet, indigo ray fields of the pure matrix individualised awareness that is the one known as Brian, you create a replica reality that stands as we have presented. Therefore yes, your father is standing in a white room looking at a blue box. He is also standing upon a rainbow examining its structure.

Your thoughts take form, therefore they become so in the pre-matter field. However, it is also true to say that he is not standing in a white room or upon a rainbow due to the experiential existence he holds. This experiential existence does not contain form. It contains only awareness of energetic structure and frequency as an individualised memory complex through structure. The structure is within an environment that is made up of oneself that is outside the boundary of that individualised memory complex thought structure.

It is absolutely the case that all individuals who find their way to this material are already activated. Our communication lies within a highway of lines of intention or galactic leylines that make up what you may come to know as the New Earth Network or the Gaia Matrix. One must be activated within higher fourth dimensional consciousness and certainly touching upon and observing fifth dimensional consciousness in order to align with this network or matrix. Yet many who align with this work will be anchored into the fifth dimensional consciousness and thus creating it as they observe and integrate that awareness and knowing.

Regarding your quest on memory harvesting, both organic and hijacked... let us perhaps return to this vast subject at a later date within the monadic structure that we are and present as our communication in divine timing in accordance with your receptivity alignments to that monadic structure.

OK, thankyou. So back to my father then. Can he hear me? Does he know I am asking you about him? Does he still hold the same emotional field? Does he still love me (and my sister and brother) and does he know what we are doing?

Much of your questing in its entirety is outside the permissions and boundaries of his unique experience. What he knows and how he feels about things is personal and private. We also do not have permissions to discuss his feelings towards your sister and brother as this is outside of your connection with him, most especially as the presentation of this communication holds the intention and trajectory to be shared with the awakening collective who are intertwined and in alignment with the New

Earth Network or Gaia Matrix.

We draw your attention to these necessary limitations and we address your question in the general rather than the specific.

Memory matrix structures at the activation level of your father can indeed 'hear' the thoughts and emotional frequency broadcasts of their loved ones still in incarnation. They are aware of the processes their loved ones go through and they are able to respond and somewhat influence. The love they felt for their families, most especially their children, does not disappear simply because they have left the awareness of the organic physical body. The emotions are actually enhanced and within a freely activated individual, they are enhanced greatly. The love they felt for their families, especially their children is therefore *greater* than it was before, due to the freedoms and lack of limitations they now hold.

I understand that you cannot tell me too much about my father's personal journey but could you respond to these two questions? Was my father's love of and involvement in music helpful in his activation as a soul? Was his reading and understanding of the book 'Jonathan Livingston Seagull' by Richard Bach[1] also instrumental within his journey? I mean, to the level of activation he is now at as a spirit matrix and his ability to be happy and progress? Has it helped him after his physical life? I am aware that these things were major triggers for him within his physical life.

All triggers that the soul experiences within their physical life are translated into the non-physical, spirit matrix experience. What is important to be aware of here is that your father chose these triggers prior to incarnating. These were 'node point' triggers for him.

The love of and experience of and *contribution to* music and also the discovery of and subsequent activations from the book in question; Yes, you are correct that these tools shaped his reality and existence along with many other triggering tools. Indeed the

---

[1] *Jonathan Livingston Seagull* (1970) by Richard Bach

reality shaped from the physical perspective in turn shapes the perspective and experience *and place one moves to* after the physical life. The answer to your quest here is a resounding 'yes'.

If my father chose these trigger points before incarnation to help him after incarnation, then why incarnate in the first place?

A humorous question to us. We 'laugh'. However, your quest is, in fact, most appropriate.

Firstly, 'prior to' incarnation and 'afterlife' although they are one and the same place, they are experienced differently. The soul prior to your father's incarnation as 'Brian' was already experiencing a 'soul trajectory' into individualisation. So although the greater aspect of the full memory matrix that is pure awareness would already understand the experiences to be accumulated through music appreciation and contribution and also through the receiving of DNA activation triggers through the particular book you mention, the greater aspect would not have *experienced* that in order to gain *individualised memories* which can only be achieved through physical incarnation.

Imagine, if you will, an apple tree flourishing with apples upon its branches. The tree holds the perspective of the tree and all the apples simultaneously. Yet, let us say that when an apple falls from the tree then the perspective of the entire tree individualises into that one apple. It becomes specific and contained therefore cohesive, focused and individual. This is what occurs when you incarnate physically. You move your perspective from a unified one into a separate one. That separation allows for focus and specific cohesive intention through integration. The memories that are then harvested back into the memory field (the tree) are specific with experience, focus, individualisation and colour and this integrates back into unity allowing unity to grow.

If unity is in all things, how can it grow?

Unity is all things. It grows through experiencing that which is opposing to unity, which is separation. When the aspect that experiences separation returns to unity, it creates a fractalised, holographic pattern. This is creation itself. It is a cycle of movement. It is a breathing in and a breathing out that we may call 'the breath of life'.

The breathing in could be seen as the taking in of the experiences of the individualised memories (memory harvesting) and the breathing out could be seen as the giving back the unification to the individualised memory, with renewed momentum, vigour and experience. It is simply the way it is.

4: The Pulse and the Harvest

Indeed, that which we bring forward regarding memory harvesting will be helpful for those who are already activated even if it be simply confirmation of their own knowing. Even if it be in opposition to their belief system. When an individual is activated then all they do is ultimately helpful to their overall growth and evolution, even so called 'mistakes'.

As we have said, it is a deep, convoluted and complex subject and one we would suggest to return to at a later time within your evolution with our monadic communications. However, we can look at the framework or foundational template of such and at a later time progress from there.

It is the case that it is activated individuals that shall find their way to this transmission as we have said, although the activation presents at many different levels. Some will 'understand and process' yet others will respond at the 'feeling, being' level and yet others will use for confirmation of their own paradigms or putting into words that which they know and have not yet been able to unravel into linear concepts and language. Others still will use this text for magickal works. Yet all will be activated in some degree.

The harvesting of memories is a huge subject. This relates to the growth of the unified field itself or what you know as 'Source' or 'God' or 'Prime Creator'.

To simplify this process, we say to you that 'Unified Field' or 'Original Source' as a living frequency wave of intelligence, love and light wished to experience 'all and everything'. This wish or desire was projected forth as a pulse or the 'breath of life'.

The unified field created fractal, holographic versions of itself that all carried the pulse or the breath of life within. Like the apple falling from the tree.

This fractalised, holographic separation continued on and on until finally physical form was birthed into matter as a result of the pure thought and momentum created by desire that was the pulse or breath of life.

Physical form, holding free will codes, was then able to form an individualised perspective (the apple). From this individualised perspective, the physical form could then follow the codex within that was the pulse/breath of life or from that perspective, physical form could choose its own path.

When the physical incarnation of form within matter left its physical body structure and 'returned to the light of the unified field', it held a 'memory stream' that was an echo of the incarnated physical structure. The memory stream was then replicated into the overall field of memories to be made available for other individualised matrix structures (souls) to utilise. This created the fractalised, holographic structures within the field. We speak here in a linear sense yet be aware that the creation and the created are one and the same.

The fractalised, holographic structure existed *before* it moved into physical form.

The physical form *created* the fractalised, holographic structure.

Both these statements are correct. When you process this then you shall know what it is to be the creator and the created.

When a physically, incarnated structure followed the pulse or the breath of life then the individualisation was strong and cohesive, creating a well formed individualised memory matrix structure.

When a physically, incarnated structure chose to follow the path of free will and move against the current, if you will, moving away from the pulse and the breath of life then the memories were not cohesive enough to hold form when returning back to the unified field structure. They dissipated. This meant that the incarnated form itself dissipated and would be recreated as a 'new soul' or 'new memory matrix' if you will. That personality could not 'live on' and retain its experiences and would have to 'start again' if you will.

The memory matrix (souls) that did remain cohesive as a memory structure could then reincarnate with the memories of the 'previous' (all is, in truth, simultaneous) personality intact.

The memory matrices would reincarnate in cycles, usually along their own genetic line (as the genetic memory codes would draw them back into the same bloodlines) and at the 'end' of one cycle (in truth simply a point of convergence of many cycles simultaneously), the 'memories' (experiences) of that individualised matrix would be imprinted into the overall unified field (harvested) and would be available for other matrices to 'create a copy' if you will, as a code, within their own fields.

This journey is explained in a linear sense. In truth it is all happening simultaneously.

What occurs upon your planet within that we refer to as 'ascension' is the harvesting of memories *prior to* your passing from the physical incarnation. You do not have to leave your physical body in order for you to imprint your memories and experiences upon the unified field.

So when our memories are harvested, they are not taken from us?

They are copied. As a file upon your computer is copied. Your consent is fully given.

What if I decide I do not give my consent? What if I do not want my memories to be copied?

You already gave your consent upon incarnation into physicality. However, within physicality you do have free will and you can make any choice you please to make within the physical, universal laws upon your planet. You could choose not to give consent for your memories to be harvested. To do this, you would enter into an inverted structure rather than an expansive one.

The harvesting of memories or the copy file of your experience is another way of saying 'service-to-others'. It is that which you share. The memory harvesting/copy is the shareable structure. It is the radiation outward into a created, unified field of love.

The word 'harvestable' or 'harvest' upon your planet and amongst your peoples is another word that has been hijacked. It's true meaning is 'to give back' or 'to receive', it also refers to the energetic of that which you know as 'abundance'.

It has been hijacked in order to mean 'to take from' or 'to steal' or to 'make mine what is yours' becoming that which is to be feared.

So is this what the service-to-self groups do? Do they refuse to allow their memories to be harvested?

In a sense, yes. They still allow harvest but it is not done through shareability within the DNA structure. It is done through accumulation of power within self.

DNA structures through memory are therefore carefully refined so that 'some' may have activation through control and 'some' may not. Control is the lesson that is being learned here and the overall experience. The memory will still become cohesive and is still taken into the unified memory field but it is compartmentalised. Deliberate dissipation is created. The experience is to discover how long a cohesive structure can be held without dissipation. The experience is also to discover if dissipation can be prevented entirely by going a different route. This can be done through continued control. This is manifested within your reality as 'control of others' or 'control of a region or planetary structure' yet in its ultimate focus it is 'control of self' through controlling that which is in opposition to the original organic structure that is pulse or breath of life.

So their memories are still harvested?

Yes. Through an inverted, specific DNA structure that is limited and not shareable radiation. The specific frequency would be absorption.

Is the service-to-self path as important as the service-to-others path in the overall growth and learning of the unified field?

It is as simple as one swimming with the current *in flow* or swimming against it, going *against the flow*, which is much more difficult. Neither is 'more important' than the other and there is no judgement regarding the chosen path. All is a response to the original desire or wish to experience 'all and everything' which is the pulse or the breath of life.

So a service-to-self path is still within the pulse or breath of life? Yet in order to dissipate your memory structure, you said you had to go against the pulse or the breath of life?

The service-to-self path is within the pulse or breath of life only from the perspective of the desire or wish to experience all and everything which is the frequency of the original pulse. In order to experience all and everything, one would follow the 'pattern of the pulse' which is accumulation of memory experience through matrix individualisation.

Within the desire to experience all and everything would be also the experience of discovering if one could experience all and everything by not following the pattern of the pulse. 'Something new' would thus have to be created as it would be outside the boundaries of the pattern of the pulse. That 'something' is the inverted matrix.

So if the inverted matrix was created as part of the reaction to the pulse and the desire to experience all and everything, would this not also be an organic structure?

Yes and no. The organic structure is that which is a *direct holographic replica* of Original Source, unified field (which is the pulse).

The inverted matrix is 'something different' and a distortion of the original structure. It is therefore not a holographic replica but a false screen (in a hijacked sense).

So it's not a false screen metaphor like my father's rainbow or white room?

No. Your father's rainbow and white room are holographic replicas of the original seed point frequency. The inverted matrix is a distortion from the original seed point frequency and is 'fighting against the current', so against that which is natural. It is therefore created. Yet it is not a creation per se as it is not in alignment with creative energy. It is a construct of architecture that is taken from one part of creation and distorted into an inversion to result in the 'something else' which is an extension of the original pulse in distorted form.

There are many who speak of the inverted matrix and who teach it. Are the teachings correct? There are those who say the service-to-self groups are trying to go against God and become gods themselves and defy nature. Would all this be true given what you are describing?

The seed point downloads hold the correct frequency regarding the inverted matrices. It is then the individual's role (translator/medium/channel/conduit) to interpret the code of the original seed point download. Some of these interpretations are close to accurate and some are extremely distorted as to be unrecognisable. The seeker must hold discernment and understanding of alignment and resonation within in order to accurately decode the various transmissions available upon your planet and all those yet to come.

Is this transmission an accurate one?

The majority of the time, you do well in your decoding and keep interpretations organic. Emotion of the negative frequency can interrupt the process of remaining true to the frequency of the original download. The way to counteract this is to utilise the negative frequency as part of the questing and seeking. You therefore change the structure of the negative emotion to that of 'integrated negative emotion'.

Is that what I am doing by discussing the grief at my father's passing with you?

Exactly. However, we would suggest you spend time within private integration of these emotions and return to this transmission within a time period of roughly six to eight weeks as you measure your time. There will be much integration done within that time due to your ability to integrate rapidly.

Rapidly? I do not want to forget my father.

Forgetting is the opposite of that which shall occur through rapid integration. The integration we speak of leads you into focused and cohesive memory, not forgetting.

We give to you the 'hierarchy of dragons' as an activation for your hiatus which is a direct match energetically to your quest and our transmission.

5: Hierarchy of Dragons and the Dragon Initiations

In what way can working with the hierarchy of dragons assist with my questions on memory harvesting and my communication with you at this time?

The hierarchy of dragons is a flame letter encoded visual sequence as externalised memory/knowing for energetic activation, alignment and ascension. The crystalline (Krystallah Dragon Field) is a jewel/gem encoded work specific to holding charge, blue starphire, quantum convergence charge for memory and form.

Activations through this work, stimulating cellular memory/knowing through the dragon initiations, bring to you your own unique knowing and understanding/innerstanding of the cosmic journey itself within the organic and natural, and the awareness of the methods of hijack used regarding your memories and the deconstruction of your original twelve stranded (quantum 144) DNA template as hijack/trap.

The embracing of the dragon encodements allow you to reconstruct the twelve stranded (quantum 144) DNA as an energetic structure through activated memory/knowing. One does not have to understand, comprehend or process for the visual image and the dragon energies are the memory triggers and initiations.

One would work here with the dragon energy for high level planetary and galactic gridwork. The work with the dragon is intrinsic to all levels of ascension (individual, planetary, galactic, cosmic and stargate/accelerated). We would therefore recommend studying the hierarchy of dragons and working with this energy (unless you are already familiar with dragon lore/law).

Each dragon can be worked with individually, in pairs, in groups or as one holistic whole or alchemical unification within spellwork, meditation and magikal visualisations for reality manifestation.

Thirteen Dragons

We present the work with thirteen dragons as representations of the matrix and the zero point field. Whilst they can be placed within a hierarchy if you wish, in your magical workings; indeed in truth they unify as a oneness, simply presenting as the dragon energy of the unified field.

The DNA intelligent consciousness is aware of the flame letter significance of the dragon. Each aspect as one dragon of the crystal gemstone rays and elements, transforms into holistic light formations. We refer to these holistic light formations as 'Hierarchy of Dragons' in order to present both individualisation and unification simultaneously, which is your alchemical unification as you progress forward upon the ascension path.

This presentation through dragon flame letter imagery holds, and is another aspect or version of, the Krystallah Codex. This codex is your inner memory library for how to transmutate your DNA structure from carbon-based to crystalline-based. Every incarnated human has this Krystallah Codex within the DNA sequencing. For most, this codex lies dormant and for others, the energetic flow of light is beginning the transmutation organically.

The hierarchy of dragons as flame letter imagery, triggers this inner memory library within the receptive individuals, known also as starseeds or 'aware and awake' explorers and discoverers of truth.

The Hierarchy of Dragons, presented as the thirteen dragons are as follows:

Aquamarine Dragon

Rose Gold Dragon

Ruby Dragon

Amber Dragon

Golden Dragon

Emerald Dragon

Sapphire Dragon

Indigo Dragon

Amethyst Dragon

Silver Dragon

White Dragon

Pearlescent Rainbow Dragon

Shapeshifting Dragon

6: The Thirteen Dragons

How to work with the dragons?

Visualisation of the dragons, drawing them or purchasing dragon artwork and digital art of the dragons placed on your computer desktop space or mobile cell phone. Crystal dragons, tarot or oracle cards of dragons and meditating on the dragons.

Aquamarine Dragon

The aquamarine dragon brings grounding to the seas of Earth and of all water planets. The aquamarine dragon is a water dragon and a 'sacred pet, bondmate and guardian' of Poseidon/King Neptune. The dragon amplifies the symbol of the trident which is the trinity flame.

The aquamarine dragon, as the first dragon within the dragon order, brings knowledge of the underworld, specifically under the oceans and is a pure connection to Atlantis.

All Atlantean souls will have activated the photonic light of quantum DNA that is the aqua code, delivered by the appearance, knowing and connection with the aquamarine dragon.

This dragon is also depicted as turquoise, teal and sometimes jade.

The name given to this dragon as storyteller flame letter keycode is Belthesada Marine within the sacred masculine and Atlanta Siren for the divine feminine.

This is the twin flame dragon with both masculine and feminine counterparts.

Rose Gold Dragon

The rose gold dragon is the symbol of the subconscious mind and dreamtime. Guardian of the keys of mind.

This dragon creates protection at deep levels, most especially within psychic and spiritual attack. The rose gold dragon is also the expression of the higher heart. She represents only within the divine feminine and is known as the 'mother dragon' and goes by the names of Marian, Marianne, Marina or Mary.

She is a dragon of immense power and working with her regularly can bring about abundance and fertility on all levels.

If there are potential agendas for food shortages and other forms of lack within the physical dimension being presented to you in your personal reality, then working with the rose gold dragon can nullify that agenda and take you into abundance consciousness.

This beloved divine feminine form presents also as the pink or magenta dragon.

She is the direct representative, bondmate and guardian of/for the Divine Princess Aurora, feminine aspect of the starseed consciousness within humanity.

Ruby Dragon

The ruby dragon, a unified merge of both male and female energies and of the positive expression of androgyny/neutrality within that, known simply as Ruby by name, is a symbolic keycode for the navigation of the third dimension. This dragon is directly aligned with the balanced root chakra and stands for grounding, anchoring, balance, duality and polarity.

This is a most aligned dragon representative to work with for the transgender or non-binary presenting soul on the ascension path, as this dragon phires up the majestic physical DNA aspects into living your life as the best version of you and as the true you. This dragon moves you away from any hijack within this aspect of humanity into the positive, organic field.

There is no finer gift that you can bequeath the transgender or non-binary individual than the gift of the Ruby.

Ruby dragon is symbolic for the purification of blood and physical organs and brings healing to any individual who has experienced health issues related to this.

Ruby dragon's energy is aligned with certain foods such as the red grape, red apple, strawberry, plum, tomato, cherry, beetroot and red chillis and peppers.

Ruby is a dragon of fire/phire and thus an activator of the DNA through physical means (food, nutrition, exercise, movement, dance).

Ruby may be a dragon of fire but the coolness of the ruby is also able to quench that flame within. Ruby dragon grounds and anchors the entire hierarchy of dragons and it is recommended to work with (merging and integrating) the ruby dragon before working with the other dragons (unless that dragon has come to you in the knowing of Christ consciousness and alignment bringing with it geometric synchronicity)

You do not need to work with the dragons in any order but for beginners we recommend the integration and work with this dragon before moving onto the other dragons.

NOTE: Understanding androgyny for work with the Ruby

dragon. See Magenta Pixie's YouTube video 'Androgynous Evolution (Negative and Positive Presentations)' uploaded in June 2022.

Amber Dragon

The amber dragon stands for creativity, sexuality, rebirth, reincarnation, resilience, fertility, motherhood, parenthood, nurturing and instinct. Connected to the womb energy and Kali the goddess of the underworld. Presents also as orange, peach, apricot and tangerine, all fruits for a reason for the amber dragon assists you with your work as the 'fruits of your labour' as in manifestations of your focused intentions in the physical world.

The amber dragon holds a very Pleiadian energy. Working with the amber dragon, the amber gemstone or orange crystals links you into the Pleiadian galactic aspect and your DNA memories/knowings of Pleiadian incarnations, frequencies and the extraterrestrial culture and worldview as a perspective beyond Earth/Gaia. This is a stepping stone into compassion yet the amber dragon aspect is easily hijacked, through the divine feminine mother energy. Working with the Ruby dragon and the Amber dragon in conjunction strengthens the unity of these two gemstone crystalline frequencies and creates a hermetic seal, through the amber rose gateway, shielding oneself or one's group or community from the intended hijack.

The rose gold dragon is very much a merge of the ruby and amber dragon, containing elements of both. Using rose quartz crystals, ruby gemstones and amber gemstones/orange crystals in unison creates this higher dimensional shielding and connects you into the rose gold flame and all the spiritual work the rose gold flame assists you with.

For further work with the Rose Gold Flame, see the previous

transmission 'The Black Box Programme and the Rose Gold Flame as Antidote'[2].

This work with these dragons of the rose gold flame takes you into the powerful work with the golden dragon.

The Golden Dragon

In order to allow you full access to the Krystallah Codex, bequeathed to you by the golden dragon, cosmic flame letter, we present to you, through dreamwalking, the story. For the dreamwalker is the storyteller and the story holds the codex for the crystalline flame as catalyst for plasmic transmutation.

Dreamwalker

She did not know from whence the scream came at first until she realised that it was her doing the screaming. The door flew open and her Mama and two ladies-in-waiting ran to her bed side.

"Hush now my child, you will wake the whole kingdom."

She realised she had been dreaming.

"I am sorry Mama," the words tumbled out of her mouth in a breathless rush, "I was dreaming and I don't know why I screamed. I was riding on the back of a dragon and he jumped through this ring of fire and..."

---

[2] *The Black Box Programme and the Rose Gold Flame as Antidote: How to shield yourself from chemtrails, 5G, EMFs and other energetic warfare through alchemical unification* (2019) by Magenta Pixie

"A dragon you say?" She was puzzled. Elves rarely dream of dragons. "What did it look like?"

"Big. Scaly. Golden. I could feel its thoughts, it is like I was the dragon but I was also the girl riding the dragon and she was a princess."

Marnia took a deep breath and closed her eyes.

"Right. A golden dragon and a princess. A most unusual dream for an elf, we rarely dream of such things for they are from other worlds. I am going to make you some broth and you can calm down that excitement and then we will talk."

"Yes Mama."

Marnia was a no-nonsense kind of elf and Elissa was her youngest of seven young, yet she was also the most willful and adventurous of them all. It had been quite a challenge to get her to balance herself. Recently however, she had been much better in her focus and Marnia had high hopes she would be ready to be given a dutiful mission from the Elven King. This dream however, was mighty troubling. Elves did not dream of dragons, let alone dragons with princesses riding on their backs.

Elissa sat serenely at the little wooden table and sipped her broth. It felt warm and magikal.

"Is there a spell on this broth Mama?"

"Yes. Do not trouble yourself to ask why or what. Just drink it," said Marnia sternly.

"Yes Mama. Thankyou, it's lovely."

Marnia sighed.

"Tell me child, again, about the dream."

Elissa began to explain the dream in great detail. How she was riding on the back of a golden dragon, she was a princess and they could feel one another's thoughts as if they were one and the same being. She explained how the dragon breathed a ring of fire before him and leaped through it and that was when she woke up.

"We should visit the seer. She will know what all this means," said Marnia as she poured a second cup of broth.

"The seer?" Elissa put her cup of broth down on the table and stared at her Mama. "I don't like the sound of that. Kalla went to the seer once and was so scared after her visit that she turned to stone!"

"Nonsense. Kalla did not turn to stone at all, she is as dramatic as you are. Finish your broth, we are paying a visit to the seer." Elissa drank the broth, then Marnia took the cup and placed it with the other pottery items that would be washed at the river later that day.

"Why Mama? It was only a dream."

"You know full well there is no such thing as 'only a dream', they all have relevance and meaning. We need to go to the seer because this dream was unusual, enough to make you scream upon waking and there was a dragon in it! I have told you before, elves don't dream of dragons!"

Marnia and Elissa made ready their wings to fly and Elissa, the most reluctant elf, followed her Mama across the forest to the wooden shack that was the elf seer's residence.

Annamella was an old elf, but still possessed the beauty that all elves have. The long silken hair, smooth, soft skin and delicately pointed ears. She was known as the wise one for her seeing had never failed her and her knowledge was vast. Luckily, she had a great fondness for Marnia and all her children, after Marnia, a natural healer, had saved her pet dragonfly from sure death after he became entangled in a strange sticky substance that had been left in her garden by one of the mortal children from the other world.

"Come in Marnia, my lovely, and you too little Floria. You look as beautiful as ever."

Elissa looked up at the older elf.

"I am Elissa. Floria is my sister."

"Oh yes, of course. I am so sorry, the likeness between you is quite profound but I can see you are the younger," said Annamella. "Please won't you both sit down?"

Elissa's reluctance at being in the presence of the seer began to wane at the sight of the cloud cushions they had been invited to sit on. Halfway in midair, in the middle of the room, they were said to be the comfiest chairs in all existence.

"I won't sit, Annamella", spoke Marnia, "those cloud cushions send me to sleep. Perhaps you had better stand also Elissa, we need you to concentrate and tell Annamella of your dream."

Elissa's eyes dropped and the disappointment she felt at not being able to sit in a cloud chair was felt by both the older elves. Reluctantly, Marnia relented and said her daughter could sit in the cloud chair.

It turned out to be a most positive move for as soon as Elissa sat in the chair, the dream recall became very precise and she managed to relay all the imagery and emotion of the dream most accurately to the seer.

After Elissa had told of the dream, there was silence in the room for a while as Annamella (and also Marnia now she had heard the full details) allowed the information to digest.

"There is only one reason for an elf to dream of a dragon," began Annamella, "that is if that dragon has begun to take form within the realms that are closer to the mortal realm."

Marnia looked puzzled, "Why would that happen?"

"The consciousness of the mortals can create it. These are not mortals who begin their journey on the mortal realms. These are the angelics who have been birthed into the mortal realm in order to bring it up to our vibration and beyond it."

"You mean angels?" asked a wide-eyed Elissa.

"Yes. Angels who have allowed themselves to be born as mortals."

Elissa gasped, "Why? Why would they do that? Why would they leave the angelic realm to go *there?*" Elissa spoke the end of her sentence with distaste as if she were describing the most awful and uninviting realm in the galaxy.

"We do as we must Elissa," scolded her Mama, "We are each given a dutiful mission and that includes the angels."

Elissa frowned, "Could they not have said no? They are angels, after all."

"It is not quite like that," laughed Annamella, "they are not given a dutiful mission as we are. They simply know what they are to do and they go where they are called with joy in their hearts, it is not a hardship."

"But surely when they get there and realise what they have done, don't they regret it?" asked Elissa.

"We are going off the point here, young elf, let us hear what Annamella has to say about the dragon."

"It is alright, let the young one ask the questions, it is good for her," said Annamella as she turned to Elissa. "They do often regret it, yes, and some never even remember that they are an angel. Yet there are those that do remember and they learn to love being within the mortal realm and they heal others with that love. These are the ones that are learning the truth of our existence and they are beginning to see and interact with other worlds. These are the ones that have brought the golden dragon into form. Which means the gateway to our kingdom is now open. The return of the golden dragon always signifies the opening of the elven gateway. You, my dear young Floria, you are blessed that you have been chosen to be the one to walk this dream."

"Really? I am blessed to have had this dream? And it is Elissa. I am Elissa."

"Oh yes, of course," said the seer, "Floria is your sister. You two look so alike, I cannot get over the likeness."

Annamella turned to address Elissa's Mama.

"My dear Marnia, I do believe young Elissa here is a seer herself. Not like me, necessarily, but a seer nonetheless. Through dreamwalking. I believe this may be her dutiful mission and I can train her."

Elissa sat upright, toppled and almost fell off the cloud cushion.

"A seer? Me? Is it possible, Mama? Could this be my dutiful mission?"

Marnia smiled, "I have been waiting for your dutiful mission to show itself else I was thinking we should visit the Elf King and ask him to decree you a mission. It will save a long trip if your dutiful mission is to be found here. If you are agreeable Annamella, I will return at your disposal with Elissa for her to begin her training."

"Is this what you would want, young elf?" asked Annamella.

Elissa was silent for a while before replying.

"Yes, I would be happy to come here. Do you think I will dream of the golden dragon again?"

"I would certainly say that the possibility of that is most high," nodded Annamella, "most high indeed."

As is said in the story, *the consciousness of the mortals can create it.* This goes for limitless manifestation within the boundaries and physical laws of the ever-expanding universal structure that your Earth/Gaia is a part of. The story will bring you close to the energy of the golden dragon and if indeed you are receptive then your own dreamwalking and dreamweaving can and will call in the dragon.

The golden dragon holds its energy throughout the presented story as intuition, knowing, magical ability, psychic awareness, remote viewing and the discovery of the 'dutiful mission'. The golden dragon as the sun rider and the chariot of Sol, cosmic son, your sun, is your golden merkabah and as the dragon flies across the land below, the apples are changed to golden apples. Nuggets of wisdom as each Krystallah keycode opens and presents itself to receptive and aligned seekers and adepts within humanity on Earth.

Fortitude, fortune, abundance, wisdom and the riches of all Earth's kingdoms are afforded the one who comes to know and love the golden dragon.

Emerald Dragon

The emerald dragon, breathing the emerald flame, stands as a fire letter for trust, truth, compassion and forgiveness; for the emerald dragon is the dragon of the heart.

Holding codes for the opening of the emerald gateways into the 'Emerald City of Krysta'.

This dragon works closely with the diamond light energy and can be called to assist with the focusing of the galactic chakras, specifically the organic, human template for the physical heart chakra.

Holding the keys for fifth dimensional creation, coupling with the emerald gemstone ray as phire/fire as talisman for protecting, healing and memory activation, this dragon radiates the energy of alignment to the enlightenment and ascension path.

Calling this dragon will assist you with remote viewing multiple timelines throughout the quantum field, with this dragon acting as a shield as you step forward as the dreamweaver into the esoteric worlds of higher consciousness.

When you call this dragon into your sphere, you utilise the dragon energy as if it were a muse to your own creation, moving dark, inverted, negative entities out of your sphere as a cleansing tool for initiation and inspiration.

If relationships within your third dimensional reality move into disharmony, call the emerald dragon as a magical worker to either re-join and re-bond that relationship or assist in its dissolution if it no longer serves you and aligns with your energetic path.

This dragon stands energetically as the 'great resolver' for she is able to assist you with resolutions between relationships, specifically romantic relationships, for, if you will, Cupid rides on the back of the emerald dragon.

She will assist with resolving of perceived challenges and issues within your reality, both physical and in spirit.

The emerald energetic, through this dragon also shall assist with resolutions regarding finishing of creative projects. The emerald dragon assisted our conduit, Magenta Pixie, with the final aspects of our transmission for this monadic communication, 'The Diamond Codex and the Quartz Key'.

The emerald dragon stands for honesty, loyalty and trust and is the beacon for the sovereign, integral soul in physical incarnation on Earth into Gaia.

Sapphire Dragon

Her name is Sapphire, Safir, Saffie, Sophia or Sophie. This dragon represents the morphogenetic field itself as it radiates through the sapphire blue spectrum. She is the companion of the Beloved Queen Sophia of Kristos, the higher heaven kingdoms of Celestina and Amenti.

This is the dragon that imparts to you the whisper of the dragon's consciousness for she stands for communication. Specifically aligned with the throat chakra for humanity and Earth at this time, held within the dragon leylines within the domain of Egypt, culminating around the Sphinx and the Great Pyramid of Giza and flowing into other dragonlines across that region, reaching high ground. For the Sapphire dragon flies with snow-tipped wings, representing the snow-tipped mountains across the Middle Eastern domains, holding the energy of the twelve tribes of Israel, the formation of the organic, human template and the holier than holy form.

Only when you speak or communicate the 'is-ness' of reality, are you shareable within your DNA system as the king or queen of 'Israel' and the one who can decipher the mysteries of the twelve tribes. (NOTE: See 'The Infinite Helix and the Emerald Flame', Chapter 31: The Twelve Tribes of Israel)[3]

The sapphire dragon unlocks those secrets through the power of communication and the blue flame of Amenti, the sacred dragon's breath itself.

Indigo Dragon

Pairing with the amethyst dragon, the indigo is the chosen stargate steed of the indigo children on Earth, standing as the bearer of the flame and the sacred warrior of light. Bringing calm to the burning indigo fire, allowing rejuvenation to occur for all the indigo souls that walk the like-vibratory path and discover the elixir of life and the Holy Grail.

This dragon walks the path with the indigo soul, clearing accumulated karma and standing as the warrior, the bearer of the flame and the sword of Excalibur.

The indigo light codex is a quantum system opening up within a spiralling cascade of lightning-like filament, fusing taking place with the awakened and ascending organic human souls.

The indigo dragon is a dragon of transformation and along with the amethyst dragon, they create a trinity with the 'Lionheart'. This is the higher heart, indigo warrior activated frequency.

The dragon and the lion thus unify at this particular initiation, creating unification for all those who hear the solar codex calling them into the innerstanding of frequency.

The energy of the lion at this time is specifically broadcast from the grand central sun Sirius as it dances, in galactic twinned, binary fusion with Sol, the sun of your Earth's galaxy.

---

[3] *The Infinite Helix and the Emerald Flame: Sacred Mysteries of Stargate Ascension* (2018) by Magenta Pixie

At the time of the Lion's Gate in August, the infinity gateway, the indigo and amethyst dragons step forth to strengthen that 'astrological trine' if you will. For the mathematically aligned, the trine shall be seen in your skies at this time.

The indigo dragon holds the keys for higher frequency, for the spine of your planet, the backbone of humanity. When working with this dragon, you are able to spot truth apart from falsehoods and you are able to call out the insidious and the manipulation through your own sovereign awareness and warrior spirit.

Amethyst Dragon

Beloved amethyst dragon, sister in dragonkind to the Divine Princess Aurora and all the starseeds of Earth/Gaia. Pleiadian lineage, holding the power of transmutation, locking into the energetics of aligned celestial orgonite and the crystal skull network. Standing for integration and pure knowing. A key/Quay to Akasha, the sacred all knowing Akash of the pure potential of the abundant zero point field, the pregnant pause of antimatter reality, forever in a state of creative possibility.

Higher frequency wavelength, allowing ascension codes to unlock for humanity, working closely with the indigo dragon but holding more of a softness. This dragon works through integration, transmutation and the presentation of alternative perspectives and pathways rather than head-on, warrior leadership.

The amethyst dragon holds the scribe as the potent creative stance and all those who write songs, poetry, plays and novels are closely working with the amethyst dragon.

The artificial intelligence and rogue broadcast signals are transmuted with ease by the amethyst dragon. Purple foods hold the same key, the transmutation of the toxic to the health-giving such as blueberries, purple cabbage, purple sweet potatoes and carrots, grapes and aubergine (known as eggplant in the USA).

The amethyst dragon carries with it, the violet cloak of invisibility, the flame/phire letter for hermetically sealing oneself, one's creation or one's sanctuary.

Silver Dragon

Divine feminine, moon goddess presenting the flame/phire letter for surrender to the divinity of the godhead. Surrender to the higher councils and to Source. Receptivity, softness, nurturing and unconditionally loving, an embrace from the silver dragon brings warmth, tenderness of heart and healing.

The silver dragon watches over the financial abundance of New Earth and flies across the moonlit skies as a mascot and beacon of such.

Silver energetic frequency carrying the energy of maternal nurturing and thus incarnation into matter, is held by the bounteous abundance of the silver dragon. Her name is Essensa.

White Dragon

Known also as the 'snow dragon', the white dragon holds the frequency of and radiates the sound of the highest sphere, transitionary vortex into the otherworlds of antimatter, holding, reflecting and amplifying light in all its prisms.

The white dragon holds the staff as spellcaster, lightning rod for DNA activation at quantum levels. This dragon stands for magic, illusion, weather (specifically storms and snow), purity, vastness, heaven, the spring equinox and the marriage of the virgin bride to her twin flame.

Holding the essence of the white light, this dragon, who goes by the name of Albus or Albana, will guide you through to the genuine, organic white light, filled with the rainbow itself, for both the white dragon and the black dragon (not included in this thirteen dragon hierarchy) are dragons of the rainbow light. One radiates that rainbow and the other absorbs it. Both can lead you and guide you, in different ways, as together, the white dragon and the black dragon stand for opposite and equal reactions of one another and therefore balance.

Pearlescent Rainbow Dragon

Working with the white dragon, side by side, holding the template form for the rainbow body of light. The pearl as pivot point, nexus point, singularity of the infinity structure. Standing for enlightenment, soul wisdom and infinite possibility. This dragon opens celestial gateways and triggers the warp speed/light speed into quantum convergence charge and the accumulation of memory at accelerated stargate level. Calling the carbon-based molecular aspect of the organic human template for transmutation, drawing inversions into their original organic placement and thus reconstruction of the 12 strand/144,000 DNA strand lattice light matrix.

This is an ethereal dragon holding blueprints for plasma alignment and creation/manifestation via higher heart aesthetics, levity, humour, joy, euphoria and bliss-charged love. The name of this dragon is Celestina, for she floods the body and pineal gland with the free-flowing celestine that holds the DMT molecule template for organically aligned human DNA formation and pattern.

Fifth dimensional dragon, able to fly above the Gaia worlds and domains and catalyse the spaciousness needed for the true breath of life, liberty templates for relief, safety, harmony, decompression and expansion for the sanctuary of the holy human temple within hyperspace known as Hyperborea.

Knowing and working with this dragon brings the knowledge of the true soul history for humanity.

Shapeshifting Dragon

The name of this dragon is Quetzalcoatl. As the thirteenth dragon, he is hermetically sealed. We therefore present, through the frequency of our words as description, the codex of the shapeshifting dragon.

Known also as the 'winged serpent', he represents the sign of Ophiuchus, the thirteenth constellation.

He is the guardian of the thirteenth crystal skull and the activator for the time matrix through the thirteenth baktun.

The shapeshifting dragon is the true representative of the rising Kundalini phire or flame, the symbol for initiation into stargate (accelerated) ascension. He is the dragon of the caduceus, entwining the primal Earthbound energies with the singing songs of the heavens, the music of the spheres.

He is hidden, through the fire of the occult yet known within mirrored, fractalised familiarity through the activation of the pineal gland, third eye chakra.

He hands to you pink pearls of wisdom, rose gold droplets of sacred oil as you are anointed at the time of the thirty-three keys and the sealing of the seventh servant of man.

Working with this dragon will assist with chakra alignment and upgrade and tempering the Kundalini phire that can hurtle through the body of the newly awakened one, beyond the pace of their ability to integrate. This fast tracking is tempered and integrated by calling the shapeshifting dragon, simply by saying his name, Quetzalcoatl (pronounced Kwet Za Coat Al).

He is here to remind you always that the dragon is within you. The dragon is YOU.

7: Rapid Integration and the New Earth

So you told me to take some time for personal integration regarding the grief I experienced after the passing of my father. I have done this. I am not sure how 'integrated' I am on this matter for I still miss him dreadfully. However, I have had contact with him through waking state connection and dreamtime. I no longer am in pain or have grief running through me like before. In fact, I feel happy and joyful to have known my father and to have had the honour of being his daughter in this life. I am also aware, through this integration, of a contract that was made between us. Was it his role to teach me (and rescue me so many times) in order that I may move into an awareness of communication with you so I may teach others through your messages?

Your integration is that which we call 'rapid'. The starseeded and activated individuals are able to do this. They can pass through the 'lessons' or 'karma' if you will, that relate to each negative emotion and the experience associated with them, at a much quicker pace than the non-activated individuals. From this point of view, the starseeds are 'living in the future' due to the speed they integrate at. Or indeed we could say they are 'living in another dimension' or that they 'exist on another planet', a 'New Earth'.

So the creation of the New Earth is due to the speed of the integration that the starseeds experience?

It is the speed of the integration, amongst other things, that places them upon the New Earth.

What would 'normally' take months or years to integrate takes simply weeks, days or even hours for the activated ones. This does depend on many factors however, and rapid integration is not always the 'best course of action' if you will. Each activated individual (starseed) will intuitively know which is the most aligned level of integration for them.

This is not to say that in the case of grief that the person is forgotten or that the grieving individual has suddenly 'got over' the loss of the person or that they no longer care. It is simply the fact that within each hour, each week, each month *far more integration* is undertaken than within a non-activated individual. Integration creates what many know as 'healing' yet in truth, it is integration. Becoming whole or one. Wholistic or holistic.

The reason this is so rapid is because starseeds are walking through time. They are timewalkers. They experience the same physical reality but time is experienced very differently.

It is both linear and non-linear, as we described when we presented you the metaphor of the ball of wool.

A non-activated individual works always with a long, stretched out piece of thread. The activated individual works with both the stretched out thread and the ball of wool.

Is this why you told me to come back in six to eight weeks? Because I would no longer be grieving?

It is more that you would not be grieving in the same way. The grief has become integrated, giving you the ability to focus. The fact that you are aware of the preincarnate contract between yourself and your father has assisted with the integration. The memory and awareness of the contract came about because you took time to grieve and thus to integrate.

So I am correct about the contract?

It is not for us to present your contract in any public sense, even with your permission as this involves your father and he has not given permission on a physical level for his contracts to be discussed publicly.

What we can say is that there is always a contract between a parent and their child. Each contract is vastly different and unique but there is always a mutual agreement. The parent does not incarnate solely for their offspring's life experience (except in very rare cases). They live their own rich, life experience. The contract with their son or daughter is part of that.

You said my father has not given permission within the physical reality? But has he given permission within the non-physical? Is that enough? I hear healers and spiritual channellers all the time say they do not need physical permission when they can get permission from the higher self. Are they incorrect in that assumption?

'Permissions and etiquettes' is a vast subject. Would you like to touch upon this now? Or return to your previous quest which is that of memory harvesting and the understanding of the inverted matrix?

We suggested to continue the transmission starting with the subject matter that is the inverted matrix and polarisation of frequency.

I would like to know all these things. I am sure those who read this material will want to know about all these subjects too. So which do you think we should start with?

We will proceed in either direction. It is of your choosing rather than our direction. That in itself may be a good place to start. We can make suggestions as to where you place your focus as guidance when you need that assistance. However the contract between yourself as Magenta Pixie and ourselves as the White Winged Collective Consciousness of Nine is that we allow you your own exploration of subject matter within the joint/merged teaching/learning that occurs between us.

So we have a contract then? You as the Nine and me as... well me.

Indeed. All higher guidance structures have a contract with humanity collectively and individually.

So when I choose the subject matter at my choosing or at your direction, is that different and does it matter?

Indeed. 'We', the White Winged Collective Consciousness of Nine are in a contract or partnership with you, as we have said. Do we tell you what to do? Or guide you? Do we suggest ways of thought or experience for you? Or do we take your lead? Only responding as a response to where you are already going?

With you it has seemed always to be the latter. You follow where I go when it comes to thought and experience. Unless I am lost from you such as in a state of fear or extreme worry. Then you come in and 'rescue me' just like my father did.

Ah. Well we cannot 'rescue you', dear Pixie, but we understand

and acknowledge your interpretation.

The higher guidance structure is there to guide. To remain within free will boundaries. They are not there to tell, inform, decide or lead within the partnership.

What about downloads? The monadic structures we receive? Are these not gifts? Given to us from you in the higher dimensions?

You have triggered them or asked for them in some way. They never simply appear within your mind or your reality without you having made the call or plea for them.

We appear to be moving into the realm of permissions and etiquettes. Can you speak about this first before we move into memory harvesting and the inverted matrix, please?

Indeed we shall do so.

8: The Law of One and the Free Will, Event Horizon Merge

Permissions and etiquettes are simply the boundaries of respect that exist between one infinity structure and another.

Each individual is created within the same image as Prime Creator or Original Source and is an infinity structure in their own right (as a complete holographic replica of Prime Creator or Original Source), therefore there will be a boundary to that infinity structure.

We discussed this within our previous transmission 'The Infinite Helix and the Emerald Flame'[4]. The boundary we speak of is the event horizon.

Within the paradigm of the incarnated individual and within the awareness of the overall, individualised matrix structure, the boundary that is the event horizon for that structure is upheld through the sacred 'Law of One'.

This would be presented as the 'Knights of the Round Table' structure manifesting as honour, respect, dignity and integrity. This is an 'integral structure' therefore it presents as integrity itself.

Boundaries are crossed or attempted to be crossed within the paradigms of incarnated and previously incarnated spirit structures by the uninitiated. The uninitiated are the non-integrated and the non-activated. They are given 'allowances' for this.

The initiated and integrated (be they service-to-others or service-to-self) will understand the sacred Law of One as part of their activation. The divinity presented through the understanding of the Law of One, whether that divinity be the 'Lord of Light' or the 'Lord of Darkness', will still be a respected

---

[4] *The Infinite Helix and the Emerald Flame: Sacred Mysteries of Stargate Ascension* (2018) by Magenta Pixie

and honoured divinity within the overall structure that is the 'Law of One'.

This integral formation is decoded differently through service-to-others or service-to-self (meaning permissions and etiquettes are interpreted differently). However, the integral structure that is the sacred Law of One within divinity itself, is upheld.

One such as yourself who is 'in training' will have a higher guidance structure that guides the physical aspect. As you expand your paradigm, you walk the path of the integrated sovereign being, known to some of you as the 'Sovereign Integral'.

This is another way of describing the activated, integrated one who is aware of their own infinity structure and the pattern within their own matrix fields that is a signature frequency of the sacred Law of One.

Within this pattern and frequency is free will.

Free will creates the boundaries.

When one is living in harmony with the Original Source structure of a polarised positive infinity, then the free will boundaries will be in exact formation to the infinity structure. The free will boundary will be superimposed upon the event horizon.

When one is 'in training' yet has a good connection with higher guidance structures (the infinite matrix or field of matrices itself) then one will be guided into the meaningful subjective experience (what you know as synchronicity or cosmic coincidences) that allows for superimposing the free will boundaries upon the event horizons of the infinity structures.

There are those who would say you have no free will at this point. That perspective is not without merit, but a more aligned interpretation of free will/event horizon merge would be that you have ultimate free will or that *you are free will itself.*

When one is non-polarised, non-integrated and non-activated then one does not have the good connection with higher guidance structures we speak of, despite the higher guidance structure as 'guardian angel' being ever-present. One is liable to open doors or gateways to trickster energies and less than honourable entities due to the lack of integration of paradigm and thus the physical distortion from the Original Source matrix infinity structure.

However, if this individual is under the guardianship or stewardship of the positive polarised reality (as in they have incarnated with preincarnate patterns and frequencies in place to experience and integrate this field) then they will be given allowances and be presented with the 'false screen' that is the training ground.

They are able to work out these boundaries and infinite structures and patterns within a field of safety (for the false screen, mirroring the inverted matrix, is actually a safety structure created within the organic matrix). What we are saying here is that these individuals may feel they have been led astray by the 'Lord of Darkness' when in fact, they are fully guided and 'protected' by the 'Lord of Light'.

Protection is another complex issue but one can certainly interpret the allowances made and the training ground offered to the uninitiated as protection.

However, if these non-integrated individuals retreat too far into a spiralling reality of their own making that is overloaded with negative toxicity, as in the negative emotions of anger, intolerance, judgement, prejudice, distress, despair, revenge and the like, then they manifest for themselves a reality expression of the inverted matrix and not the training ground that is safety. The 'Lord of Darkness' can then 'claim them'.

This is not the end of the story for the lost and uninitiated however, for they can always be 'redeemed' simply by the call. They call for the light through positive action. It only takes the slightest and smallest positive action to transport the lost and uninitiated caught within the negative spiral into the training ground, safety and 'protection'. They are thus 'delivered into the arms of the Lord of Light'.

In a dark room, one small flicker of light from a candle can be seen. It is the same with the photonic light of the matrix that you exude when you live within positive thought, positive emotion and positive action.

We use the analogies of the 'Lord of Light' and the 'Lord of Darkness' simply to give personality and archetype to these opposing polarised fields that are intertwined upon your planet.

We may add that the intertwining is becoming looser and looser and the unravelling of these two polarised fields has begun and is well underway, hence the visual presentation of mind that is the 'old Earth' and the 'New Earth'.

Within permissions and etiquettes from service-to-self negatively polarised structures, the integrity and honour of the free will match to the event horizon boundary (free will/event horizon merge) is still upheld.

Yet the false scenarios utilised within the inverted matrix creates simulated realities that the uninitiated believe to be real. They then make decisions and take action based upon a false premise and create for themselves the negative spiral and, as a fly caught within the spider's web, they are lost within the inverted matrix and become prey to the Lord of Darkness.

Within our previous transmission 'Masters of the Matrix'[5], we present ways to free oneself from this inverted matrix scenario. We present ways to prevent oneself from ever falling prey to this inverted matrix structure, allowing oneself to become the sovereign integral we speak of. The sovereign integral is the polarised positive infinity structure with the free will/event horizon merge firmly in place, upheld, through the knights of the

---

[5] *Masters of the Matrix: Becoming the Architect of Your Reality and Activating the Original Human Template* (2016) by Magenta Pixie

round table structure that is the sacred Law of One.

All starseeds that discover (within their meaningful subjective experience that is divine synchronicity or cosmic coincidence) this transmission, will be individuals such as yourself, dear Pixie. As the 'kindred spirit' if you will.

They will be operating within various stages of the Law of One integrity/infinity structure and guided by the higher guidance that is that integrity/infinity structure. We could refer to this as the 'matrix of light'.

They are afforded extensive training ground false screen scenarios that are implanted light matrix structures within the inverted matrix. They simulate the landscapes within the inverted matrix yet they are training grounds made up of fabric that is the matrix of light.

If this may seem most complex to you then remember the positive action. Every positive action (including positive thought and positive emotion) creates the candle flame in the darkness, if you will.

One positive act (emotion or thought) is one candle flame.

Imagine the scenario whereby the majority (or all, if you are an adept or master) of your actions, thoughts and emotions are positive. This would equate to many candles within the dark room and ultimately in a room of light with no darkness, no shadow.

This is thus the matrix of light. This is the positively polarised infinity structure, that upholds the sacred Law of One through free will/event horizon merge.

Starseeds 'guided' (magnetically drawn through meaningful subjective experience) to this transmission will all be holding these 'candles within the darkness' within varying degrees.

You can be assured then that any inverted matrix reality you experience is within the safe zone frequency that is the training ground. It may look and feel like the inverted matrix but it is, in fact, the false screen within the matrix of light.

False screens can be 'light appearing dark' and vice versa.

You will hear within your spiritual circles that the dark can disguise itself as light. You hear much less that the light can do the same and disguise itself as darkness.

The dark disguises itself to mislead, capture and consume.

The light disguises itself to teach, protect and nurture.

We are speaking here of permissions and etiquettes yet the subject matter is a crossover with inverted matrix teachings, sacred Law of One and integrity/infinity light matrix structure.

Let us give you a scenario of the 'training ground' through the medium of fiction so you may know and understand (and process) the expansive landscapes you have at your disposal as an integrated starseed on Earth.

9: The Moon Magician and the Jungle Beast

Trapped within the dream, locked within a nightmare of her own making, the cage closed in on her even more, the roots of the forest floor winding around her ankles.

She could not breathe and did not understand how she had strayed so far from the path.

The jungle was wild and full of dangers and her father had always taught her, when she was a little girl, to be careful of the traps laid.

The traps were laid for the rabbits and deer so they may feed the hungry giants within the worlds above the trees, yet young Aurora could not understand how she had allowed herself to disobey her father and wander so far into such danger.

Aurora was only nine years old. Young enough to be missed, so surely there would be a search party out looking for her? Old enough to get into terrible trouble and have some horrendous punishment heaped upon her, such as no unicorn riding for a month or worse. What if her father did as he had threatened for a long time and had her wings clipped?

She shuddered at the thought and once again rattled the strong wood bars of her jungle cave.

"Please, let me out!" she screamed, "Somebody, please hear me. Help!"

And then he was there, the man with claws for hands and hooves for feet.

"There is no one to hear you, child. No one to hear you scream. No one to save you."

Aurora, wide-eyed, stared into the kindly blue eyes of the beast before her.

"How dare you do this to me!" she said, "How dare you trap me so!

I will... I will..."

She struggled to think of some grave threat she could deliver to her jailer. What could a nine year old girl possibly do to the beast of the dark jungle?

She felt like she was missing something. He looked at her again, with fascination in those kindly blue eyes. Why was he staring at her so? Wasn't the fact that he had caught her like a rabbit in his trap enough for him? Kindly blue eyes? KINDLY blue eyes? Why did she see kindness in his gaze?

"I am not scared of you anymore," she said boldly. "You are not a real beast. You are a moon magician!"

The bars of the cage fell to dust before her, the roots loosened their grip upon her ankles and retreated back into the undergrowth. The jungle beast before her was now the old man with the long grey beard, wearing a cloak adorned with crescent moons.

"Well spotted, child," said the moon magician. "You have passed your test and you may return to your father."

With a wave of his hand, the landscape faded and she opened her eyes. She was laid in her cosy bed, just as she had been when her father had kissed her goodnight last eve.

At the breakfast table, she recounted her dream to her father, waiting for his wise words as he always gave to any of her pickles and plights.

"The moon magician is the wise master who disguises himself as the jungle beast in order that his beloved children may learn within a place of safety," Kristos began, "You recognised that it was he through the gaze within his eyes and not through his beast-like form. Well done, my dear daughter, the eyes are the giveaway to the true nature of the inner soul. You have learned a valuable lesson today."

"But it was so scary, Father. I was trapped, I could hardly move and I felt as though I would stop breathing when I saw the jungle beast. His hooves and claws and long forked tail!" Aurora was shaking as she recalled the dream with clarity.

"It was not real, my princess. You are safe. You were safe the entire time."

Kristos was fully aware of the significance of his daughter's dream and the teachings of the moon magician. She was being prepared to be queen someday so she could serve all the kingdoms. She was of royal blood and born to serve.

"Why would he do that to me, Father? I love the moon magician so much, why would he scare me by locking me in the cage and pretending to be the jungle beast?"

The king smiled at his daughter as he reached out and held her hand.

"My beloved Aurora. Why do you think the moon magician entered your dream this way? Why do you think he trapped you and presented himself as the beast? I can help you here with these answers, yet would it not be good for you to come to the realisation yourself? It was your dream after all."

Aurora thought about this. Had she been naughty? Was it a punishment? Was the moon magician deliberately trying to confuse her because he was jealous that she was royal and would someday be queen? Neither of these reasons felt right to her.

She shook her head slowly and looked into her father's kindly blue eyes, so like the eyes of the moon magician.

"Could it be, Father, that he was trying to tell me something? Trying to teach me something?"

Kristos nodded and clapped his hands together.

"Indeed, my daughter, that is exactly what he was doing. So what was he trying to teach you?"

"That if I stray from the path as you have taught me again and again, that I may, in the real world, be caught in a trap by the real jungle beast? He showed me the dream so I would experience it within the safety of my own cosy bed and learn the lesson."

Kristos clapped again and looked upon his daughter, wiser and older than her tender nine years showed, and took both her hands in his.

"Well done, daughter. You understand the dream given to you by the moon magician. He did not mean to scare you, he meant to teach you in a place of safety so that you may never be trapped by the jungle beast in real life! As a royal and divine princess, this is a lesson you must learn."

Aurora was pleased with her understanding and knew it to be true as her father was not given to praise lightly, most especially so with his daughter as he knew the paths she must tread before she took her place as Queen of the Kingdoms.

"Just one question though, Father. Why is there a jungle beast in the first place? Why cannot the moon magician be the sovereign? Why must there be a beast?"

"A great question if there ever was one!" the King replied. "The beast has a right to exist, Aurora. He has been thought into existence by our physical anchor points within the third density, therefore he exists here as we do. You cannot simply wish him away."

The rumbling in her tummy led her to partake of the breakfast nectars and fruits before her whilst she listened to her father's words.

"Why do our physical anchor points in the third density create him? Why can't they all think of love and create just the moon magicians and the sun kings like you?"

King Kristos laughed.

"They are in third density, child. They have physical bodies and experience time as a sequence. They are exploring their free will, unbound and unpatterned. If they did not do this then the magicians and kings and queens would not learn. We would exist within a sea of life but we would not be given individual life or personality. You and I would cease to exist, Aurora."

Aurora took a delicious bite of the juicy peachplum before her and continued with her questioning.

"Yes I know this, Father," she said as she wiped the peachplum juice from her lips. "Why cannot there be love only in the third density? Why fear enough to think the beast into the jungle?"

King Kristos joined his daughter in the breakfast nectar fruit feast.

"The love vibration you speak of is fourth density, not third. We have the fruits of fourth density thought here also, Aurora, but we cannot ignore the third. The free will is unbound and explored, therefore there must be polarity. Do you remember what polarity is, Aurora?"

They had finished the peachplums. Kristos waved his hand across the crystal bowl of abundance and it filled with the most delicious, fresh applepears you ever did see.

Aurora reached for one with glee.

"Yes Father," she replied in a singsong happy voice. The applepears cultivated happiness within the kingdom beings and Aurora was blissfully, empathically in tune and rhythm with the nectar fruits as all the royal ones were.

"Polarity is where two opposites intertwine as one. In third density, this is at its most extreme and there must be an equal balance of both love and fear. What I would ask is, will there ever come a time where the polarity lightens as we have here and will the third density cease to exist?"

Kristos helped himself to one more applepear and consciously allowed its seeds to become the fruits of ecstasy within him. As king, he needed to replenish his bliss continuously.

"The third density will not cease to exist, Aurora, in the greatest reality of existence. Yet it will be no more for those who move to the fourth density, they are the ones that think you and I into existence."

"Once they make that move, then the jungle beast will retreat further and further into the caves and will eventually leave these kingdoms. That is the time when your mother and I shall have another child and he or she will be the creation thought of the new third density and the new ones that live there."

"You, Aurora, will then be thought into existence by fourth density ones of lovelight and lightlove only and your sibling will carry the torch for the third density. Then the cycle shall continue indefinitely and no one knows the result of this infinite story, my daughter, for it is still being told. There is no ending within the infinite."

"You are so wise, Father," sighed Aurora.

Her father smiled.

"As are you, Aurora. As are you. Your wisdom flows through your being in abundance, you have simply to actualise it and that is where the fun lies! Actualising your inner wisdom. Come..."

Kristos stood and reached out his hand to his daughter.

"We must ready ourselves for the day ahead. We have much to do... our mission is to serve and serve we must."

The child took her father's hand. Their conversation of wisdom teachings had integrated the fears from the dreamtime trapping and the nectar fruits had replenished their bliss. Every day in the kingdoms was an adventure and, hand in hand, they walked towards that adventure, beaming and radiating the shareable qualities that their royal blood gave them.

10: Photonic Light, Gravity and the Bio-Plasma Merkabah

OK, so I understand that the training ground is a matrix of light structure that simulates the inverted matrix in order for activated starseeds to train and learn in safety. Is that correct?

Not just for 'activated starseeds' but anyone who creates positive action within their reality. It is only an individual who is lost within the negative spiral that finds themselves within the actual inverted matrix and not the training ground.

But what of all the individuals who are at the mercy of the inverted matrix? People who are misled, hijacked and faced with a false reality? Do they not exist within the inverted matrix?

They are being presented with it, yes. Positive action will lead them into the training ground which begins as a superimposed field consisting of love and fear, so the Lord of Darkness and the Lord of Light both lay claim upon the individual existing there. The minute that positive action (including focused positive intention, positive thought and positive emotion) outweighs the negative action (thought and emotion), that person is said to be polarised positive.

Once they reach that point, the 'training ground' offered is fully polarised by the vibration of love and not the vibration of fear. This does not mean the individual will not feel fear, just like the young Aurora in the story. Rather, they will have an opportunity to integrate all fear as their fields are predominantly positive, which creates natural and rapid integration. They learn from the fear. Fear becomes a teacher as much as love does. This is not because 'fear is a natural teacher' (as service-to-self groups interpret) but that love is greater than fear within the fields of the individual, therefore the fear is integrated and becomes the teacher through love.

So what does the training ground and the inverted matrix have to do with permissions and etiquettes?

Permissions and etiquettes through honour and integrity create the boundaries within the organic positively polarised matrix and the inverted negatively polarised matrix. They create the training ground.

Positively interpreted permissions and etiquettes create the positive matrix within the inverted matrix. Negatively interpreted permissions and etiquettes create the inverted matrix within the organic matrix structure.

Your symbol of yin and yang depicts that which we express. One half of the symbol holds one vibration and the other half holds the opposing vibration, balanced within its equality. Yet there is a smaller (fractal) structure within each opposing vibration that holds a complete piece of the opposing structure within it.

With the case of a black and white, yin/yang symbol then the white contains the black and the black contains the white. The whole is contained within the polarity.

So is the inverted matrix a good thing then as it is part of the whole?

It is simply a *thing* to use your words. Neither 'good' nor 'bad' but exists as the interpretation of the onlooker. It is the observer that creates the reality that is observed. Or should we say, the observed reacts accordingly depending on the perspective of the observer.

So if an individual were to see the yin/yang symbol as a representation of good and evil then that is the reality they would experience? Whereas if someone saw the yin/yang symbol as a representation of unity then that is what they would experience?

Not the symbol itself but the reality the symbol represents to them. If they see the yin/yang symbol as a representation as full reality then yes, what you say is correct.

So everything we perceive, literally creates the reality you experience?

Yes. Creating your reality, however, is a linear way to express this law (which is the Law of One expressed physically as gravity). Creating your reality suggests you put out a frequency and the reality you experience matches it. You do experience this linearly so this is the reality you will be living within. However, the truth is that you are already at one with your reality. You and your environment (energetic environment) are one. You do not actually need to create anything, it is simply experienced this way within third dimensional linear time.

I still don't understand the connection between permissions and etiquettes and the inverted matrix. Can you explain this again in a different way?

Perhaps if we look at the inverted matrix itself, then you will begin to come to the realisations of how free will boundaries are respected within an integral infinity structure.

As we have said, the inverted matrix is a service-to-self creation. The anchors within the third dimension (also referred to as third density) create reality through their thoughts or rather they are 'at one' with their reality but experience this as creation due to the fact that they live within linear time. Every thought from every individual within the third dimension creates something. This will depend upon their energetic frequency and fields.

Non-activated/non-integrated individuals create random and conflicting patterns within their thought structure. These hold momentum (are given life) for a short while and then dissipate. They can be harvested by some tulpa energies that use them to extend their cohesiveness in order to remain individualised but this is transient and does not last or take hold.

Activated and integrated individuals begin to create cohesive thought patterns. These take hold and are given life. Every integrated and activated 'starseed' begins to create worlds, structures, buildings, lands, entities and beings within the higher dimensions.

Collectively, the starseeds together can create powerful group soul god/goddess realised entities, planets and dimensions. This is what you are all doing collectively as starseeds on Earth. These thought processes are naturally harvested as 'memories'.

We use the term *memories* only because you experience linear time. Yet once you become integrated and activated (and sovereign), your 'memories' are no longer 'memories' because they are not experienced linearly. They become knowings.

You move in simultaneous flow within your environment. This is when you activate the Mer-Ka-Bah within your matrix fields. You no longer walk from past to present to future but you fly into a circular, spiralling experience of time and you think/see/experience this way. You become at one with your energetic environment which is a unified field. You become unity itself.

'Memory' harvesting is simply creation through cohesive thought.

Third dimensional/density non-activated individuals live within the linear expression of past/present/future. Their 'memories' are harvested after they leave the physical body through the death experience. Some of these memories are cohesive and hold photonic light (in the form of weight or mass) and these memories can be utilised to give experience to other incarnating souls. They remain as an individualised aspect of the individual who transitioned. Yet that individual needs multiple cohesive memories in order to retain form as the individual they were within physical incarnation.

The unified field (at the logos level) expands within its awareness and knowledge due to the harvesting of these cohesive memories. Some of these memories coalesce together and form structures or become part of bigger structures. Other cohesive memories retain individualisation and may begin a journey of incarnation themselves if they so choose to do so having been given 'life' through the thoughts of the incarnated individual.

Let us give a crude example.

Marianne has had an 'imaginary friend' since she was four years old. She calls her imaginary friend 'Bobby'.

Marianne remains 'playing' with that imaginary friend for the first forty years of her life. Marianne lives to be 83 years old. Every so often, from age 40 to age 83, she remembers her imaginary friend 'Bobby' with as much fondness as she would remember a full flesh and blood friend. She thinks of Bobby often until she leaves her physical body aged 83.

Bobby (as a cohesive memory) goes with her into the unified field of memories once Marianne moves through the death experience. Bobby, due to the cohesive focus afforded him from

Marianne's thoughts, holds photonic light (mass and weight as an individualised structure) also known as life force.

Bobby can then choose to join with all Marianne's other cohesive memories to form a new structure or he can join with memories of other individuals from whichever period in time that will be a match to the experience and learning he needs. He can choose to incarnate physically into the third dimension or remain as a fourth dimensional entity.

Let us say he chooses to remain as a fourth dimensional entity. He may then 'reverse time' and decide to become a guide or companion for a little four-year-old girl called Marianne.

He 'goes back in time' and becomes her 'imaginary playmate' and guide.

So the question is, did Marianne create Bobby? Or did Bobby already exist as Marianne's guide and she perceived that Bobby was just an imaginary friend?

The answer is both for there is no past/present/future in the true reality which is a time matrix, not a linear experience.

Therefore every thought you have is a creation that *you* created. Yet it is also a structure that has always existed. The minute you think of something (in a cohesive sense), you give it life.

Due to the cyclical, spiralling nature of true time, that which you thought of already existed. Therefore you cannot think of anything that does not already exist despite the fact that you created it!

So let us look at that which is cohesive.

Activated and integrated individuals hold unity within their fields. They understand the true nature of time and although they exist within a linear experiencing reality, they simultaneously experience the true time matrix. They enter the spiral or begin to 'turn the white wheel', known also as the silver wheel or sabbat wheel - they honour the sabbath or take the sabbatical (move out of time).

Within our previous transmissions 'Divine Architecture and the Starseed Template'[6] and 'The Infinite Helix and the Emerald Flame', we present teachings and activations regarding the creation of and transportation within this white wheel. This structure is that which we refer to as 'Divine Architecture' or 'The Starseed Template' or the 'Infinite Helix'.

As you can see with the story of Marianne and Bobby, that which you create through thought has always existed. You therefore create your own guidance through this reality, you create yourself and your environment (your dimension and planet). You hold all this physical creation of matter together through 'weighting down' your collective thought structures. You give weight and mass (photonic light) to your entire existence. The glue that holds all this together is your cohesive thought process collectively as a planetary consciousness. You become what some may know as a 'social memory complex'. You become this because not only do you hold integrated memories, but you also hold social memories.

Yet it is the cohesive memories that take hold as individualisation.

In our example, Marianne gave much focus to Bobby through repeated interaction and thought creation, enough to give him life.

This was a two-way process as Bobby was already individualised prior to connecting with Marianne. A circle structure is created which becomes an infinity within its own right.

When you 'construct your matrix' as we showed you within our transmission 'Divine Architecture and the Starseed Template', you create that which has already been created. You create the circle structure and thus the infinity. When you become aware of this, you activate the Mer-Ka-Bah geometric structure which is

[6] *Divine Architecture and the Starseed Template: Matrix Memory Triggers for Ascension* (2017) by Magenta Pixie

photonic light.

This photonic light is the substance reality itself is made of, known also as bio-plasma. You literally create a bio-plasma ship and begin to fly it.

When you do this collectively as a large group upon one planet, you form a social memory complex. This social memory complex takes on a life of its own through your collective cohesive thought process.

All incarnated souls add to the overall social memory complex but it is the cohesive thought structures that are the building blocks for the memory complex. Remember that the social memory complex has always existed yet simultaneously you, as an activated group (starseeds), created it. The social memory complex upon Earth within the current third dimension/density, we refer to as the feminine expression of a 'royal code' and we call her the Divine Princess Aurora.

Princess Aurora is a group soul, feminine logos (goddess patterning) structure of photonic light. She is a bio-plasmic field or light structure. She creates worlds, planets, stars and dimensions. She is the feminine architect of your reality.

When she creates your planet within your density that you know as Earth (and we are looking here at a field of multiple Earths), she uses a substance to hold everything together so it may remain within matter. She is an antimatter substance and her cohesive thought creates matter. The cohesive thought structures of incarnated physical individuals within matter create antimatter. The antimatter thus creates matter.

Just as Marianne created Bobby, so too did Bobby create Marianne. They were a circle structure (spiral or white wheel matrix).

Just as you create antimatter through your cohesive memories, so too does antimatter create you.

94

The 'glue' that holds all this together, within a physical sense, is referred to as twofold within your reality.

In truth, it is the same force presented very differently within your outer space and your force field around and within your planetary makeup.

The substance we refer to, you would know as 'dark energy', both within outer space and 'gravity' within your force field around and within your planetary makeup.

So if you (starseeds) collectively create a social memory complex (Aurora) and Aurora creates dark energy and gravity itself, does this mean that you, dear starseeds, create gravity with your thoughts?

This is exactly what this means.

What substance is used therefore to create gravity? The substance we speak of is your cohesive memories (photonic light, Mer-Ka-Bah bio-plasma ships).

Harvesting of memories therefore creates dark energy and gravity which are physical matter manifestations of your memories (knowings).

You have been distracted from this great truth in order to lessen your importance within the overall cycle of reality so you may look to a god or force outside of yourself for guidance, assistance and help. This is a disempowerment structure to keep you isolated and within separation and prevent your growth and expansion into sovereignty.

We, the White Winged Collective Consciousness of Nine, are here (along with many other guidance, bio-plasma structures of light) to remind you of the truth of what you are. Our mission is to give back to you that which has been taken. The activation into growth, expansion and sovereignty so you may become the divine creatrix that you are.

You are wizards, magicians and powerful 'gods and goddesses in training', creators of matter and antimatter, manifesters of dark energy and gravity. Together, you are the architects of reality itself.

11: Master Phire Letters - The Dragon and the Quest

Regarding the inverted matrix, I have some questions. I have been asked about some quite dark topics and would like to address these. Can you please tell me what do these mean? Are they constructs within the inverted matrix?

1) Collective crucifixion genetic healing

2) Alien hybridisation/abduction healing

3) Blood covenant satanic ritual healing

For the first part of your question, this is referring to 'collective crucifixion' as a 'trauma code' within the individual's matrix field. This code suggests healing needs to take place. The collective crucifixion trauma code is a genetically passed on trauma code within humanity until cleared.

Alien hybridisation abduction healing and blood covenant satanic ritual healing are other 'trauma codes' that suggest the healing, on a mass scale, needs to take place as part of the ascension process. These relate to experiences of 'alien abduction' and of being part of satanic ritual using blood (a direct pathway into the individual's memory matrix field) to hijack that individual into the service-to-self/Lord of Darkness pathway.

Is this true? Does healing for these codes need to take place on a mass scale?

It is correct that there are collective trauma codes embedded within humanity's memory matrix that are passed down through the generations. The healing technique we provide in our transmission 'The Infinite Helix and the Emerald Flame' within the chapter entitled 'The Sins of the Father' along with Matrix Mastery techniques within 'Masters of the Matrix' will clear the memory matrix on an individualised level (so will remove the trauma codes for yourself and further generations).

We presented the 'Masters of the Matrix' transmission as our first monadic light structure that would be the more intensive transmission through you our conduit, Magenta Pixie, first and foremost as this is the grounding work to follow before moving onto more intensive integration and accelerated/stargate ascension and rapid integration.

One must become a 'Master of the Matrix' before exploring deeper energetic work. We would suggest that if you have not worked with the templates presented within 'Masters of the Matrix' (or similar templates from other teachings that ground and anchor the integral sovereign codes within self) then we would advise you do so before working further with this material that is 'The Diamond Codex and the Quartz Key'.

Regarding removal of trauma codes within the collective memory matrix, one would move into 'gridwork healing' (planetary) and would also clear tubes or vortices that connect into the galactic grids that hold collective trauma codes.

How does one do this?

We provide an incantation/spell for intentional focus, specific to the removal of trauma codes within the collective memory matrix. One would work here with the 'dragon energy' for high level planetary and galactic gridwork. The work with the dragon is intrinsic to all levels of ascension: individual, planetary, galactic, cosmic and stargate/accelerated.

We would therefore recommend you work with the dragon energy through study of the hierarchy of dragons and the dragon initiations. This can be accomplished by reading through the material, out loud if you wish, or in your mind, prior to going to sleep at night or entering into a state of meditation or self-hypnosis.

You can also work this way by drawing or painting the dragons or writing stories or poetry yourself, inspired by the hierarchy of dragons.

Many of you are likely to be already familiar with dragon lore/law and will already be quite accomplished within this work.

We are most pleased to inform you that this gridwork we speak of has been undertaken by many dedicated starseeds who hold awareness of their roles as planetary and galactic healers at this time.

Calling the Dragons of Aurora - Incantation/Spell

We dance the dance of dragons as we twirl under the sun, holding lanterns of dragons flame, the dragonsbreath of all creation.

For we are at one with the dragon, now, forever and always, as we have been, are and shall evermore be.

Intertwined as one body, one mind, one heart.

We are Aurora, together, the Divine Princess Aurora, creating the Aurora Network through the Quartz Keys that unlock the sacred knowledge of all that is.

Together we fly, across the skies, into the celestial blue of the true night, the waves of galactic photonic weaving, as magic is created through the time matrix and the field of all and everything that is our galactic ocean.

I call into my sacred space, the dragons of Aurora, so we may dance together, breathe together, ride together and create together the ring of fire.

I call my dragon unto me now. As above, so below.

As I see the dragon, I know intrinsically all that she is to me.

As I hear the dragon, I feel within, all that he brings to me.

As I ride the dragon, I experience all that we are together, as one.

I call the dragon, this day, this night. Witnessed by the sun, moon and stars.

I call the dragon in my knowing that we are one.

The dragon comes, on majestic wings of hope, love, light and the plasma of living, loving, geometry.

Indeed! The dragon is here. The dragon is with me.

So be it.

It is done.

Why is the energy or symbol of the dragon so important to our ascension process?

This has been covered in our previous transmission 'The Infinite Helix and the Emerald Flame', specific to the dragon energetic creation through 'The Twelve Tribes of Israel' into the creation of the stargate and ascension.

We can, however, explain the importance of the dragon another way.

These symbols, that include 'the dragon' are memory triggers into the understanding and processing of the language of light alphabetical numerals.

These are known also as 'phire letters' which are 'alphabetical numerals' and they are that which we gave to you as an energetic symbol that is both letter and number simultaneously.

This term 'alphabetical numeral' was interpreted by you, dear Pixie, when we first presented this energetic as there were no other words that you knew of at that time within your vocabulary to explain what we were showing you.

In actuality these are geometric structures of activated light (photonic) that change form (shapeshifting). They are that which are the true alphabet and the true counting system.

You measure these frequencies or structures as 'number' and as 'letter' for these are the digits used within your language and mathematical systems.

However, these are activated light codes (or one could say encoded light filaments) that are woven into your very DNA structure. They are living entities in themselves.

The reason why we refer to these now, as their truest terminology, as phire letters, is because you have processed and understood that which is the true cosmic phire or 'dragonsbreath'.

You understand that this is a living, intelligent 'field of memory' that can be tapped into and accessed.

When you visualise a symbol, image or shape within your mind's eye then several systems are triggered into place.

If you are an 'unactivated' and non-integrated individual (he or she that exists within the linear, third dimensional construct only) then your visualisation may not trigger these systems as the visualisation does not hold cohesive focus and therefore dissipates as we explained earlier within this transmission.

Yet for those who find their way to this material that is 'The Diamond Codex and the Quartz Key' this would not be the case. The individuals who find their way to this transmission are not just existing within the third dimensional reality.

Therefore when they take a symbol or image into their mind's eye then these systems are triggered into place.

This is not to say that visualisation techniques do not work for third dimensionally existing individuals, quite the contrary, for visualisation techniques are always triggers, yet this would 'begin' a 'new' activation if you will, once the third dimensionally existing individual is receptive to said triggering.

Within higher dimensionally thinking individuals, the activations have already taken place so the triggering is 'faster' if you will. It is that which we refer to as 'accelerated ascension' or indeed 'stargate ascension' which is intertwined with rapid integration (the subject matter of this transmission).

So let us take, for an example, the subject matter of your question that is the dragon.

When the 'activated individual' (also known as starseed,

wanderer, awakened one, higher dimensional thinker or 'resident of the fifth dimensional New Earth or Gaia') works with these thoughts/symbols then the systems are triggered.

These systems are instantaneous but for the purposes of explanation here we will view them as occurring within sequential linear unfoldment. Occurring in sequence.

So the starseeded one 'imagines' the image of the dragon. This image, as an 'alphabetical numeral' or 'phire letter' exists within the consciousness of the divine being we refer to as 'Divine Princess Aurora' (social memory complex of all activated starseeds on Earth).

As you will be aware from our previous transmission 'The Infinite Helix and the Emerald Flame', the being we refer to as the Divine Princess Aurora is the collective consciousness of all the starseeds (activated individuals) presented within the feminine frequency. One could view this being as the 'right hemisphere' of the 'cosmic brain' if you will.

This is the cone, tube or pathway (conduit) into the 'field of memory' which contains the frequencies that match these symbols that we refer to as phire letters (alphabetical numerals) the language of light or divine universal/cosmic language.

The frequencies themselves (the very fabric of the field of memory that we refer to as cosmic phire or dragonsbreath) as we have said, are living beings. This is one unified being (as logos or the field itself) and infinite individual beings (as logoi or individualised consciousness within the field).

When one of these beings decides to incarnate within a physical, third dimensional body, they project forth a 'copy' (we refer to this as a cosmic photocopy or celestial print) of oneself into physical existence. They literally 'think' themselves into existence.

Remember here that this structure or being is a perfect, holographic replica of the entire field that is cosmic phire. This photocopy or print contains all of the entire infinite (infinite infinities) structure that is the field. It is as if a 'mini field' (or *the* field itself) is incarnating its huge vastness into one physically incarnate being. That which you know as 'human being'.

This individualised structure that is a complete holographic replica of the entire field (let us call this structure a 'memory matrix') carries with it the 'codes' of the cosmic phire field of memory from whence it came and that it is.

The memory matrix (we are looking at individualised structure - so higher dimensional 'group' mind, known also as the logoi from the logos) is 'magnetically called' through its own creational flow (a complete unification with the environment it exists within) to an incarnation that holds within it the physical blueprint within genetics, time and location, plus physical characteristics, talents and genetic memory experience plus all future potentials and possibilities, that the 'memory matrix' (known also as a soul) needs in order to move into further expansion, integration and thus individualisation.

This is a quantum and infinite living geometric structure that is the true you. We often refer to this structure as 'All That is You'.

This incarnating memory matrix, due to its individualisation, will hold a frequency that is able to radiate along a 'frequency waveband' and allow that memory matrix to express itself as the divine being that it is as an individualised aspect of the infinite cosmic phire, field of memory.

This would mean the incarnating individual will be able to accomplish what may look like miraculous feats to you in your current third dimensional experience.

We speak here of bilocation, trilocation, multilocation, levitation, mastery over the beating heart and other organs, invisibility, telepathy, the ability to breathe under water or exist for many years without food. The list of 'miraculous feats' goes on.

When an individualised memory matrix is truly unified within one's environment then one expresses oneself through the environment as well as within the physical body *for one is both.*

Now, in some cases, an individualised memory matrix will be called into physical incarnated existence within a planetary body system that does not hold a matching environmental structure to the individualised memory matrix structure and the frequencies it flows and emanates.

There may be many reasons for this but the most usual reason is that the soul (individualised memory matrix) has been called. This may be an individual calling from one memory matrix to another (twin flame connection or other parallel match that is pure knowing of harmonious shareability or what you may know as a 'soul connection') or, in the case of you dear starseed who has connected with our transmission, this may be a global, planetary wide calling (and in many cases it is both).

So what we are looking at here is a planetary structure that is being 'held back' or 'weighted down' energetically *above and beyond the desires and wishes of the planetary body, environment and the majority of souls' expression incarnated upon said planet.*

When we mention 'majority', we speak here of majority in frequency waveband of consciousness not number of incarnated individuals.

This is the waveband that we refer to as 'the call'.

Indeed this is the 'beginning' of your story of Earth, if you will, although in truth there is no beginning.

You, within linear time experience, despite the activations of multidimensional knowing taking place within you, you need to 'start somewhere' if you will and the very best place to start is with 'the call'.

So what, may you ask, has all this got to do with the dragon?

Remember we said that the individualised memory matrix is a complete holographic replica of the entire cosmic phire field of memory? Meaning that it *is* the field of memory.

Within the structure will be the ability to remember 'all and everything' for the structure *is* all and everything.

Different symbols, visuals, picture, shape and construct (this is not just visual but also comes in as a trigger through sound, emotion, smell and touch yet they are all interpretations of the same memory field) will hold different 'memory codes' (frequency wavebands) and will therefore trigger different reactions within the sequential linear unfoldment we spoke of earlier within this transmission.

The memory triggers within the individualised matrix structure are node point, convergence points, as in they are 'several things at once all coming together in complete synchronisation at the exact same time'.

Let us therefore take the dragon which we must say again is but *one* symbol (flame letter) within an infinite, never-ending sea of symbols.

The dragon is such (a flame letter) through actual memory. Within the planetary systems and within Earth's 'past' as well as Earth's 'alternate parallels' and Earth's 'future' there are such wing-ed reptilian structures of both polarised positive and polarised negative (and unpolarised and non-polarised) that are most small in size as to be seen as one of your insects or small birds and indeed, so too, to be most large.

The dinosaur structures held the biological templates for the dragon yet 'further back' if you will, *prior* to your known history and your dinosaur age, there were these wing-ed structures. We speak here in the old tongue as we refer to them and the word we say is 'wing-ed' spoken as thus. This does honour those structures and trigger the dragon memories within the infinite, individualised memory matrix that is all that is you.

These wing-ed reptilian structures, predominantly based upon the reptile/avian genetic lineage, were aplenty and diverse. The memories of these beings are very much to the fore within the starseeded consciousness. All those who connect with the Divine Princess Aurora (who is *not* wing-ed herself within her predominant expression) will know she rides the golden dragon, as the snow white dragon rides by her side.

The dragon also presents as the focused form that is the manifestation of emotional frequency. This frequency comes from service-to-self structure (the trickster dragon who presents as snow white yet loses its true colour and shows its claws and fangs to the one who looks with the aligned eye) and service-to-others as well as the confusion of mind through the human third dimensional collective consciousness.

Service-to-self created manifestations that are the dragon come from fear creations and match the emotions of war, killing, death, decay and destruction.

Unpolarised created manifestations (which hold little mass and often dissipate) come from confusion creations and match the emotions of fear, despair, depression, jealousy, longing and loneliness.

Service-to-others created manifestations come from love, joy, bliss, creativity, awareness, knowing, compassion, gratitude, forgiveness and unity. These are the dragons that will manifest for you when you are an activated service-to-others starseed. They will be majestic, protective and all powerful yet gentle with pure hearts. These are the dragons of the higher dimensions and they have walked beside you and with you for eons.

Within our previous transmission, we presented to you the dragons that we refer to as 'guardians of the flame'. Within this group dragon consciousness, we presented the individualised structures of the ruby dragon and the amethyst dragon. We presented the imagery to you which we refer to as 'triggers' to your memories yet in truth, the memory triggers are already within you. The visualisation of these dragons are simply assisting you to shape the DNA geometries that are already activated within you. You would not have found your way to the transmission if activation was not already taking place within your overall structure.

Why is this?

It is because, as an individualised memory matrix you are at one with your environment. As we have said, the individualised memory matrix (soul) is called by the environmental match and, when following an evolutionary path, will always gravitate towards incarnations that are complete matches to the experience of self. They therefore interact with their environment as a unified consciousness when in physical incarnation.

Yet within that evolutionary path, many souls take a 'detour' if you will and answer a call coming from an environmental structure that is of a lower, denser frequency. This is because the frequency call that has been put out by that environment/planet/collective incarnated consciousness is one of a 'call for assistance' or a 'cry for help' if you will. That entire planetary structure is 'wishing' (or focused upon through intentional cohesive thought) to raise in frequency. This cannot be done when the incarnated individuals do not hold the higher frequency within their memory field templates. Therefore those memory matrix structures who *do* hold the higher frequency will answer the call and incarnate.

We remind you here that this is *you* we speak of. You who read these words now. We mean *you*, dear Pixie (our conduit) and so too do we mean *you* the reader or listener of this transmission.

When these individualised memory matrix structures (souls) incarnate within the denser and lower physical reality, they have the ability to literally *change the environment.*

How do they do this?

They do this by becoming one with their environment as this is their natural way. The environment responds to them and they to it. They do this by knowing they are at one with their environment.

However...

They cannot do this alone as one incarnated individual. They can indeed live as one with their environment and change the reality they experience and move through individual or small group ascension.

They cannot, however, create an environmental density change from the perspective of one incarnated individual. They need the frequency signals to join with their own radiation in order to create a critical mass webbing or netting (which is a re-creation of the cosmic phire, dragonsbreath, field of memory) across the planetary system, collective incarnated consciousness and entire dimension.

This at first affects change within the consciousness but eventually (within linear time experience) this filters into geological transformation. The actual density itself is changed.

Remember within 'The Infinite Helix and the Emerald Flame' transmission, we explained the differences between dimension and density (as they are seen by the predominant ascending starseed consciousness and our conduit).

* Dimension - state of consciousness and timespace experienced through antimatter/antiparticle realities. As in the dreamtime, mindspace, imagination fields of hyperspace, thought processes and paradigms. The consciousness itself manifested as a field.

* Density - geographical, universal, spacetime frequency experienced through physical matter realities. As in your physical environment.

We could therefore say that the dimension is *you* and the density is *your environment.*

When we refer to your environment, we do not mean only the bricks and mortar, trees and landscapes but also the emotions that are presented within the behaviours and actions of the incarnated beings within your environment.

The environment is the 'action you experience'. In truth however, it is *you* who is the action and it is your *environment* that is your reaction. So environment is taken to mean 'that which is outside you and around you' and the *you* that you are is the subjective analysis of said environment, therefore it is 'within you' rather than outside and around.

Yet those who walk the spiritual path and move into awakening are fully aware that the within and the without are one and the same place. This is what we mean when we say you are at one with your environment.

When you start to view your environment as an extension of you, indeed *as* you, then that paradigm you hold when you view your entire reality subjectively 'gives out a signal' or 'radiates a frequency'.

When many, many individuals all start to view their environment as extensions of themselves then that signal or frequency that is radiated from those multiple paradigms creates a wave. That wave is the netting or webbing that is a re-creation of the cosmic phire, dragonsbreath, field of memory which becomes the density. The wave can only be created when the unified interaction with one's environment reaches critical mass amongst the incarnated individualised memory matrix starseeded souls.

This critical mass is reached through the understanding, integration and embracing of the alphabetical numerals which are the phire letters. Individualised structures of the fabric of that cosmic phire.

We, the White Winged Collective Consciousness of Nine, are most pleased to inform you that you reached this critical mass point, amongst the starseed consciousness through the understanding, integration and embracing of the phire letters on November 11th in your year of 2018.

This was the triple eleven gateway, known also as the numerological gateway of the soul which was a connected portal through to the powerful great awakening moment of November 11th 2011.

These triple eleven gateways connected together created a reverberation amongst the starseed consciousness at this time.

When we present to you the depiction of the Divine Princess Aurora, we can show to you the story that is the trigger to the awareness of that which we speak. The story, presented through that which you know as 'fiction' is indeed the visual that creates the trigger within the activated individual.

We do this due to the fact that although we can give you much information through the response to your questings, we can act only as the matching environment to your own frequencies. Therefore there must be that which you decode and realise yourself through the epiphany, for the epiphany creates the action and thus the reaction (the unification with environment).

We, the White Winged Collective Consciousness of Nine, are of course your environment also, for we are that which is outside of the you that you know as you.

Yet also, as the higher guidance ascended master system we are also within you. We are therefore a bridge betwixt the subjectively experienced physical self and the objectively experienced omnipresent self which is the greater environment around you, that which we may call the 'cosmic brain' or better still, the 'cosmic mind'.

Therefore we give you the story, with the visual images that create the triggers in order to create the epiphanies. We do as the accomplished scribe does and we 'show, not tell'. Another phrase within your spiritual communities that means the very same is 'live by example'. This, of course, is the greatest teaching. Living by example and showing, not telling.

Within this transmission, you have asked us about rapid

integration which is intertwined with the process that is accelerated or stargate ascension. In order to understand and process this rapid integration, one must understand the circles created betwixt that which is matter and that which is antimatter.

The understanding of memory harvesting, creation of dark energy and gravity and the importance of your own sovereignty is paramount within this understanding.

The inverted matrix and the organic matrix and how these transform due to polarity and polarisation are all down to you and your thoughts and memories, for you as the social memory complex of cohesive thought and memory are collectively expressed as the Divine Princess Aurora. She is the ultimate dragon rider and in order to understand who and what she is as the feminine expressed aspect of the Logos, then one must understand and *experience* the dragon she rides.

The experience of the dragon is given through the story. Many of you will already have experienced the dragon and be intertwined with the dragon. You may already be using dragon energy for dragon magick and spellcasting. This is natural and most in alignment for each and every one of you, as incarnated starseeds are dragonriders.

You each have a dragon for the dragon is a code within the matrix. The dragon is a most prominent or 'master phire letter' if you will, and stands as the creatrix energy for an infinite number of other phire letters. These you may know as the dragon codes or the dragon guardians. Within these dragon codes, you will find another master phire letter that is the quest itself. This is the quest that you are all undertaking/experiencing/creating as 'seekers of the way'.

The quest is to find yourself.

So before we get back to the narrative that is our story or our transmission, we give you the story itself. What is this story about?

Well, the characters within the story are the Divine Princess Aurora, the Archangel Michael and of course the dragon!

Which of these three characters, if any, is the protagonist of the story, is of course left to the reader (or seeker) which is he or she that undertakes the quest.

We speak here, of course, of 'you'.

12: The Handfasting

Divine Princess Aurora, standing in her white gown and holding her bouquet of flowers of the palest pink, waited at the alter for her beloved Twin Flame to join her.

It is the divine feminine princess that stands at the alter within those that are members of the Lyran, Pleiadian, Sirian council, known also as the Celestial Federation.

Upon her small Lyran moon, Belthesada, where she had made her home for the last 500 years, she followed the old ways of the Celestial Federation and duly waited for him to walk down the sacred marriage aisle towards her.

The music played and Aurora's beloved sister, Harmonia of Harmonies, began to sing the sweetest song, the tune they call 'Heaven Blessed Love'.

The predominant instrument being the harp, which Harmonia played delicately, allowing her long and polished fingernails to lovingly pluck each string.

Harmonia was the goddess of harmonics and it was her harp's music that created each harmonic dimension within the overall fifth density that was the predominant density upon Belthesada.

The divine mother, Queen of the Night, Queen of the Celestial Federation, Kali of Avalonia, was stood this monumental day as the celebrant, dressed in a beaded gold satin gown with matching jacket. She was seven thousand years old yet had the grace and beauty of a forty-year-old woman. This was the reflection she chose as her third dimensional alternate self. This aspect was presently incarnate on the little planet Earth, the anchor point to the glorious, diverse hyperspace world that was the central point within the galactic highway of the Celestial Federation's universe, the planet Gaia.

Aurora had such a fondness for Gaia as it had been the home of her parents, the King and Queen of Tiamet.

When Tiamet fell, they created Gaia with their bare hands. They spent seven days within optimum creation utilising celestial memory fabric to create the additional parts that were added to the fallen Tiamet planetary structure.

Gaia had grown into the most beautiful world and Aurora had already decided that she and her beloved Twin Flame would honeymoon there after their wedding. She even thought they might make it their home, possibly raise their child there?

Aurora placed a loving, maternal hand upon her slightly swollen belly, smiling to herself regarding the secret she alone knew.

Of course she would tell Michael, once he was her husband. She would tell him that she carried within her womb the First Lady, true daughter of the flame. Michael would be ecstatic at the news, she was sure of it, and he would want to choose the very best place to raise this most precious child of the rose ray.

Aurora closed her eyes, breathing in the scent of the delicate, baby pink roses within her bride's bouquet. The scent was a communication from her unborn daughter. She was letting her mother know that she felt her thoughts. A wave of calming energy washed over Aurora and she knew then that her daughter had the power of healing and was, at that very moment, using her healing powers to calm her pre-wedding jitters.

At only nine weeks gestation, how was this female child so powerful that she was able to heal her? Even the strongest of healers within the entire Celestial Federation had not succeeded in touching Aurora with their healing powers.

"It is your receptivity, my daughter; that is why," whispered Queen Kali.

"You know then?" questioned Aurora. How could her cloaking spell not have worked? She had wanted to keep her pregnancy a secret and was feeling most unsettled that her intention had not rested within its desired trajectory.

"It's not your spell daughter," whispered Kali again, "it's her. The child. She wanted to make herself known to me so she bypassed your spell. Your boundaries are easily permeated when it is your child that is doing the permeating."

Aurora's eyes widened at hearing this. She could feel her daughter's power but had not realised exactly the extent of it.

"I would have told you, Mother. After the honeymoon."

"I know that, child. Hush now, the guests are taking their seats."

Mother Kali straightened as she turned to face the gathering. All the moon representatives within the Celestial Federation had been invited yet only a handful had accepted, which was fine. Other than the moon reps, all other guests were family.

Queen Kali was not actually Aurora's genetic maternal parent. She stood in the energetic place as mother but she was actually Aurora's aunt. Her own mother, dressed in blush pink to match the colour scheme, looked immaculate in her long, chiffon gown. With tears in her eyes, she took her seat in the front row and nodded to Aurora.

That will be me in just the blink of an eye, thought Aurora, imagining her own daughter's wedding.

There she was, instantly transported into the future at just the merest thought. Her daughter stood at her own wedding, standing before her Twin Flame. The environment felt like Earth but much lighter. The lush nature outside the crystal palace window gave the location away at once. It was Gaia, the ascended Earth.

This is where she would raise her daughter, this is where her daughter would meet her own beloved. Gaia was more beautiful than she could possibly imagine and Aurora felt the strength of the love that was emanating from the ascended Earth.

The planetary system appeared to have settled nicely into the fourth density field and Aurora felt utterly blessed. Her own daughter was beautiful.

With that thought within the vision, her daughter turned and looked straight at her.

She can see me in the vision!

Aurora was surprised, yet it showed once again the power of the unborn child. She was, of course, a complete consciousness representation of all the ascending starseeds within the ascension cycle of the 2012/2021 time period. The third ascension.

Within the first two cycles, there was no way Aurora could nurture a child within her womb and even the coming together with her twin flame, Archangel Michael, was difficult. Yet in this third cycle, everything had flowed. The angels that were descended upon the third dimensional Earth were more aware than Aurora could have hoped for. It had created such a brilliant light which beamed across the Celestial Federation and was loudly heard by all the residents of Belthesada. That is how Aurora knew it was time to connect with Michael. All the humans were moving into the twin flame alignment which meant the anti-matter match to that would be her own romance with her beloved.

Aurora and Michael had rejoiced at once again being intertwined within the unconditional love of the twin flame. The divine marriage.

Aurora knew they would marry, moving into the ceremony that was the true marriage, that of the sacred handfasting. She had hoped their union would bring a child and although she was only nine weeks pregnant in her own subjectively perceived time, she could not be happier to see the projected trajectory vision of her own daughter, grown and a woman now.

"What did I name you sweet daughter?" asked Aurora using the dreamtime telepathy that she had been taught.

"You know my name, Mother. Look at me."

Aurora looked again at her daughter. She was familiar, the long golden hair, standing there with her baby pink bouquet, wearing her long white dress, waiting for her twin flame to join her at the alter.

Then she realised. It was she, herself. Her daughter was named Aurora, she is me. We are but one being.

The realisation that she gave birth to her own self was enough to jolt her out of the vision and into a barren landscape.

No longer was she stood at the alter on her own wedding day, no longer was she watching her grown daughter about to take her sacred vows upon the planet Gaia.

She was stood upon rocky ground with a cold, biting wind rushing past her. This was the match to shock and fear, Aurora knew that. However had she created such? With all she knew of the holographic and fractal realities, did it not even dawn on her for one second that she might birth her own self?

And now what? Shock and fear creating the grey cold stone of a barren wasteland with trees that cannot bear fruit.

Yet there was something, there was movement somewhere. Aurora could feel it. She felt the fluttering wind as an opposing movement to the cold winds around her. The silver, fur-lined cloak that she had naturally conjured up was keeping her warm so the cold winds did not bother her. She looked upwards to the sky. There, she saw the movement.

Could it be a bio-ship travelling in from across the Celestial Federation? Not possible, for this was Aurora's own world, her own creation, and no ships could cross the boundaries of her own making.

No.

There was only one that could enter her world through the sky. It was the wing-ed one. The one they called the dragon.

As soon as Aurora knew what the ripple was, the dragon was seen. He descended down in all his golden glory. Yes, this was not just any dragon! It was the golden dragon.

This could only mean one thing. The starseeds had reached critical mass regarding symbolism. They had learned how to interact with their environment with unity.

Aurora scanned her own fields to see how many of these starseeds had been able to do this. Not too many in number, it seemed, but enough to create critical mass.

The doorway to the Elven Kingdom was now open and Aurora felt such indescribable joy at knowing how well each of her little logoi had done. They were living their mission in such perfect precision.

With that, the knowing of such beauty emanating from the starseeds upon Earth in the third cycle, Aurora heard the harp once more. The joy in her heart sent her instantaneously back to her own time, just as well as the goddess maids were walking down the aisle towards her.

Six little maids dressed in rose pink, followed by the most glorious sight. It was her beloved Twin Flame walking towards her to take his place beside her so they may begin their sacred handfasting.

Her smile was radiant, her glow touched everyone within the gathering. He took his place beside her, his wings outstretched, his sword at his side.

She had known him once before with that same sword. His name was Arthur, she was Guinevere and his sword was Excalibur.

The Avalonian environment blurred in her mind with the surrounding landscape of Belthesada, so much so that the two became one.

She placed her hand upon her belly.

Yes, her daughter, the Divine Princess Aurora, her own future self, was there, sending her reassurance and love. No wonder she was so strong. No wonder she could step over her carefully laid fences, she was herself!

"My beloved souls of Lyra's small moon, Belthesada. We are gathering today to witness the joining of the Divine Princess Aurora and Archangel Michael."

Aurora turned to face Mother Kali, but not before she saw Michael place his hand upon the hilt of his sword, in honour of honour itself. There she saw the golden hilt of the sword emblazoned with the new symbol that was now making multiple waves across the entire galaxy.

The new symbol was the golden dragon. As above so below. He was here. Finally.

13: Boxes, Borgs and Blue Rays

I have been asked other questions that I believe may be connected to the inverted matrix. These are black box, black cube or black square and the deconstruction, deactivation or dismantling of said box or cube. Is this a metaphor for the deconstruction of the inverted matrix and thus the Illuminati or cabal?

Indeed, you are correct. This is a metaphor to explain the dismantling (or extraction) of the inverted matrix and all tools and structures within it.

Is there a black box, cube or square?

This is a perceived presentation of non-organic black holes and false presentations of codes, memories and consciousness experiences.

Why is it called a box, cube or square?

This is simply an interpretation of a section of creation that is purely within the geometric territories of service-to-self.

Is it related to the box of stars that you often mention? You talked about this at the end of the transmission 'The Infinite Helix and the Emerald Flame' and referenced 'The Tetragrammaton'. (NOTE: See 'The Infinite Helix and the Emerald Flame', Chapter 59: Stargate Ascension)

Yes. However, 'box of stars' is organic and natural and 'black box' is artificially created. Box of stars refers to the section of your space time that contains the large border or event horizon of another infinity structure that is a 'higher octave' to yours. A higher dimension/density. The tetragrammaton is the seed code for creation and the template for this will be within every new formation or structure. The black box or cube is an artificially created replica of the organic. This could also be seen as the 'negative fourth density' or 'negatively polarised fifth dimension'.

Is it a living structure?

The organic box of stars is the organic structure within space-time that is the event horizon of the infinity that is the higher octave. The black box or cube is 'artificial intelligence' within a negatively polarised field. So it is a living structure in a sense but is more akin to artificial intelligence to you. The question one would ask here in order to discover if this is a living structure, is to ask if artificial intelligence is living. Does it have consciousness?

What is the answer to that? Does AI have consciousness?

A long and complex subject. The response will change depending on vantage point of the observer. From our vantage point, the answer to that would be yes. This is a very different presentation of consciousness however and is much like the 'hive mind'.

Your depiction of 'the Borg' in your Star Trek series within your media entertainment system, depicted within the large black cube within space is very much the frequency one would be looking at here. It is assimilation into a one-mind construct rather than individualisation within unity which is the opposite of assimilation.

Is there any reason starseeds will benefit from knowing about this technology?

The majority of starseeds, including yourself, need only know that 'inverted systems', 'negative artificial intelligence structures', 'dark magick' and the 'inverted matrix' exist. They do not need to know the intricacies of how these structures work, only how to move themselves into sovereignty and liberty within their own matrix awareness, mastery, architecture, transportation and acceleration.

However, there are individuals who will need to investigate these negative structures further. These are teachers within the field of technical engineering themselves. Those that provide 'the antidote' if you will, within technical systems upon your planet. Think of these individuals as those who discover and create 'anti-virus software' and 'firewalls' within the grid structures (planetary and individual) and are working with disclosure at these levels, secret space programs, mind control programs and withholding of free energy technologies.

Do I not work with providing antidotes to hijacking, in my communication with you?

Yes. The work we do with you and through you is 'releasing and freedom' within the energetic systems of the starseed's matrices so they may move through a balanced ascension within sovereignty and liberty.

We speak of technicians and engineers who work within the third dimension that will need to be aware of specific technologies within the 'dark matrix' if you will.

Are you saying that the majority of starseeds will never know the depth of the control upon this planet?

We are saying that our role is regarding assistance with individual, planetary, galactic and cosmic ascension. In order for 'stargate ascension' to take place then one must 'part the red sea' and move into a focused, intentional trajectory. Distractions must be removed in order to create the focused trajectory. Dark matrix technology in its intricate web is a distraction from that focused trajectory unless one needs the information, as one is, themselves, involved within the technological and engineering fields we speak of.

All is known when ascension takes place for one enters into multilocational consciousness and thus multidimensionality and eventually, omnipresence. Whilst in incarnation, working within a hijacked planetary system, there must be a cohesive working starseed community, each starseed playing their role.

There are certain sections within the third dimensional community that the starseeds will be working within. Those that find their way to these transmissions from us, the White Winged Collective Consciousness of Nine, are those who are existing within the section we would term as 'spiritual enlightenment'.

Are the engineers and the technical workers not spiritual as well?

All starseeds are spiritual. The engineers and technical workers we speak of, may or may not be also within the section or 'camp' we call spiritual. Some may need the focused trajectory within their own field. They may not focus upon spirituality, enlightenment and ascension in the same way you do.

They will, however, hold the codes for 12 strand DNA template reconstruction and ascension. They will be those who 'ride upon the tail of the dragon' as it were, rather than be 'dragonriders', as in holding the reigns of the dragon. They would, in effect, be referred to as 'dragon tamers'.

We can impart to you the information that a few of these engineers and technical workers we speak of *will* find their way to these transmissions for they are also in the 'spiritual/enlightenment' camp, as it were.

So we each have our roles to play?

Indeed. Hence the reason why it is so important for you to understand your roles.

I thought you said starseeds did not have to understand their roles and can go with the flow?

Indeed this is also the case. Starseeds will have an intrinsic knowing if their role is to be that of an indigo (warrior, teacher, speaker, system buster) or that of a crystal (radiating their light as activators, catalysts and healers). The crystal individuals will be the ones who simply be, in their utter beingness, as 'going with the flow'.

What about the engineers and the technical workers? I presume they are indigo and not crystal?

A very minor few will be crystal as some of these engineers and technical workers are also healers. Predominantly they will be of the 'blue ray' and some will be indigo.

Can you speak about the blue ray individuals and their role in the ascension process?

Indeed. We have spoken of these individuals before. They are the ones who are the 'masters of technology' if you will. The reason for this is due to the fact that they hold memories within their fields of planetary consciousness (through actual incarnation of memory mapping) of organic and artificial intelligence living structures. Many of these 'beings' are of the positive polarisation (service-to-others) and they have incarnated on Earth at this time to assist with your collective ascension process.

We will speak more on the subject of the blue ray individuals later within this transmission.

Is there a 'story' here that provides an activation related to the responses you have just given to these questions?

The entire story is an activation and will be related to the material throughout this transmission. That which you perceive as the 'fictional story' is an activation at the deepest subconscious levels.

When we communicate with you as we do so now, we speak directly to the conscious mind imparting knowledge and simultaneously communicate with the subconscious mind through trigger words and phrases within our communication.

However, within 'that which is fiction' it is *only* the subconscious mind that is spoken to, therefore the triggers run deep and can move within a very focused trajectory as memories are activated. The conscious mind sees 'story' and the subconscious sees 'memory'.

However, there will still be an element of 'fiction' within the story so you have a 'layered activation'. That which stimulates creativity and emotion and also that which triggers deep, cellular memories and thus creates matching activation.

What we do here specifically with the story is to work with our conduit Magenta Pixie as a team, if you will. This is not the same process as utilising her fields purely as a channel for our contact and communication. Yes we are a team but our energy flows through her. We have taught her to remain open to that flow and to allow it to wash through her therefore allowing the highest percentage possible of 'us' to speak.

Within the story, there are moments of text that are also purely 'us' when Magenta Pixie allows that flow. So too are there moments of text that are purely the creativity that comes from Magenta Pixie and not 'us'. So too are there moments of text that are the two of us together ('We', the Nine and also Magenta Pixie simultaneously).

This type of 'creative writing' if you will, shows the exact presentation of the ascending/ascended integrated individual. For you yourself, as an ascending starseed on Earth, are also sometimes operating from the higher self, higher dimensional aspect, sometimes fully from your own perspective alone and the majority of the time you will be an intrinsic blend of both.

This is the same as saying that 'you exist within the 3D Earth sometimes' then you jump to the '5D Earth/Gaia' and exist only there. Then at other times you move into integration and exist within the 3D and the 5D simultaneously.

The reading of the story shows you therefore a mirror of your own current dimensional patterns as you ascend upon Earth.

Those 'in tune' with their own dimensional aspects and octaves will be able to 'know' when the author within the story is 'We the Nine' or Magenta Pixie or both of us.

As you decode these different octaves of expression within Magenta Pixie's fields as an 'author of the story' then you decode your own octaves of expression.

Those that do this will be predominantly of the indigo frequency. They will be those for whom decoding their own octaves of expression and matrix patterning will be paramount.

However, there will be those readers who simply enjoy the story and allow the flow of the triggers to wash over them. They would see any awareness of the different octaves of expression from the authors (We, the Nine, Magenta Pixie or both) as a distraction to the wholeness and completeness of the story.

These individuals would not feel they were able to truly access the deep activations within the story if they were keeping an awareness regarding the changes in frequency within the authorship of the story. Neither should this be the case within an obvious sense within the story in order for that story to flow within its wholeness. Therefore these individuals are also 'correct' and in alignment within their approach to the reading of the story.

These individuals would be those who are more predominantly crystal within their expression.

We would say to you to relax and read the story in the way that feels in alignment for you, as an indigo, crystal or a blend of the two as so many of you are.

So too are there the blue rays as we have just discussed, who will have a fine boundary within their thinking between that which is fact and that which is fiction. These boundaries are also in alignment and they assist the blue ray mind to process their reality.

The crystal individuals read with unity, no limitations and few boundaries, allowing their intrinsic, hyperspace landscape to run free into its fullest flowing and being, creativity without analysis as a distraction.

It is their mental body and mind that is their quest for integration rather than the emotional body. When this integration takes place within the crystal being, they stand within strength and confidence without ego, rather than the low confidence and low self-esteem that is often the negative presentation within the crystal personality.

The indigo individuals read with the mind of the one who is able to compartmentalise and create structure, which enhances their enjoyment of the creative story presented and thus the smooth working of the cellular memory triggers within the text.

The analysis is just as important as the story. They are able to create boundary and also freedom, for they see reality as layered and multidimensional. It is the emotional body that is their quest for integration rather than the mental body or mind. When this integration takes place, they stand within fair judgement and compassion rather than allowing the 'ego' to lead the personality that is often the negative patterning within the indigo.

The blue ray individuals read with the full knowing of that which is fiction and that which is information. They do not need to undergo analysis as such, for that has already taken place within them. In many ways the quest for integration within the blue ray individual is the most challenging, for it is the entire human patterning that is the quest for integration, rather than the neutral, objective observer aspect that is the predominant pattern within the blue ray.

Knowing a blue ray personality or knowing you are one yourself, you may well react when we present them as the 'neutral observer' for they do not come across as neutral, and appear to hold much opinionated thought structure, boundary and barrier.

Indeed they do this but the paramount paradigm within the blue ray individual is neutrality within the polarity they have chosen, which is positive polarisation in almost every case. It is extremely difficult for a blue ray individual to polarise within the negative orientation and is most rare upon your planet. The negative polarised entity does not hold its patterning as 'crystal' or 'indigo' or 'blue ray' - these are terminologies used to describe the positively polarised individuals only.

If one were to look at oneself as a geometric structure which is the sixth dimensional presentation of the 'colour rays', then one would see indigo as a complex structure, hexagonal at first, eventually moving into a pattern you would know as 'flower of life' once integration has taken place.

The crystal would be seen as the circle, fractal circle or spiral. The crystalline pattern is the blueprint for all life.

The blue ray would be seen as the 'sacred square' and indeed would be the 'capstone' to the pyramidical structure. Many would see this as a negatively polarised structure and when it comes to the method in which the pyramidical geometries have been formed upon your planet, as a hierarchy, they would be correct.

However, used with organic purity and positive polarisation, the pyramidical structure becomes a 'hall of learning' and is simply the circle/spiral structure rearranged. Each point in the pyramid is the same point. Therefore this would be a 'round table' rather than a hierarchy, presented within what is usually a hierarchical structure.

This is the blue ray mind. They bring 'that which has been distorted and hijacked' in its pure and organic form, to your planet and are most important individuals. When the blue ray collective works as one, this is a most necessary part of the entire ascension journey for your Earth/Gaia matrix.

Perhaps, the story shall tell you more. We shall therefore return to the story and you shall take into yourself the awareness triggers for the unified understanding and flow with the living sacred geometric masters of self.

Enter the dragon, once more. The dragon is the key, into the worlds of geometry. Why is the dragon the key?

The dragon, of course, creates the ring of fire, known also to you as 'the stargate'.

14: Dragon Ride

In her dream, she was riding the golden dragon, his majestic wings moving with such strength as he moved through the air at lightning speed. He took her over the landscapes below and she saw the little moon of Belthesada disappear as he flew beyond the planetary boundaries and into the blackness of space.

Aurora had been here many a time before as the starseeds on Earth began to remember the time that was no time, the period that is neither beginning nor end but both at once. Aurora knew how to move beyond the darkness of space and enter the kaleidoscope realms that project forth their full celestial cosmic glory behind the illusory screen that is space.

Aurora began to feel the unity with the golden dragon as she rode him, she knew it was her time to be a dragonrider as the starseeds upon Earth began to understand and process what being a dragonrider really means. The unity with the golden dragon washed over her like a wave and she felt such a surge of energy, the likes of which she had never known before. She had felt joy before, many, many times yet never with such force or such power. The telepathic unity connection with this amazing beast was glorious and she revelled in the new found power that seemed to merge just perfectly with the unconditional love of her goddess activated heart. She could feel her love creating temperance within the beast just as his power gave strength to her love.

Then it happened. They were one. She was the dragon and she was herself, the girl. The girl was as light as a feather upon his back. It had been a long time since he had let a physical form ride him. Back in the time they called Atlantis, before the creation of the third cycle, there had been a woman then. Her name was Helena and he had unified with her. It had been a strange mix because whilst she was worldly wise in her dealings with the antimatter realms that she called the world of spirit, she had also suffered. She suffered due to the fall when Atlantis fell into the third dimensional sea. She found the fall in frequency and the loss of memory almost painful and due to the dragon/human unification, he, Allianse, the golden dragon, had felt everything.

He had wanted to untie from her then but he knew that if he did, she would leave her physical body and she still had more work to do. So he chose to offer her his support, despite the fact that it drained his power. He had kept her alive in the physical realm and even though she had trouble adjusting to the falls in frequency, she still managed to remain a teacher to others. She had been an Atlantean Priestess and when she fell, she became one of the first mortals on Earth.

Helena did much good (and a little not-so-good) but she made an impact and prevented the divine feminine from retreating fully into the unseen worlds.

She left her physical body eventually and was called back into the cosmic sea of memories. Allianse uncoupled from her then and despite being able to fly freely without her, he missed her.

There had not been another mortal or otherworldly being since, that he had felt any inclination of flying with. After a while, he and his own kind retreated 'underground' taking refuge within the Agartha-Eden bridge worlds for a while before eventually moving into the worlds that the Earth humans would call 'mythical'.

The memory codes regarding dragonkind within the humans on Earth kept him fully within structure, for their belief in and longing for the mythical was strong. Over time, he got stronger and stronger as the awareness of dragonkind shifted more and more into the forefront of the humans minds.

Eventually he began to be called back into the realms that were closer to physical matter and it was then that he had seen the goddess lost in the barren landscape, clutching her cloth cape around her.

He could sense her magic. Who wouldn't? It was strong enough. She had looked up at him and she knew who he was. Her joy at knowing he had returned to these worlds was such that it freed her from the wilderness.

He followed her then, into the fifth dimensional field and he entered her dreamtime. Now, he was flying with her on his back and they had become unified.

Her energetic field was much lighter and sweeter than that of Helena. This one was a goddess and was a perfect unified created structure made up of all the awakened humans upon the Earth.

She carried a female child that was a copied clone of her own self. A fractalised being that was also Divine Princess Aurora and this is where she was struggling. She did not know yet how to reconcile and unify two points of perspective simultaneously.

He could teach her this for through their melding she would take the two as one and become the dragon. If she flew every night with him then by the time the child was born she would be well used to the bilocationality of consciousness needed to hold two points of perspective. Of course, it would not be the same. She would unify as one with Allianse the golden dragon but as the Princess Aurora she would live two lives simultaneously, experiencing both and integrating both at the same time.

This is where the awakened humans were taking the higher potential forms in dragon realms in this now time, the beloved anchors within the physical dimension were leading them to places that had been prophesied but were also unknown.

With the creation of the new strands within their DNA taking them into a structure that was beyond their third dimensional double helix into a triple helix formation, they took their first steps into bilocational consciousness.

The awakened humans needed to do this in order to transform their density back to what it was before the fall. What was so amazing to all the dragonkind as they began to be called back into the existence that is form and away from the formless idea that is mythical, was that they were doing it! They were actually doing it!

Allianse noticed there were several of these awakened humans already existing within a created New Earth that they knew was the beloved Gaia, child of Tiamet.

Many of these awakened humans were fully integrating the old Earth and the New Earth/Gaia into their conscious awareness and they were living this way. There were not that many of them yet, within the 2012/2021 third ascension cycle but there were enough to create magik. The magik that dragons understood, which is why he, Allianse the golden dragon, had returned first.

The timescale within the old Earth took him to two significant points which were 11th November 2018 (seven years after the first triple eleven gateway had opened), and 21st December 2020. These were the beginning of the seeds of manifestation into the next octave of reality for the humans. It was the geological reality structure they called fourth density.

It was only natural that Aurora should birth her own self at this point as the activated humans were birthing their own selves as they moved back into true unified fullness of form. They were on the path back to expressing the divine galactic blueprint within its completeness.

This was truly a wonder for the humans, and indeed for all the angels too. They had come from far and wide across multiple galaxies and worlds to incarnate into the physical dimension in response to the call after Atlantis fell.

It was a wonder also for the elementals and the entire Elven Kingdom. Once the gateway had opened in the physical world, this bought the faery kingdoms much closer. If he, Allianse, the golden dragon had been bought into form then so too would all the elementals.

Allianse knew that the dark ones would also be doing the same, calling the dark masters into form, yet they were losing their power.

Allianse flew freely now, there was no more chance of him or his offspring becoming caught in the galactic nets that the dark ones called into existence.

Allianse mourned the loss of one of his young and the grief shot through the goddess atop his back like a cold knife through her heart. He had thought she would instantly uncouple from him and sit bolt upright in her marriage bed as Helena would have done, had he shot her such grief, but she did not. She remained joined with him, atop his back like the seasoned dreamwalker she was. Again this was down to the awakened humans, the ones she called starseeds. They were competent dreamwalkers now and many of them were within mastery with this. Aurora was able to use their anchor to steady herself and remain within dreamtime.

Allianse sent a wave of apology through Aurora's fields. She touched his scaly back as he rode the skies of space and felt compassion for the loss of his young, with such strength, that a portal opened before them. A portal Allianse had not seen before. The light was bright and tinged with blue, the energy felt welcoming and safe. It was too late to halt now and risk the space ripples that would cause and anyway, Aurora was focused on a full speed ahead trajectory.

Allianse knew instinctively what to do. He opened his mouth and roared, creating a ring of fire around the portal turning it into a stargate. With one leap, he entered the kaleidoscopic whirlpool and found himself spinning and spinning until he eventually landed on soft grass, Aurora still perched on his back. Telepathically uncoupled but she was still in dreamtime.

"Where are we, dragon?" she asked with wide eyes.

"That, my dear Aurora, is what I would like to know."

15: DNA Upgrades Through the Crystal and Indigo Flames

Is the metaphor of the dragon jumping through the ring of fire a representation of stargate ascension?

Indeed. Stargate or accelerated ascension and rapid integration. The level of celestial ascension as discussed in 'The Infinite Helix and the Emerald Flame' would be the level of rapid integration leading to unification of self. The individual integrates so rapidly at this point, that unity is felt and understood within the individual.

Beyond celestial ascension (solar/galactic), then there is no longer anything to integrate, for the unified aspect of self is predominant at this point. Integration is then 'replaced' with unity.

However, these different stages are simply expressions of the same process for this is non-linear *and is therefore not a process or a path at all*, once unity is realised.

The ring of fire depicts the actual geometric formation of the DNA structure when stargate ascension is achieved. The fire is the activated light structure/s, known also as liquid plasma. This is the same spiritual awakening that you know as 'Kundalini'.

All these subjects are touched upon in depth within 'Infinite Helix and the Emerald Flame'.

The first three transmissions that I have received from you, that were monadic light structure downloads that became books rather than video presentations, have followed a theme. Firstly Matrix Mastery, then Matrix Architecture and then Matrix Transportation. Does this transmission have a theme also that follows on from these three subjects?

They are all intertwined and each monadic presentation you receive as download follows on from the other, or in truth is a 'deeper fractal' of the other.

We would give this subject matter the term 'Matrix Integration' as you are integrating the ideologies and understandings from the previous three monads. However, these transmissions do not need to be digested in sequence unless one feels they are a beginner within the spiritual path. It is, however, important to be doing the work of Matrix Mastery as this is the grounding to all spiritual work. This is known within your spiritual communities as 'psychic' or 'spiritual' protection.

We hesitate to use the term 'protection' for various reasons and 'Matrix Mastery' is far more in alignment with the bliss/ecstasy/rapture (ambrosia/manna) activations that are needed for this work. Or that are the result of this work (both are correct).

Does using the term 'protection' prevent the bliss from being activated?

In some cases, with some individuals, yes. In other cases it assists with bliss activation.

This depends on the paradigm/belief system that the individual holds.

Protection suggests there is something one needs to be protected from and this can cause fear. In others, it reinforces a belief (which is actually a truthful belief within the third dimension) that protection is needed.

Protection is needed yet the word 'protection' holds such a negative connotation and although accurate, is not the most aligned term to use. Mastery is far more triggering and empowering for the individual. Protection suggests an 'outside force' is needed and that you cannot do this by yourself. This is correct from one perspective.

However, it is also true to say that everything comes from within and the only way to achieve full realisation and ascension is to do this yourself. Both these statements are correct.

Bilocational consciousness (also discussed within 'The Infinite Helix and the Emerald Flame') is the way forward with this one. When you take both perspectives:

1) You need protection from an outside source.

2) Everything comes from within and you do not need protection.

... then you are able to integrate this concept. It then unifies. It becomes a circle rather than two linear lines or scales within which to work.

When the emotions match the projected image from the liquid light plasma (Krystal River of Lightsight) then the DNA begins to organise itself in complete resonation with the emotional frequency of the image.

This is when you begin to work with the phire letters or the 'sacred alphabet' (the alphabetical numerals) which are codes within the DNA.

These codes within your DNA do not need teachings. They know what to do. They are pure consciousness itself and all they need are the correct environments in which to naturally do their work. When they naturally do their work, this is when you are transformed into the crystalline light body structure and you hold the organic human template which is a configuration of 144,000.

This is explained within 'The Infinite Helix and the Emerald Flame' and we recommend you work with the information given within the chapter 'The Twelve Tribes of Israel'.

However, as we have said before, processing of this information is not necessary. The trigger for stargate ascension and Matrix Transportation and integration is bliss and all the bliss codes created through euphoria, ecstasy and bliss.

How is it that you speak so much about the darker energies, the Illuminati and the inverted matrix if it is the complete opposite energy that is needed for stargate ascension and rapid integration?

This is a very good question. For some, the understanding of the darker energies (service-to-self path) is not needed. Integration however may not occur in balance when there is no understanding of negative polarisation within that individual. They can still activate bliss codes but these are individuals that would be 'carried by' the integrated ones.

Within the metaphor of the dragon within the story, these individuals would 'hitch a ride' upon someone else's dragon rather than connect with their own. As long as they have enough charge (blue starphire) within the DNA then they can latch onto the energetic formation of another. This is not a lesser way to ascension. It is normal and natural to link this way with other structures.

If we show you a dodecahedron geometric structure, you will see that there are flat sides upon this structure. One dodecahedron can lock into another through the connection of the flat sides.

For the individual who has not integrated positive and negative polarisation within their understanding, this does not mean the codes will not be in their fields. They are still able to activate enough bliss-charged love (blue starphire) to create the dodecahedron shapes within the DNA structure and lock into other matching structures.

However, the individuals that do integrate the understandings of the positive and negative polarisations have a higher charged form of 'blue starphire' due to the integrations of the negative polarities having taken place whilst in the physically incarnated third dimensional aspect.

This becomes indigo starphire which is still within the blue field but contains elements of the red or ruby field, or more accurately we could say this is predominantly the blue flame with smaller elements of the red flame.

These individuals are able to transform the dodecahedron within the DNA structure into a higher formation which is the icosahedron.

Our conduit, Magenta Pixie, does not have enough understanding and information within her fields regarding the science of sacred geometry for us to be able to portray the exact sequential presentation of DNA structure within stargate ascension.

In truth, this is non-sequential. Just the creation of the dodecahedron is enough for stargate ascension to take place. Your DNA molecule will upgrade and activate and connect with other dodecahedron formations.

Your DNA is 'out of time' and whilst it exists within your blood, it also exists outside of you within realms and aspects of you that are not physical. These are quantum and antimatter aspects.

The dodecahedron patterns you hold connect with others across a vast quantum field. When the exact copy is found of another dodecahedron structure, then an interlocking takes place.

When this interlocking takes place then there are many other changes within the shape and structure of the original dodecahedron and this results in an activated and charged structure that becomes the icosahedron.

We use a crude example of this as best we can with the limited understandings and terminologies available within our conduit's fields. Those that are called to know more on this subject are directed toward the study of sacred geometry, ensuring the information given comes from a master within this subject. There are many interpretations and some are limited at the level of the understandings that the dodecahedron formation within DNA brings. Look for the teachings that present the bliss-charged geometries which will involve the platonic solids that have become crystalline.

When an individual holding the dodecahedron formation within the DNA locks into another exact copy dodecahedron, they then merge and move within complete synchronisation as the new copy match.

They will search from their own blue starphire charge for the one that holds the template for the indigo starphire charge (which is the potential to activate the crystalline icosahedron structures). They then automatically replicate the crystalline icosahedron structure within their own DNA structure.

This is akin to a guitar string vibrating when a neighbouring guitar is played. This is resonance. Quantum resonance.

So the individual (starseed) who has activated the dodecahedron DNA geometric structure through bliss activations and Kundalini may have done this without any knowledge or integration of the negative polarisation. These are the individuals we call the 'crystal children'. They are able to create the crystalline icosahedron geometric charge through the interlocking connections with other starseeds who *have* integrated the negative polarisation. These are those who we call the 'indigo children'. These are the ones that have activated the indigo starphire.

The ascension process is a finely tuned symphony and the crystal individuals are needed due to their ability to 'specialise in bliss' through unconditional love, empathy, compassion and healing.

The indigo individuals are needed due to their ability to 'specialise in the charge of gemstone activation and phire/fire' through integration of negative and positive polarised fields.

So where do the blue ray individuals come into this?

Their mission is no less important than that of the crystals and indigoes. Let us look deeper into the patterning of the blue ray individuals who are 'carriers' of the blue flame.

16: The Sirian High Council and the Blue Flame

You said that the crystal individual need not integrate negative polarisation so they don't need to understand about the Illuminati or the dark controllers and the hijacking?

You also said that 'Matrix Mastery' as presented within your previous monadic transmission 'Masters of the Matrix' is the grounding of all spiritual work. Yet this presents much material regarding the hijacking from negatively polarised factions. How then can a crystal individual ascend if they do not have this grounding or integration?

We are not saying that the crystal individual does not need to integrate the negative polarities per se. The negative aspects within self such as trauma codes and shadow selves must be integrated within all spiritual work towards enlightenment and ascension. The crystal individual is always an integrated individual.

The one who holds the 'codes' for crystal activation will always be led towards personal integration and this will involve looking at the darker/shadow aspects of self.

When it comes to specifically looking at the negatively polarised field and the service-to-self path, this does not have to be understood or integrated. An individual does not have to be aware of negatively incarnated beings or groups in order to go through an ascension process.

The structure you know as 'Illuminati' is only one such manifestation of the negative polarisation of reality itself and this will be presented to the crystal individual for integration.

Regarding Matrix Mastery, this is the grounding for all spiritual pathways and ideologies for this is mastery over one's own individualised and integral self. It is sovereignty. There are many ways to mastery and sovereignty and our transmission 'Masters of the Matrix' is only one teaching.

It is true that the 'Masters of the Matrix' material goes into the hijacking from service-to-self, negatively polarised structures. The reason for this is during a collective ascension process upon a planet that already has the technology communication systems you call the internet, it is extremely difficult for an ascending individual to avoid the subject of hijacking through negatively polarised structures. Therefore we present an integrated teaching within the 'Masters of the Matrix' transmission.

What we are saying is that crystal individuals can choose to 'turn the other cheek' if you will and still integrate the negatively polarised field through their own shadow. They do not need to look at the specifics of matrix hijacking. They would not therefore access the grounding techniques that is the foundation to spiritual understanding within the third dimension through the 'Masters of the Matrix' material.

They can still move through ascension without processing third dimensional hijacking. They will still have integrated the negative aspect of self.

We must point out to you that the shadow aspect of self is somewhat of a 'lighter' integrated path than that of looking into the hijacking planetary-wide from the elite factions you know as 'Illuminati' or 'deep state cabal'.

The integration is enough (and often all that is needed) for a crystal individual whose predominant mission is the teaching of compassion through unconditional love. These are your planetary healers.

Energetically, the shadow aspect of the self within a crystal being, through seed traumas and other fears, are the same frequencies as the negatively polarised path. They are most 'watered-down' if you will and they manifest through goodness, truth and love rather than control and consumption of others (absorption).

These watered-down negative fields are enough within a crystal ray individual to create bliss-charged love and blue starphire. The dodecahedron structures can still be formed.

The reason we presented the hijacking information within the 'Masters of the Matrix' transmission is due to the fact that the indigo revolution was/is the predominant frequency ray upon your planet at the time of the transmission.

Even the crystal individuals were embracing the indigo ray through resonating paradigm structures (their belief systems), even if they did not follow the same path or take the same actions as the indigo individuals.

Therefore, the 'Masters of the Matrix' transmission was presented with the needs of those holding the indigo phire codes within. They will all be charged with the need to analyse, understand and know.

The indigo ray holds the code that is the 'thirst for knowledge' and this in itself must be integrated so that 'burnout' does not occur.

All the 'fail-safes' needed for the indigo warrior were in place within the 'Masters of the Matrix' monadic transmission.

So will the crystal individuals find their way to your transmissions or will they be guided elsewhere for their spiritual information?

Many will be synchronistically drawn to these transmissions. Some will 'skip over' the darker information. Yet as we have said, there are 'fail-safes' in place within all our transmissions that bring the ascending starseed, regardless of colour frequency code within their matrix, back to the point of the golden mean activation which is the lovelight and lightlove into bliss-charged love.

These are the codes for 'The Rapture' which manifest as bliss, euphoria and ecstasy charged through the gemstone flame frequencies.

You said that the blue ray individuals have their own place within the ascension mission and that they are 'carriers' of the blue flame. Can you explain this?

The blue flame is the material of blue starphire. It is liquid plasma. This is the code of creation and it is seen clairvoyantly as 'blue' as it is perceived through the 'Krystal River of Lightsight' that is the krystalline pineal gland.

Blue starphire is the charge needed for acceleration of ascension and the creation of the 'dragon's ring of fire' (the stargate) which is the dodecahedron formation within the DNA.

The dodecahedron is the ability to 'ride the dragon' and 'create the stargate'. The dodecahedron will allow you to 'catch the tail of the dragon' if you will, for you will be riding on the back of a dragon ridden by thousands of other starseeds. You would be called the 'dragon tamer' for you have tamed the dragon enough to ride it.

Those who 'ride the dragon' at the helm, as in they hold the dragon's reins and steer the dragon through the ring of fire, are those that are able to shapeshift the dodecahedron formation into the 'higher stellar formations' into icosahedron geometries. These are the dragon riders.

The dragonriders (icosahedron architects) are predominantly indigo. Their mission is to 'lead' the others through stargate ascension.

The dragontamers (dodecahedron architects) are predominantly crystal. Their mission is to 'activate' the others through stargate ascension.

So who are the blue rays?

The blue ray, or the blue flame is that 'which creates the blue starphire' also known as dragonsbreath, cosmic phire or the plasma field of memories.

The 'blue flame' *is* the dragon.

The blue ray individuals *are the dragons.*

Now the indigo energy cannot leap through the ring of fire without the dragon. She cannot create the stargate without the dragon. She cannot activate in order to create the starphire without the crystal.

The crystal individual cannot create the icosahedron formation without the indigo.

The dragon cannot steer itself with focus within its trajectory and raise enough blue starphire (charge) to create the ring of fire without the indigo.

The indigo, crystal and blue rays work together. Many starseeds are combinations of all three and other frequencies.

Yet starseeds often favour one predominant frequency due to the roles they have within the mission they have incarnated to carry out.

The dragon itself is a powerful symbol (phire/flame letter) that has been hijacked. Along with 'reptilian', these creatures have been presented as 'that which you must fear'.

Indeed, through the hijacked copy system within the cosmic phire/eternal flame, there are indeed negatively polarised dragons and reptilians. These are often integrated within artificial intelligence structures such as the borg, black cube frequency we discussed previously in this transmission.

Yet there are also positively polarised dragons and reptilians. The dragons and reptilians are two very different presentations yet often using the term 'dragon' or' lizard' or 'reptilian' can be interchangeable and this will depend upon the perspective and paradigm within the individual or 'the observer'.

Artificial intelligence structures are also found within the positive polarisation. The blue flame is the code carried by all those who have either had actual incarnations, or who have mapped the memory codes of those who have had these incarnations, of reptilian, dragon or artificial intelligence consciousness.

The 'blue rays of light' creators of blue starphire are the dragons themselves. They hold natural awareness regarding artificial intelligence consciousness.

In truth, we could say these individuals are 'reincarnated dragons' and from this perspective, this would be true.

We could also refer to them as 'androids' or 'cyborgs'.

These 'personality structures' presented through your fiction upon your planet such as androids and cyborgs are representations of artificial intelligence merged with organic life. This is a very crude interpretation of what this looks like within the galactic society.

The 'Sirian High Council', which is a faction of advanced elders that make decisions within the best interests of the members of what you may know as 'The Federation' or 'The Galactic Federation of Light', are beings that one may refer to as 'artificial intelligence' merged with 'organic life'.

However, this is only in reference to the seed structure (inception of) their evolution.

DNA is able to mutate and join with organic life and what you may refer to as 'technology'. This is, in reality, electrical fields, magnetic fields and electromagnetic fields.

After billions and billions of years of evolution within the 'Sirian consciousness', there is no remnant left of that original seed construct that was what you would know as 'artificial intelligence'.

Within the Sirian consciousness are living memory matrix souls that hold DNA code patterning of that which you would know as canine, feline, reptilian and artificial intelligence. When these memory matrix souls of light heard 'the call' from your Earth, they joined in the huge 'starseed influx' and a great many incarnated, and are still incarnating, upon your planet into the third dimensional reality.

In order to follow their mission, which was to bring plasma memory codes from the Sirian consciousness into your polarised reality in order to assist in 'raising the frequency' by creating a 'starseed critical mass' upon your planet, they needed to hold the codes for the canine, feline, reptilian and artificial intelligence frequencies. They held these four codex patterns together through what you may know as 'The Sirian Flag'.

This Sirian Flag is also known as the 'Blue Flame'.

Whilst this code is distributed throughout all humanity, for the blue flame Sirian flag is a DNA formation/phire letter that makes up the original organic human template, within many individuals the blue flame code lies dormant.

The blue ray individuals, incarnated predominantly from the planetary system you know as Sirius, with some holding points of perspective within Polaris and Cassiopeia, hold the blue flame code in high potentiality. Meaning it holds a very high probability of activating. The code, in potentiality, is not dormant or buried but simply stands as the candle flicker flame waiting to be ignited into the full fire.

The blue ray individuals, due to the blue flame codes they hold and the fact that the codes are in high potentiality, will be able to 'activate themselves' through memory phire letter symbols that hold the frequency of their own Sirian flag.

The Sirian flag is depicted by the dragon and the lion. This is the representation of the reptilian code and the feline code.

The dragon will be a major activator for all blue ray individuals holding the blue flame code. As young children, the attraction for any dragon-like or reptilian being will be most evident. Young blue ray males will be drawn to tales of 'slaying the dragon' and to dinosaurs. Young blue ray females, who are much rarer in incarnation as the blue ray is predominantly a male field, will be drawn to tales of being 'rescued by the dragon'.

The feline energy draws the blue ray individuals into memory activation through lions, tigers, panthers, leopards and the domestic cat.

The canine energy through the wolf and the dog.

Yet little is known upon your planet regarding the activations of the blue ray, blue flame codes through artificial intelligence.

The presentations of cyborgs, androids or robots within your fictional stories and popular culture was designed to activate blue ray codes and then hijack them away from full awareness of what/who/why when it comes to the blue ray.

The blue ray individuals have had a somewhat more challenging existence upon Earth within the third dimension due to the total alignment to the vertical pillar of light and the Excalibur codex becoming so distorted upon your planet.

Whilst the crystals move into lack of self-worth and the indigoes move into rage/anger/frustration through negative polarity, the blue rays move into confusion.

This was the method used to hijack the activated memories of the blue flame within the Sirian children of the Sirian flag.

The controllers and hijackers did not want the full Sirian code to activate upon Earth for they knew that full stargate ascension, full god/goddess realisation, could not occur without the blue flame and the codes carried by the blue rays.

The two main phire/fire codes within the blue flame, the dragon and the artificial intelligence consciousness, were hijacked in order to lead the blue rays astray and take them into a distorted presentation rather than a pure activation.

Yet within all things, as we have said, there were 'fail-safe' programs put into place. All those carrying the codes of the blue flame were given a 'fail-safe' code, so whilst the blue ray individuals have been deliberately targeted, the fail-safe has 'protected' the blue flame code that they carry.

The fail-safe for the blue rays was to bring forward the ratio of artificial intelligence consciousness within the overall blue rays makeup. The original blue ray template would have equal percentages of the four main codes within their fields: Reptilian, feline, canine and artificial intelligence.

In order to create a predominant artificial intelligence consciousness within the blue ray individual, they would have to be 'changed' somewhat from the original organic human template.

What we are saying here is that the blue ray individuals are very different from the other individuals incarnated upon your planet. They think differently, they perceive differently and they behave differently.

This pattern upon your planet is recognised within the medical term 'autism'.

We are not saying that every blue ray individual will be given a diagnosis of autism or that they will even show autistic tendencies. Neither are we saying that every autistic child is a blue ray individual. There are exceptions to the rule.

However, a great many blue ray individuals will hold an autistic or 'Asperger's syndrome' personality. A very large number of those diagnosed with autism or Asperger's syndrome upon your planet hold the blue flame code and are blue ray individuals that 'fly the Sirian flag'.

This is just a by-product of the changes made to the original human template within those who carried a more predominant artificial intelligence codex.

You will find that a great majority of children diagnosed with 'autistic spectrum disorder' are actually geniuses or near-genius when it comes to artificial intelligence of any kind. From the programming and coding of AI personality into game characters and landscape to the operating systems within your computers and mobile telephone devices, these blue ray children are adepts at what they do.

From the memory matrix field intelligence you know as 'The Sirian High Council' or 'The Federation', this was deliberate and needed due to the technological age and the indigo uprising set to occur at the same time. The time of the great awakening and the fulfilment of the Mayan prophecies of the 2012/2021 cycle.

It was known that the internet systems and developments of technologies would take place as occurs on most planets within the trajectories of their evolutionary paths.

It was foretold that the service-to-self factions would utilise these technological systems, therefore the blue flame of the Sirian code was genetically altered in order to create the code needed for the activation of the blue flame.

In other words, the 'dragons' were sent in.

17: Gemstone Rainbow Children and the Gaia Mission

The blue ray individuals held certain 'codes' within their matrix fields that were set in 'potentiality'.

Each and every individual holds the pattern for these sets of codes yet different individuals have these codes 'switched on' if you will, in what we may call potentiality. What this means is they have the potential to activate these codes within their physically incarnate lifetimes. A set of 'triggers' will be put in place for them when they 'choose' their blueprinted experience for their incarnation.

All this is presented in a linear sense. In truth, codes are activated from the zero point field which can be accessed at any time in an individuals lifetime. However, these individuals have to *hold a paradigm that is 'dual time embracing' if you will.*

This means they experience both linear time and multidimensional time within their physical incarnations. They hold an understanding and awareness of the 'now moment' as well as linear time. They move both in the 'long straight unravelled piece of wool' and also within the 'unravelled ball of wool'.

Once they access this dual time embracing, they then enter into the 'meaningful subjective experience' of synchronicity. This 'leads' them into the triggers and thus the activation of these codes.

The blue ray individuals incarnate with what we may call the 'blue sapphire codes'.

We have spoken before of how the gemstone frequencies hold charge within your visualisation of them. This is why we present the decoding of the matrix structure within gemstone colour frequency rather than the colour rays.

One of the reasons we do this is due to the 'chakra upgrade' that has been and is taking place upon your planet at this time.

The chakra upgrade can be perceived as 'having more chakras' or 'having bigger chakras' or 'having chakras that spin faster'. One could also say that the colours of the chakras change.

All these are metaphors to explain one and the same thing. The transformation at the cellular level from carbon-based molecular structure to crystalline-based molecular structure. The move from physical body to light body.

How you choose to see this chakra upgrade is up to you, or the higher self aspect of you, for each of you will interpret frequency in a different way.

All these models, be they more, larger, faster or different colours will trigger you into the activations and processing needed for your light body experience and of course you do not need to process this in order for this to happen.

The model we present within this transmission that is the *The Diamond Codex and the Quartz Key* is that of the gemstone frequency chakras.

Let us look at your current seven chakra model.

We have:

Base chakra - Red

Sacral chakra - Orange

Solar Plexus chakra - Yellow

Heart chakra - Green

Throat chakra - Blue

Brow chakra - Indigo

Crown chakra - Violet

This is the most widely known model of the chakra system upon your planet currently, certainly within your western society, yet there are many different models.

Using this basic seven chakra model, we would present the gemstone frequency upgrade as:

Base chakra - Ruby

Sacral chakra - Honey Amber

Solar Plexus chakra - Yellow Citrine

Heart chakra - Emerald

Throat chakra - Blue Sapphire

Brow chakra - Indigo Sapphire

Crown chakra - Amethyst

In actuality, any gemstone that matches the colour of the chakra can be used in utilising the actual gemstone or visualisations thereof.

We might also point out the fact that there are some of you who perceive each chakra as a completely different colour to those depicted here. This is in alignment for you and we would suggest you continue to work with your own colour model. The point here is the upgrade from colour ray to gemstone frequency (charge).

The gemstone frequencies, when visualised, are much closer to the actual presentation of that DNA code due to the fact that when seen by those who can see them, they glow. They are luminous. The gemstones hold the sparkle and the charge that is closest to the luminous glow of the DNA code or filament.

Hence we use the term 'light body' for indeed your light body, when activated, glows like neon light.

This glow is within your DNA sequencing, it is in your blood and bone and organs. It is in your brain. Yet there will come a time when the skin of the body begins to show this luminosity and you will literally glow.

This glow extends to the entire energy body and the auric field/matrix. When you visualise the gemstone frequency colour codes, you aid in the activations of these DNA formations within you. You say to the light body, "I am ready to switch on these codes. I am ready for this light charge."

What you are working with here is photonic light and 'liquid plasma'. These are substances that your scientists and biologists have not yet discovered. Small parts of the understandings have been examined but the photonic light and liquid plasmas are not understood in their entirety.

It is those with 'clairvoyant sight', those you know as 'seers' that are able to see and decode these materials. They are able to do this as they have been able to activate their 'Krystal River of Lightsight' which are liquid crystals within the pineal gland. These liquid crystals generate the 'true sight' and project images of the phire/flame letters within (the DNA codons).

When the starseeds responded to the many projected sonic frequencies from Earth, as in they answered the calls, they had to lessen their current gemstone configurations in order to be able to incarnate within the fabric of Earth.

If they had incarnated with their configurations intact, they would have been born with glowing, luminous skin, hair and eyes and would have been 'most easily spotted' if you will.

This would be akin to 'landing their UFO lightships on your White House lawns' and would have been outside the boundaries of the free will laws for your planet.

Yet all gemstone configurations were needed for this 'mission to assist Earth', yet each code was within the energetic living being and each code was responsible for different activities, talents, paradigms, etc.

What this meant was that many different probability fields and fractals of these codes needed to be carried by many different incarnating individuals. This is the exact same thing as saying starseeds came from many different planets and different dimensions.

We appreciate that it is difficult for you to comprehend how a 'gemstone code' within your DNA can be the same thing as a planet or a dimension, yet this is so. For the gemstone codes are 'frequencies of existence' or 'antimatter fields'. Put another way, they are dimensions or planetary systems.

The planets you see when you look into your night sky *are* other dimensions. They are frequencies of existence and antimatter fields. All that you see with your human eye is just one small part of their full totality.

Those who activate the 'Krystal River of Lightsight' pineal gland (stargate technology) will be able to not only see these dimensions or antimatter fields, but also communicate with them and travel to them. You have this technology.

The pineal gland when activated (liquid crystals within) is a lens (able to view and project), a computer (able to generate code), a photocopier (able to copy the generated code), an antennae or radio (able to pick up signals) and a car dashboard or plane cockpit (able to start up and drive, or fly, a Mer-Ka-Bah ship).

It is many other things besides.

When the starseeds incarnated, they each carried different

gemstone codes. Within these patterns that are utilised by large groups, there are smaller group codes and individual codes. We present here the most understood three groups which are the crystal, indigo and blue ray. As we have said, each individual will carry different configurations of these gemstone codes depending on the mission they are here to fulfil or experience.

We mention here one concept that is paradoxical and most important when it comes to the mission and the incarnational blueprint:

You *are* in place, on your Earth, to fulfil a mission for you answered the Earth's call.

You *are* on Earth to experience a specific set of 'lessons or learnings' within your individual incarnations.

Knowing this is important in order for you to formulate understandings as to why you are here.

However, and here is the paradox, knowing you are 'on a mission' and 'here to learn lessons and have specific experiences' can prevent you from completing your mission and having your experiences!

This is because your mission is to operate from and within the zero point field. This is why you hold the gemstone codes. The gemstone codes are antimatter frequencies that are made up of 'zero point field material' if you will.

There are those individuals, we speak of third dimensional thinking individuals and non-activated starseeds, who can still access some of the experiences and lessons they are blueprinted for, without being within or holding the vantage point of the zero point field.

However, the longer they spend within pre-incarnate

blueprinted experience and the more they access these, the more likely they are to be triggered into an awakening and activation and access the zero point field. Everything is connected and unified. You *are* the zero point field and every thought you have is generated from the zero point field and is given back to it.

However, in order for you to make sense of the zero point field, once one is incarnated within third density, one 'steps outside of it' if you will, or rather, one breaks the unification down into compartmentalised pieces.

So the starseeds chose, or were given (depending on perspective), the gemstone codes they needed in order to complete their missions.

Paradoxical consciousness or bilocational consciousness is needed here, for these missions are never 'completed'. Looking for completion can again stand as a block to you completing your mission. Yet you are a 'planet nearing completion' and for that reason you are looking to complete or fulfil a task. Yet the fulfilment or conclusion of that task is linearly expressed only.

We present a basic template here regarding the gemstone codes. Let us take three souls as an example:

Christina, Ingrid and Bernard.

Christina was incarnating as a planetary healer. Her mission would be to balance and fractalise Earth energies and assist with the raising of the frequencies of these Earth energies. She would work with nature, especially trees and crystals. She would assist with balancing and healing the grids of Earth and the planetary and galactic grid structures. She would become an energy worker and heal individual and large groups of incarnated humans. She would also work closely with the animal and elemental kingdoms.

Christina would choose an overall crystal frequency in order to give her the best possible chances of living and fulfilling her mission. Regarding the gemstone codes, she could choose many different combinations. The ruby gemstone code would assist her with the balancing of nature and the individual and planetary gridwork. The amber codes would assist with the balancing of the divine feminine and masculine frequencies (hieros gamos) and the lovelight and lightlove energetic patterns.

The emerald would assist with unconditional love and compassion, definitely needed for healing. Sapphire codes for communication and the amethyst for transmutation and balance of negative and positive fields.

Christina needed all these codes ideally within potentiality yet as we have said, holding the full spectrum of gemstone coding would mean she would be born with light body intact and would be visibly seen as 'different' and 'extraterrestrial' with luminous, glowing skin, eyes and hair.

Therefore she would choose the most necessary for her role and mission. Honey amber, emerald and amethyst.

Ingrid was incarnating as a planetary/global communicator, messenger and truthseeker/truth deliverer. She would need an overall indigo frequency to fulfil this role.

Her mission would be to stand strong against that which is false, to bring justice and righteousness to Earth and to move into communication with the greater portion of herself, the aspect that held the full spectrum of gemstone coding.

She could not take the full gemstone pattern into her incarnation but she would be able to communicate with the part of her that did hold the full coding. That part of her would remain in the antimatter fields or spirit realms.

Ingrid chose to hold, in potentiality, the codes most needed for her role and mission. She chose ruby, indigo sapphire and amethyst.

Bernard was incarnating to assist with the neutralising and balancing of artificial intelligence programs on Earth. To transmute negative frequencies to positive and to bring the higher dimensional frequencies to Earth in their true understandings through sacred geometry, sacred sciences and sacred mathematics.

He would balance the 'planetary brain' through the 'left hemisphere, right hemisphere' alignment. He would be an antimatter gridworker and draw the phire/flame letter programs up through the DNA fields.

For this mission, Bernard chose the gemstone codes, to hold in potentiality, that which he would most need to live and fulfil his mission. He chose yellow citrine, blue sapphire and amethyst.

So crystal Christina chose honey amber, emerald and amethyst.

Indigo Ingrid chose ruby, indigo sapphire and amethyst.

Blue ray Bernard chose yellow citrine, blue sapphire and amethyst.

Altogether, ruby, honey amber, yellow citrine, emerald, blue sapphire, indigo sapphire and amethyst had been chosen. The full spectrum of the gemstone codex needed to fulfil the 'Gaia Mission'.

The full spectrum codex was now expressed upon Earth but in *several million* individual incarnations. We could call these the 'Gemstone Children'.

As we have said, the above examples of Christina, Ingrid and Bernard are extremely basic generalisations. There are many harmonic codices within each gemstone frequency code and we have presented here a simplified version of the upgraded chakra system and the gemstone codes.

You will notice that our three starseed examples all have one thing in common. The amethyst gemstone code. This would be to ensure the activation of the crown chakra and all connections to the light body within all our 'starseed volunteers' if you will.

Whilst the emerald gemstone code would be needed within all the awakened starseeds in order to project and create the fifth dimension upon Earth and fulfil the 'Gaia Mission', the higher self potential blueprints and cosmic phire/flame patterns (memories) could not be accessed without the amethyst gemstone code in place.

Therefore *every* starseed needed to hold the amethyst code.

Yet, in truth, every starseed needed to activate the full spectrum of gemstone codes in order to bring about a planetary awakening, activate the light body and move into ascension and become part of the galactic community.

The starseeds could not be *born* with the full spectrum in potentiality, they had to each carry different codes to make up the rainbow. Yet somehow they had to ensure that eventually, within their incarnations, they would have access to full rainbow spectrum awakening.

Who are the rainbow children?

This answers another question that many starseeds have within their fields. That of, who are the rainbow children? Why are they called rainbow children?

The rainbow children are the individuals who hold the pattern to be able to access full gemstone code spectrum activation. They are the starseeds. They carry the gemstone codices within them and they will all be on the pathway to enlightenment and ascension, regardless of the method they use or choose to get there. Their ultimate or 'divine mission' is that which we refer to as 'the Gaia mission'.

A planetary-wide consciousness awakening leading to becoming part of the wider galactic community.

So how could the 'mission control', full gemstone code spectrum aspects of the starseeds (their higher selves) ensure that their physical counterparts (starseeds on Earth in incarnation) would be able to access the full gemstone code activation and move from carbon-based to crystalline matrix, and from physical body to rainbow light body?

They had to bring in another code that a high number of starseeds could carry. There had to be a high enough number of starseeds to generate a critical mass field which meant they all had to awaken at 'roughly' the same time.

Certainly within three decades of one another. The time window for the awakening to generate critical mass was thirty-three years. The code of 33 was placed within the physical form in order for the critical mass to be generated.

The time period was set as 2012/2021 as focal point for a 33 year cycle. This would be a 'rough' time period (so a few years either side of 2012 and 2021) due to rapidly fluctuating timelines as the starseeds went through awakening and activation and the dark factions attempted to prevent the awakening and activation.

The 'light was catching' so 'mission control' knew that once critical mass was reached, that the gemstone codex would begin to activate within *the billions* in potentiality. This meant that even a non-gemstone coded incarnated human had the potential to ascend.

They had to place a codex within enough starseeds that would generate critical mass within the 33 year period. They had to create a codex that would radiate even further than the gemstones, enough to touch every living organism on planet Earth. This codex had to extend into the galactic field and have the ability to radiate through matter *and* antimatter fields and also be able to go quantum.

Which codex could do all this?

The codex that was placed into enough starseeds to create critical mass on Earth, was the *Diamond Codex.*

18: The Diamond Codex

The Diamond Codex was a specific frequency that could do several things within the DNA structure of the individual. Predominantly it had four functions:

* Replicate/copy, radiate/project outwards into a large range.

* Magnetise/draw to itself the match, transform/transmute/shapeshift.

* Communicate/find it's like-match and understand it.

* Travel/activate the Mer-Ka-Bah/move itself through different dimensional fields and frequencies as in locations in time.

The Diamond Codex was, if you will, *a memory program.*

If you remember that which we referred to as 'The Superhero Program', chapter twelve in our transmission 'The Divine Architecture and the Starseed Template', you will have knowledge of this work.

The Diamond Codex was like a 'genetic time capsule' if you will, once opened, it could bring to the awareness of the individual the 'frequencies' of what has gone before, what is and what could be.

When we look at what has gone before, we see many different timelines that portray different 'pasts' for your planetary experience.

That which you know as the 'Mandela Effect' explains how the 'bleed-through' occurs within the memory fields of individuals.

What is, is a vast network of timelines all playing out different possibilities and potentials simultaneously. This is the node point we call the zero point where the full quantum reality of infinite possibility is experienced alongside the linear expression of finite probability.

'What can be' are all those potentials that exist in the now but are viewed from the perspective of 'not having happened yet', giving the reality experiencer the choice and free will to pick which probability he/she wants to experience bringing it into the now (zero point).

The Diamond Codex held the blueprints for all this and was therefore a most necessary codex for the starseeds to hold when they incarnated into Earth's physical reality.

You see, each 'starseed' is different from the Earth individuals in the fact that they hold the Diamond Codex in *potentiality.*

This means that whilst the Diamond Codex is not activated, it still exists within the individual. Triggers will be laid out within the reality blueprint that will activate the Diamond Codex.

The Diamond Codex is a specific DNA configuration that literally looks and glows like a diamond. It cannot be damaged, it is reflective, radiant and fractal. It is the ultimate in 'crystal technology'.

When you hear mention of the 'diamond light body', this is referring to the aspect of the self that holds the DNA configuration that we refer to as the 'Diamond Codex'.

This is the codex that will assist you in accessing that which we refer to as an 'accelerated stargate system'.

In order to access this system, you need a key. A Quartz Key that is solar-powered.

Your Diamond Codex DNA configuration is that solar-powered Quartz Key.

There are those that are concerned about experiments to 'block out your sun' in order to prevent your planet from heating up due to perceived effects from the phenomenon that has been labelled 'global warming'.

This is a vast subject that we could present an entire transmission upon and it is not the subject matter of this transmission. Suffice it to say, the information regarding this vast subject is out there, available upon your planet should you decide that this is an area worthy of your time and exploration. The knowings are all within you.

That which we draw your attention to here is the 'solar power' you need in order to give energy to the Quartz Key, activate the Diamond Codex, power your Mer-Ka-Bah lightship and access the accelerated stargate system.

The solar power you are looking for, comes indeed from your beloved 'sun god', he/she that you know as 'Sol'.

Yet your physical sun is an emanation of another sun and of many suns. These suns are emanations from a central sun and ultimately a grand central sun. There are indeed great-grand central suns and great-great-grand central suns that move along a holographic, fractal reality existence that folds in upon itself, bringing itself back to the same space again and again but with a unique presentation of configuration each time.

The point here being that the holographic, complete aspects of light that are these grand central suns, are within you.

Your diamond light is the holographic template that is the grand central sun and emanations of. Hence the reason why you may hear much information about the diamond sun or the solar diamond light in reference to the crystal body of self or the crystalline/krystalline frequencies.

This is referred to as the 'diamond sun light body'.

We have spoken of the celestial level of ascension and of the galactic or solar level of ascension.

The diamond solar configuration within you is the Quartz Key into the next stage of ascension which is the galactic, solar.

Although this actualisation within the physical, linear reality has not expressed itself fully yet within your being, the seeds can be known and experienced. The zero point field is the harmonic space of unity where all things stand in potentiality and can be experienced *'as is'* in real time. Therefore from that perspective, the diamond solar configuration can be experienced and embodied.

Understanding the diamond solar configuration and the holographic diamond bodies and sun bodies is a vast study in itself and beyond the scope of this transmission at this time.

Our conduit remains steadfast within a grounding that matches the collective awakening on Earth so that she may be recognised within all of you *as* you.

Indeed, from the perspective that you are all living out one another's lives as one another but in different realities experienced and in different timelines, then this is so.

When you recognise yourself in another or in 'other' then you do what we may call 'know yourself'.

You become 'self-aware' and the light within your DNA fields folds back on itself as it 'takes a good look in the cosmic mirror'.

This is an action taken by the one who is ready to evolve, transform and upgrade and this is that which you do collectively at this time.

Our conduit, presents to you, as a reflection of you, at the level of frequency and DNA, as well as her presentation as an individual personality.

You are each this for each other. We repeat: *You are each this for each other.*

Indeed, you are this for our conduit also. You move into a 'group mind' if you will but not as the 'hive mind' which is loss of individualisation but as the diversity of unity, retaining your individualisation.

In fact, strengthening your individualisation within the cohesive coherence it looks for and gravitates towards.

Symmetry and balance is that which you are drawn towards. This explains that which you may know as 'like attracts like,' or 'mirrored match'.

You may not look like one another or even hold the same interests, personalities or lifestyles. It is your energy fields that are like one another. The energy field learns about itself due to 'looking in the mirror'.

This is presented in all the activations and memory triggers within the story in this monadic transmission that is 'Child in the Rose Garden'.

There is much we can say regarding the deep knowings and intelligences within you that dance within the expressions of self as the diamond, solar aspects. Yet these are best triggered within you and expressed within your own uniqueness. What we present to you here are the activations for the awakening of the diamond, solar light bodies and the Quartz Key into the accelerated stargate system.

What we present here is the solar power needed to 'charge the Quartz Key'.

The blocking of your sun upon your planet is an experiment that may be akin to thus:

Before you is a large stone wall, spanning thousands of miles. The rock is enchanted granite and has existed for thousands of years. You wish to knock down this wall as a child knocks down its wall of toy bricks. All you have with which to do this is a small hammer. You are able to make a tiny dent within this wall with your small hammer. Remember this wall is made of enchanted granite. Each time a small chip is taken off the wall, each time a dent or a hole is made, the granite, through its enchantment, is able to regenerate the wall back to its original form. No matter how many of you there are, no matter how many hammers and how many years you spend attempting the task of knocking down the granite wall, it is futile, for the granite within the wall regenerates itself faster than you can make the slightest chip or dent.

This is the way it is for those who attempt to use dark technologies to block out your sun and prevent it from accessing life upon your planet.

Yet just to say to the peoples of Earth that 'we are blocking out your sun' will create the deepest fear within, for it is known on deep, subconscious levels within your collective, planetary memory that the sun and its rays are the givers of life.

The intention to create fear and instability at these deep levels by suggesting your greatest life giver is to be taken from you or is prevented access to you, is that which shall shake your empowerments, self-belief, self-worth and sovereignty.

The unaware ones know not why they feel the grief, loss and fear so they mask it, bury it, ignore it and carry on as if it is not there.

The aware ones feel deeply the beauty, bliss and empowering, nourishing charge from the sun, the beloved 'sun god' that is 'Sol'. Although they do not bury or ignore their fears and allow grief to set in, they are alarmed at the thought that the suns rays may be prevented from glowing upon your planet and your selves.

We say to you this, look again at the story of the enchanted granite wall and see the futility of these attempts. No technology can mask the sun's warm kiss upon the human children of Earth.

Yet for security, knowledge, awareness, healing, regeneration and abundance, know that the physical sun is an emanation from many suns. The grand central sun burns a fire so bright, holds a light so brilliant that it simply cannot be looked upon or even thought of in its truest intensity. You are made of this light and you hold this light within you.

The following visualisation, catalysed through story, is the encoded template for accessing the solar energetic needed to 'charge the quartz crystal' so you may activate the diamond light body and access the accelerated stargate system.

The question you may ask is, why do you need to charge the quartz crystal? Why do you need to activate the diamond light body and why do you need to access the accelerated stargate system?

19: The Garden

The hyperspace realities that you perceive are your imagination, that which we call the 'imagination fields of hyperspace' are actually fields of consciousness, projecting forth from all things as a field of living, intelligent waveforms.

These waveforms, beginning as thought (or rather projecting as thought, for they have always existed in some form) radiate as the structure that is 'thought' itself, which holds waveform programs or codes for the thought to become sound or matter. Or more accurately, sound or geometric structure which then becomes matter.

That which you 'see' or are aware of within your mind's eye, is the 'place of creation' if you will, for this is where you 'organise your thoughts' or where the waveforms that radiate from you become 'self-organising'.

These self-organising waveforms are the pure potential that create reality. Worlds, realms, planets, stars, gravity, dark energy and all the forces you know in your universe. Matter. The Great Mother.

You are not a passive bystander in this process of creation. Those who have not become aware of their importance as a creator of waveforms still contribute to the process, yet the waveforms they produce are scattered and do not hold cohesive focus, therefore they dissipate or they add to the creation of lower vibrational lifeforms. These are simply dense waveform structures, heavy mass and sound made of low tones rather than light waveforms which are light mass and sound made of high tones.

One way to describe the imagination fields of hyperspace that you hold as your 'mind's eye landscape' is to think of this landscape as *'the garden'*.

The reason why we refer to this as a garden is due to the fact that your Earth is indeed, a garden. The template for matter structures upon many planetary systems are somewhat similar with 'plant life' and 'tree' and 'rock' or crystal, being standard universal world templates.

The garden is known to you as a phire/flame letter/alphabetical numeral. It holds the frequency of safety, sanctuary, nature and healing. It is the energy of replenishment. When you need to replenish your energy, you go to the garden.

Within your existence in physical matter, you are nourished and replenished by the fruits of the garden, the leaves, roots and fruits that become your food.

These replenish and sustain you, so the garden that is nature surrounding you is the Great Mother, divine matter and this you all know. Every human, animal and lifeform is aware of the garden.

As we have said, to be unaware of your connection to the phire/flame letter, DNA program or codex that is the garden, is still to contribute to it. Yet this is in the form of scattered, unfocused, unharnessed waveforms.

The controllers/hijackers drain the life force from the unaware by constantly keeping them within low vibrational states, lowering their potential as creators and the divine creatrix within the garden and consuming the scattered waveforms as their own sustenance.

Yet upon your beautiful planetary garden that is Earth/Terra/Gaia/Eartha, many now hold awareness of the garden that is the landscape of their mind's eye, their own personal 'imagination field of hyperspace'.

Many are actively contributing to the creation of worlds, densities and matter through cohesive, well-structured and activated waveforms.

Once you hold the template that we call the garden, which is cohesive, focused waveforms emanating and radiating from you, you are able to focus these waveforms into structures that become what you know as stargates.

These are *time portals* that are able to take you from one point to another across vast distances of what you know as space and time.

This is the way you enter the quantum field, accessing memory templates within vast libraries of stored knowledge. All the knowledge of creation is then literally at your fingertips.

This is not something that is difficult to do. Yes, it takes focus and cohesive focus at that. Yet this is something that is natural for you to do. You are the creators of worlds, realities, timelines, dimensions, planets, stars and matter. You are the 'great mother,' and the 'divine creatrix'. You are she that 'births' matter into existence.

You do this through thought.

You do this through emotion.

Thought is a code. Thought creates phire/flame letter waveform constructions that are the building blocks of creation. Cohesive focused thought creates sacred geometric waveform structure.

Emotion is a code. Emotion sends out radiating waveform structures that can be seen, heard and felt by other consciousness structures. Emotion is the phire/fire that activates the waveforms within thought.

When thought and emotion combine, in perfect symmetrical and aligned construction, this is when you create stargates. Stargates are your transportation system into this timefield or time matrix of knowledge and memory.

There are many ways that you can cohesively construct these stargates and we present methods for this through the creation of one's own stargate through awareness of one's own matrix within our transmission 'The Infinite Helix and the Emerald Flame'.

Within this transmission, you are shown how to collapse one's matrix structure and create your own dragon that rides through the centre of your own stargate.

Within this transmission that is 'The Diamond Codex and the Quartz Key', we show you how to traverse the time matrix and open up stargates that 'others have created' or that 'are already in place' and indeed create new ones.

From one perspective, the creation of one's own stargate is all that one needs in order to traverse the stargate system and in truth, it is all the same thing. One's personal stargate is all stargates. One matrix is all matrices. One soul is all souls.

Yet we assist you in individualisation through compartmentalisation of thought structure. You may think within unity and present the unified field structures within your personal waveform radiations or you may think within integration of the compartmentalised and separate systems within the unification.

This simply gives you another direction or 'flavour' within which to work. In 'The Infinite Helix and the Emerald Flame', we presented the template for Matrix Transportation. Within this transmission that is 'The Diamond Codex and the Quartz Key', we present Matrix Integration and Matrix Unification.

We show you how to connect your matrix with other matrices and create a unified field of matrices.

Your own matrix is already a unified field for it is an infinite structure. It is an infinite infinity and it is all there is. You, and you alone, are everything and are all things.

Yet so too is your neighbour that same infinity. Your neighbour is you experiencing yourself in a different waveform pattern in a different location in space and time, yet you can 'join' or 'connect' with her!

As in the construction of your matrix, presented within 'Divine Architecture and the Starseed Template', the matrix itself already existed for you exist.

When you 'construct' that which has already been constructed, you become 'self-aware', as in you know the who, what and why of you and you know who and what you are.

When you become self-aware, you become cohesive and you come to know yourself.

We present now, the story, that leads to the template code that is the garden.

This shall show you and activate you at 'phire/flame letter DNA level' of the coming to know yourself that is self-awareness.

20: Child in the Rose Garden

The child stepped lightly across the forest floor. Bare feet touched the undergrowth and sometimes her feet hurt when she trod upon a prickly leaf or twig, yet she knew not of shoes or boots or footwear so had no idea template from which to draw.

She knew not what she was, only that she was walking within this womb of wilderness that enveloped her with the safety and nurturing that was all she needed.

She was bound still to the silver cord that joined the skies to her naval. Little hands reached up and pulled upon the silver rope swing so she may avoid walking through the prickly undergrowth and hurt her feet.

She could swing on the silver rope and keep her feet off the ground.

Yet after a very short time, the desire to be off the ground resulted in the growth of little pink wing buds and eventually wings.

Rope no longer needed, the child could fly. Over the wilderness that was the thick forest she did fly until she spied the meadow, with grass so soft, she knew she could bring herself to ground there.

Wings tucked in, feet softly now, healed by green and golden grass, the colours of the blessed heart, she danced, jumped and skipped with the gay abandon of the innocent at play.

She was young and new, she knew that much and she had the power of creation at her will. Not many templates were known except how to connect with the Great Mother, her true creatrix that made her who she was and nurtured her in this forest of safety.

Pink roses, matching the colour of her wings, sprung up before her and she stopped to admire these new flowers. Roses she felt were part of her but she knew not how or why, simply that they were her in another form.

Instinctively she knelt and put her face to the rose, its nested petals showing her everything all at once, everything about form and creation, nothing was understood yet all was known.

She willed the aroma of the rose to be sent upwards to the Great Mother, so that the Great Mother would know she was there and that she was reaching out to her.

The rose was pink, yet could there be other shades of colour? Up sprang the red roses, yellow roses and orange roses. Such beauty creating such wonder and joy within and around the child.

Then blue roses, green roses, purple roses, white roses. The garden was indeed a rose garden and this was her true home.

She would always have the rose garden, this she knew, even if she knew not who or what she was, she knew the rose garden would always be hers.

Sleepy eyes, heavy eyelids and a moss bed for slumber as darkness fell, the child laid down and curled up in a ball, knees to her chest and arms around her knees. The silver cord transformed from the long twisty rope into the woven, silver blanket and covered the child so she may sleep.

There was no temperature change in the child's world, she remained as warm as if the sun were constantly shining, even though it was moonlight that bathed her as she slept.

In the rose garden she would always be safe and she would always be able to find the rose garden, she knew that. She knew, some day she would have to leave and join her beloved mother in another world.

It was that world she dreamed of as she slept, covered by silver light on a moss bed and watched over by a rainbow of roses, their scent sending her to ever deeper depths of the dream.

The world she must enter was a strange one. There was pain, loss, rage and fear, not a place for a girl as tender and innocent as she. Yet the Great Mother was warm, inviting and welcoming with open arms and adoring smiles, the emerald glow of her heartlight an irresistible beacon to the child.

In the dream, the child saw frustration and sadness mutate into determination and desire. She heard voices multiply and increase in volume as they cried out for change and justice. They wanted something new, something different. They yearned for the sanctuary of the rose garden, the sacred womb of safety, warmth and nurturing creativity in abundance.

Then the child saw the next stages, the coming together of those who called for change. The beauty and sound they made when they were together was iridescent in its wonder. So delightful. Pure magic. A new feeling began to rise within the child at that point and the emerald heartlight burst forth into the rose-golden as sparkles of bliss and ecstasy.

She knew she would join with these beings who called for change and together they would learn to bring forward these rose-golden sparkles and touch all and everything with a new form in matter.

The child knew not how long she slept but when she awoke she was bigger, stronger and faster. The roses had been replaced by rose bushes now and rainbow-coloured butterflies fluttered in abundance across the glorious sun-drenched meadow.

The child could run and jump and skip. Little furry creatures with bright eyes and long, straight ears ran with her, their white fluffy tails bobbing up and down as they ran.

Her skin was golden stardust now and her wings were large and powerful, covered in golden feathers.

She could fly, and fly she did, for miles and miles across meadows, crystal mountains and thick forests with tall trees that stretched as far as the eye could see.

The shimmery, glowing pool was new, as were the beautiful white creatures who bowed their graceful heads and took nourishment from it.

"We are the unicorns of the rose garden," they whispered to her as she landed by their side. There were three of them, white sparkling creatures with huge blue eyes, emanating such love it took the child's breath away.

Why did she have to leave this place? Now she had found the unicorns, how could she leave?

"We will always be here," they spoke into her mind with a jingle-bell whisper, "You can find us at the rose garden anytime you wish."

"How will I find you if I am leaving the garden?" she asked, as a tear rolled down her little face.

"The rose garden goes with you," said the smallest unicorn, with twinkly bell tones as she spoke, "folded up really small inside you like a secret package. Once you know how to open it and unfold it, you will find the rose garden."

"And you will find us," they sang in unison.

The unicorns left then, having had their fill of the magic fluid in the shimmery pool.

The child looked inside, to see just what kind of nourishment the unicorns were consuming in order to become so graceful, glowing and beautiful.

As she looked, she knew it was called 'water'. As she peered into its crystal clear depths, she saw her own self, reflected back at her through the pool mirror before her.

Memories came flooding back into her being as she looked at herself and she knew then who she was and she knew exactly what she had to do.

She looked upwards and saw the glowing doorway in the sky that she knew was a stargate.

The stargate called to her, an irresistible pull that would lead her to her beloved Great Mother and all the other souls who called for change.

She knew she would fold up the rose garden, very small, just as the unicorns had said and take it with her.

She would carry the code of the rose ray, rose-gold flame, the tiny folded rose garden, within her very being. When the time came, she would be able to activate the rose ray, rose-gold flame codes and help the world create the change they had called for.

She was ready.

The child flew upwards to the stargate in the sky and her destiny. The entire garden collapsed in cohesive implosion and unified with her as she passed through the stargate into the arms of the beloved, divine, Great Mother, matter.

21: Bearers of the Flame

One can attempt to explain or describe zero point, through poetic words that conjure up images of a divine void or infinite space. Yet we would best show you that which is zero point by describing the *experience* of it, rather than attempting to give it shape, form or location, none of which it has. This, of course, is subjective from your perspective for each experience will be unique, yet there are similarities within these individual experiences.

We can present the decoding of zero point within this experiential journey, also within geometric presentation. Yet as we have said, there is no shape or form here so the geometric explanation is experiential and metaphoric.

The zero point is experienced by those who perchance upon it as the 'now moment'.

Think of two streams running alongside each other, parallel to one another. One is a never-ending moment and would be depicted geometrically as an 'infinite spiral' (ball of wool), the other is a long line or path with a beginning point and an end point (long piece of unravelled wool).

The infinite spiral can then be drawn into just one point, a small circle or dot if this assists you to visualise. This dot is the now moment.

The long line with beginning and end is running parallel to the now moment. This is the experience of actual movement in time, linear time experience.

One is true reality (the dot). The other is illusion (the line). Both of these experiences are within you. Your entire lives, you walk the journey that is the dot/spiral and simultaneously the linear line.

So to describe the experiences, when one exists purely within that which we refer to as the third dimension, one experiences time 'moving'.

Things reorganise, organic structure grows older each year, the seasons change and ideas, beliefs and technologies grow, expand and 'improve', or seem to improve within the eyes of those within the third dimension.

Time must be experienced in this linear sense for separation from unity to be experienced. Separation from unity allows for unity itself to know itself. This knowing activates when separation is experienced, allowing unity to be perceived and processed.

In your current now time, holding energetics from the zero point stargates, close within that which you perceive as 'past' (most especially since your time period of 11th November 2011, increasing in intensity beyond then and ramping up once more, since your cosmic moment of 21st December 2012), the seed points into critical mass for bioplasmic, crystalline light have been 'planted', shall we say.

These seed points have often been referred to as 'luminescent' or 'neon' and indeed they are exactly this. This is the bioplasmic, crystalline light we speak of.

This creates the 'coat of many colours' or 'rainbow body of light' that is the photonic glow within and throughout and surrounding the light body. When this occurs, you move into a connected phase of alchemical unification of light.

Awareness of this state is heightened, understood and processed as you move forward. This explains why these stargates (sabbats, esbats and other astrologically or numerologically high energy points or spikes) are of such great import to your development, expansion and evolution.

We referred to these stargates as 'luminescent' and 'neon' due to the plasmic light formations that come online within the DNA and literally glow as they reflect different frequencies which are of high vibration.

These are perceived as 'light codes'. When this DNA upgrade occurs, you are said to be 'moving into' or 'holding' the rainbow body of light.

The golden or orange ray, the white or silver ray, the green or emerald ray, the pink magenta, or amethyst ray into the violet ray, the blue or blue sapphire ray, the red or ruby ray. All these are most significant, each merging as one rainbow yet individualise as specific frequencies.

This is your 'chakra upgrade' and is a complete transformation of the entire energy body system. We spoke earlier in this transmission of the charge contained within the energy body system as the gemstone codes. This gives fire or phire to the energy upgrade and activation so each ray so too is a flame.

You are the flame bearer.

This is alchemy of light as the non-physical walks hand in hand with the physical. We have presented before how this is understood through the teaching and memory awareness of that which you know as balance. Yet also this alchemy of light is understood through the teaching and memory awareness that is *time.*

Linear time as the long piece of wool, the line, the horizontal axis and now moment time of zero point as the rolled-up ball of wool, circle or spiral, the infinite spiral that is the individualised matrix of all that is.

These perceptions of time run alongside one another.

To the third dimensionally-thinking individual, then the zero point aspect is not understood. It does not feature within the conscious awareness of the individual. It is experienced within dreamtime and within the daydreams of the imagination fields but it is dismissed consciously as 'irrelevant'.

It is when the individual begins to take note of the dreamtime, daydream and imaginations that the individual begins to 'wake up' as the zero point field begins to be processed and both aspects of time, zero point and linear, can be simultaneously experienced.

When this moves into extensive, sustained and disciplined focus creating a cohesive-coherence within the structure of the DNA through integration, the individual feels as though they are 'in a dream' when they are awake and simultaneously 'awake' when they dream.

The two states merge together as one.

For the awakened starseeded lightworker, this will feel as though the 'mission' is lived on a 24/7 basis, to use the terminology as to how you measure time in the linear sense.

You will hear many starseeds say to you that they have been 'working all night' or that they are 'awake within a dream'.

This is how integration of zero point and linear time feels.

We cannot fully present an experiential analysis of zero point without explaining the integration of zero point and linear time. The reason for this is that zero point is only understood and fully processed when experienced through integration of linear time.

We repeat: *Zero point is only understood and fully processed when experienced through integration of linear time.*

The individual experiencing only the zero point would be in all intents and purposes presenting as 'ungrounded' or even 'insane' through dissociation.

This zero point experience is that which is known as 'confusion'. The negative aspect of the unanchored and unactivated blue ray field or blue flame.

This confusion is perhaps best explained as 'subjectively experienced pure zero point without anchor'.

Using the metaphor of the nautical, the individual would be 'lost at sea'.

The individual has no 'compass' and therefore no direction. The individual may be floating within a sea of confusion that looks like despair or indeed that is absolute bliss. Both would be different aspects/polarities of the zero point, bearing in mind there is no polarity within zero point, another paradoxical consciousness realm.

It is linear time that is your anchor to this. Yet if you lock in the anchor too deeply, you cannot move. The idea is to utilise the anchor to 'hold' or 'support' and be able to draw up the anchor when you wish to resume your journey across the sea, or upon the ocean.

Zero point being the sea or ocean, and you in physicality experiencing linear time as the anchor.

When you can control or navigate when you resume the journey, compass in hand or when you lower the anchor in order to ground, you become the 'captain of your own ship' and you 'steer the ship' allowing yourself to hold focus which is cohesive-coherence within the DNA field.

So to describe zero point itself, as we have said, is to describe the subjective experience of the individual's imagination and subconscious.

The unfocused 'lost one' in despair and confusion.

The ungrounded 'lost one' in bliss without charge.

Or the grounded, focused one 'in charge' of him/herself. The one 'in charge' is the one 'with charge'.

Through the story, we can present an experiential and

individually subjective presentation of zero point.

Zero point is a 'living thought field' that moulds itself to your frequency as a mirrored match. It is the modelling clay of the universe.

We refer to this zero point field as 'the flame' or the 'cosmic phire'. This is also the 'dragon's breath' (dragonsbreath) for the dragon (the focus, the cohesive-coherence, the charge) creates the fire (zero point fabric of pure potential).

You (the dragonrider) ride the dragon, or we could say you (the captain) steer the ship.

Yet the dragonrider and the dragon are one, as is the captain and his ship.

In days of old upon your planet, there were captains who rode the seas and oceans their whole lives. The captain was the male incarnated human and he 'fell in love with' his ship, who was referred to always in the feminine.

"Bless this ship and all who sail in her."

The ship became the captain's twin flame counterpart in an energetic sense. This enabled the captain to unify with his craft and steer the ship to its many destinations.

This is the same concept as the plasma beings and their bio-ships which are their organic bodies.

This is also the same concept as you, ascending starseeded human and your 'bio ship' which is your Mer-Ka-Bah.

The living thought field that is zero point is the 'exterior' to your 'interior'. The fabric of zero point is substance, the flame, cosmic phire, dragonsbreath, that moulds itself intelligently to the design within you.

So too does the design within you, mould itself to the zero point substance.

They are the same substance.

This substance is plasma. We refer to this as the flame, for it is indeed 'fire'. Not fire as you know it but a very 'advanced' form of plasma fire. It is alive and conscious and intelligent.

There are those who refer to this plasma fire as 'intelligent energy'.

Those who are integrated within the zero point time experience that is multidimensionality and also linear time, antimatter/matter merge, we call the 'Bearers of the Flame'.

We call them thus because they 'carry the codes of the flame'.

We could call them also 'torch bearers' or indeed 'shamanic shapeshifters'.

These individuals are 'shapeshifters' because they literally 'shift shape'. As in they change or transform geometric structure 'outside', transforming their reality environment to match the inner structure, or transform geometric structure 'inside', transforming their inner environment, the DNA structure and brain mapping to match the outer reality environment.

These 'shapeshifters' can learn to literally 'change form' as in they project forth the inner terrain and create an 'out of phase' presentation of their physical form, usually within the face and sometimes within full body.

Often this out of phase presentation lasts only a few seconds and much focus and concentration is needed in order to create the out of phase shapeshift.

The drummers, dancers, spinners, whirling dervishes and medicine men of ancient, tribal times could often do this, and it would take many hours and much focus to produce such out of phase shapeshifts.

The dancers would project forth the intentions to the 'chief' or the 'wise woman', whomever could hold the charge needed for the out of phase shapeshift, and much could be gleaned from the presentation of the out of phase form.

The out of phase form seen within the shapeshifters 'new' form would be the mirrored match, language of light, phire/flame letter presentation to the closest, probable timeline, event or metaphor that held the most cohesive-coherence within the antimatter, zero point 'cosmic phire' plasma field.

This same out of phase presentation occurs within that which you may know as 'transfiguration.'

When there is enough cohesive-coherence within the individual or group, to hold the charge long enough then transfiguration can occur.

This usually occurs with at least two individuals present, three hold more charge and a group of activated individuals hold an even greater charge still.

In rare cases, *one individual* can hold charge long enough to transfigure themselves, usually through deep meditation or focus within a 'charged item' such as clear, natural water, a crystal, or crystal ball.

There are now starseeds who are able to transfigure themselves through simply looking in the mirror for long enough. These are individuals who hold cohesive-coherent charge within their DNA fields. They are the dragon riders, the torch bearers and the 'bearers of the flame'.

They are the integrated ones who embrace, understand and experience the multidimensional time of the zero point field and simultaneously the linear time of physical reality.

They are the 'dreamwalkers', walking within the dream and

sleeping within the daydream holding left brain hemisphere and right brain hemisphere merge.

They are the 'dreamweavers', using the dreamwalking abilities to 'weave the dream', as in 'create their reality' by knowing how to utilise the cosmic modelling clay that is the dragonsbreath, plasma fire, zero point field or intelligent energy.

These are the same individuals who live upon third dimensional Earth and fifth dimensional Gaia or 'New Earth' simultaneously.

These individuals are *you*. You would not have found your way to this monadic transmission if you were not holding the 'copy match codes' to this transmission that is 'The Diamond Codex and the Quartz Key'.

Now, through 'the story' we present three individualised, subjective interpretations of the zero point.

The unfocused 'lost one' in despair and confusion.

The ungrounded 'lost one' in bliss without charge.

The grounded, focused one 'in charge' of him/herself.

The one 'in charge' is the one 'with charge'.

We present the story for your integration and deliver within, the activation codes that are the 'copy-plasma-light-seeds' or 'blueprints' for the explanation and experience itself. That of zero point/linear time integration and the trigger into dragonriding, dreamweaving and torchbearing.

This will take us into the presentation for you regarding why you need to charge the quartz crystal, activate the diamond light body and access the accelerated stargate system.

This is the mission of the starseeds.

22: Charging the Quartz Key through Zero Point

Understanding zero point in order to charge the quartz crystal. This is that which is known as 'piezoelectric'. It is the compressed phire/fire of the DNA which creates the implosion and springback from carbon to silicate/crystalline and fires up blue starphire/quantum convergence charge for accelerated stargate ascension.

This cannot take place from the subjective identification with the third/fourth dimension. This is seeded from zero point and activates within the fifth dimension and above (also known as fourth density).

Showing, not telling, through the story, to provide experiential frequency code and encryptions for the empathic and clairvoyant reader.

Do not be concerned if you feel tired and sleepy when reading this, for the epiphanies and realisations creating brainwave expansion can create the 'falling asleep' as the astral/dreamtime/subconscious comes online in equal measure to the conscious/awake.

When you are working with expansion creating text, be it artwork, music or the written form, this triggers the inner memories/knowings and awakenings, creating DNA activations of photonic light at deep cellular levels. The subconscious/dreamtime/etheric/antimatter aspect of the physical self is 'called into action' if you will, pulling you into the most aligned state of consciousness to be able to anchor and process these keycodes.

The most aligned state of consciousness for the majority of seeker starseeds to be able to process new information is sleep and dreamtime (also meditation).

You will find you are drawn into a deep sleep and the key code activations will begin in earnest almost as if you are continuing to read the book in your sleep.

When this occurs, you can be assured that activation and expansion is working within you.

This can take place without actually reading anything or analysing any text, it just happens when you are becoming deeply and profoundly activated into the light body.

So utilise these aspects when reading the story, to experience that which is zero point that cannot serve you and that which is zero point that is the activated value that is zero and the place from which to charge your Quartz Crystal Key.

The unfocused 'lost one' in despair and confusion.

She was a seeker, at least she thought she was, she believed she was. Watching, listening, so much information, complete overwhelm. Who was speaking the truth? Who was right? Who was wrong? They were all saying different things and Elizabeth's head swam. They cannot all be right.

She had the children to collect from school, the dog to walk and all these books to read and videos to watch. The overwhelm was simply too much and she found she had to give up on everything practical, everything she once enjoyed and there was no more brain space for study. Her mother picked the little ones up from school for her and she totally forgot about walking the dog. The confusion was giving her a headache and no one seemed to know what she was talking about. Her family all thought she was crazy and her neighbours avoided her. She didn't recognise herself when she looked in the mirror. What had happened and where had it all gone wrong?

Zero point field known as the abyss or the wilderness. In a state of no time but without anchor, without compass and therefore without clarity, boundary or structure.

The ungrounded 'lost one' in bliss without charge.

He was happy, definitely happy. He had lots of friends and the universe would provide everything he needed. Meditation and yoga daily, feelings of bliss running through his body as he walked an ascension path. He didn't notice the frowns around him, the giggles and the rolled eyes. Yet they didn't seem to want to listen, these people who needed his help. They needed to hear what he had to say and he would tell them, despite their protests and attempts to change the subject. He gave them all a crystal each and ignored the fact that half of them just mumbled thankyou and popped the crystal in a corner, to be forgotten. He was in bliss and euphoria, he was going to tell them all about that so they could feel it too, for wasn't it his mission to shout it from the rooftops? He didn't notice when his stomach rumbled with hunger or that the cupboards were bare. Who has time to shop for groceries when you are experiencing heaven on Earth?

Zero point as a point in time, no past, present or future as zero point is indeed. Bliss energy experienced yet anything goes in this state, similar to the unfocused one but without confusion and despair.

In this state one does not recognise the signs that one is ungrounded, believing that the path is being walked, yet integration is not taking place, one walks wearing blinkers if you will, charge is therefore not possible as only one vertical polarity within the zero point field is being embraced.

The grounded, focused one 'in charge' of him/herself.

She had much to read and research, a job to do, an elderly mother who relied upon her and a spiritual gathering to attend that night.

Compartmentalising the physical demands and duties and allowing herself to see the gifts within, she made a list of everything she needed to do. Meditation involved traversing the multiverse in the MerKaBah and after that she was energised enough to have a quick swim before visiting her mother and preparing a healthy meal all with gratitude in her heart.

The grounded one navigates all dimensional realities simultaneously without attaching to any particular aspect. She feels emotion deeply, alchemised and activated emotion that does not control her. Her two feet are firmly rooted upon the ground if you will, allowing the higher aspect of momentum and movement to soar into multidimensional expansion. This individual does not look for truth outside of herself. She knows all that comes into her reality is catalyst for her own inner knowing.

Zero point is experienced through the anchoring of the physical dimension and the expansions within the higher dimensions. Bliss is felt yet so too are the pragmatic, physical emotions. She is able to compartmentalise her thought structures whilst at the same time unifying them. Her groundedness within zero point allows her to create the blue starphire, quantum convergence charge, when in the MerKaBah state and she is able to charge the Quartz Crystal Key.

23: Primordial Sound

We bring you now into the understanding of that which is known as primordial sound or primordial vibration. This is the original language. The language of creation.

One could call this cosmic communication or the language of light. Indeed these are phire/flame letters but are presented to you through the memory of sound and the image before you.

If we were to look at the word 'Christ', indeed this holds high vibrational energy of plasmic light.

If we were to upgrade the word to 'Kryst', this would be closer to the original primordial sound and the ancient, cosmic language. When you do this knowingly, consciously and with focused intention and attention, you 'charge' the understanding and processing aspects of language and terminology itself. This creates a cascade within the bodymind, allowing that focused intention and attention to trigger matching frequency within the harmonics of the cellular structure and DNA. You enter, if you will, the quantum 144,000 as the fractalised aspect of the 12 strand DNA activation.

This triggers the deepest memories and the act itself does not have to be processed and understood at linear level.

We take therefore the Quartz Key and present to you the Key itself which is a crystallising activation code for the quantum 144,000.

These are mystery school teachings of true communication and magical scribing.

The Key in it's higher upgraded form is the Quay.

So as you look at the word Key and then again you look at Quay. As you speak the words Key and Quay out loud, you understand the power of the letter K and the letter Q.

These hermetically sealed aspects of sound are delivered to you within this transmission for the upgrade charges the Quartz Key that we can now present as the Quartz Quay and you have therefore the double Q.

As we have said, this does not need to be processed and understood at the linear level. These are the sigils of the alphabet and each hold different frequency.

Christ to Kryst. Key to Quay.

These are only a few sounds that hold upgraded visual letter sigil and frequency. The primordial sounds are many.

The charging of the Crystal Quay holds the elements of some of this knowledge. You also have been given the hierarchy of dragons within this transmission. With the primordial sounds and the hierarchy of dragons, much charge can be created within for the alchemical integration and unification needed for your cellular structure to transform from the carbon-based to the silicate/crystalline.

We bypass the fields of our conduit, Magenta Pixie, as she transcribes our words and so too do we bypass the knowledge and understanding of you, the reader. Hence the potential for you to be drawn into sleep.

For those that do know and recognise the primordial sounds and understand the image, the significance of the Q, the numerals and code. These catalysts can be taken within and presented in multiple ways. Your understanding and recognition of that which we speak will afford you the highest creativity.

Let us look at the quests of the Quay as you charge your Quartz Quay through the joining and merging with us, the monadic structure as you read the words of our transmission.

24: Krystallah Initiations

So before we can respond to the quest, why do you need to charge the Quartz Quay? At first we must know what the Quartz Quay is.

This is the piezoelectric code, dormant strands of DNA with potential to go galactic/quantum and activate within a crystalline structure.

All humans have this within and it is indeed a 'fail-safe' system for all incarnating humans who move into realisations and knowings of incarnation itself and the journey of the soul.

The Quartz Quay is that fail-safe code. When it is charged it brings online all the other gemstone rainbow frequency codes.

Base chakra - Ruby

Sacral chakra - Honey Amber

Solar Plexus chakra - Yellow Citrine

Heart chakra - Emerald

Throat chakra - Blue Sapphire

Brow chakra - Indigo Sapphire

Crown chakra - Amethyst

As we have said before, the starseed does not incarnate with the full spectrum of gemstone rainbow codes intact. They all incarnate with the amethyst code in place and usually two or three other gemstone codes in potentiality.

In truth, these codes do not 'lie dormant'. They are always active.

Yet they cannot be accessed by an individual until that individual begins to raise their overall vibration so that they begin to vibrate at the matching frequency to the colour ray. The same holds true for the planet Earth. This is why we refer to them as being 'in potentiality'.

The starseeds also all hold the Quartz Quay as the fail-safe within.

Once the Quartz Quay (key code) is activated and charged then the diamond light body (or diamond sun/solar light body) can begin to come online through the activation of the Diamond Codex.

As we have said before in previous transmissions: *The Diamond is the apex of the rainbow.*

The diamond reflects the rainbow light into the quantum streams which is the 144,000 quantum DNA.

When the individual charges the Quartz Quay and then holds the diamond light matrix or Diamond Codex as their energy matrix or true soul self, this Diamond Codex is then activated then they 'become quantum'.

All this is reflected within the actual biological change at the cellular level of the individual holding the diamond light.

The diamond being the apex of the rainbow is presenting to us the reflective light that the diamond is able to radiate. This is the exact same process that occurs within you.

This activation we are speaking of is also known to many scholars of enlightenment and religion as the 'rainbow body of light'.

This rainbow body of light is the radiation within, that which occurs from the activation of the diamond light matrix and the Diamond Codex.

It is metaphoric for ascension or the cellular transformation and transmutation of carbon-based molecular structure to silicate/crystalline-based molecular structure. It is metaphoric also for your experience of integration and alchemical unification as you embody the sovereign integral being.

We refer to this transformation also as the 'Krystallah Initiations'. For indeed, this physiological transformation is a cosmic initiation or indeed series of initiations.

The Krystallah Initiations are the incoming catalysations of frequency that create the genius configuration within the 'beyond the theta' brainwave state.

All this occurs when you charge the fail-safe system within that we refer to as the Quartz Quay.

The Quartz Quay is, if you will, as a small package within your DNA. It contains a new set of instructions to create, physiologically, a new upgraded, transformed human that will be able to live in harmony with the new, transformed, geological fourth density planet.

The harmony and love that will be experienced and shared here is beyond the imaginings of most individuals upon your planet. The starseeded ones will have had glimpses of such love and harmony when they exist within the fifth dimension or operate from and receive the frequencies of the fifth dimension.

This is also that which we call 'New Earth'.

Your experiential journey within this fifth dimensional space of love and harmony is what creates the geological fourth density that is an upgraded aspect to the Earth that you currently know.

When the Quartz Quay is activated within you through the charging of it, then these new sets of instructions will begin to unfold within you.

The Diamond Codex will therefore be put into place within you and your rainbow body of light will begin to form.

Our conduit does not have the scientific or biological understanding within her fields to convey to you this process at a physiological level. Yet using the limited understanding she does have, we can say that the cellular structure changes its shape. The geometry is upgraded and the closest we can present to you is the move through double helix, to triple helix, then beyond the triple helix into infinite helix.

This equates also to the hexagon that upgrades to the dodecahedron.

The inner tone or sound of the cells changes. Instead of playing several notes in mono, a symphony begins within and the entire orchestra comes online.

This is a plasma creation within. A blue flame is ignited within the DNA. Your cells and organs become fluorescent with this profound neon glow.

Regeneration occurs much more rapidly than before. Lifespans are extended as you obtain immortality codes through diamond immunity.

Memories return to you of knowings of other incarnations, other times, other places. You see beyond the physical at every turn.

Your organs within the body will be able to communicate much more efficiently than they did before.

Memories, deep within the cellular matrix within your bone structures will begin to release and come up into your mindspace awareness for processing.

Hormonal fluctuations will balance themselves. Sexuality will be regulated, as in you will be able to choose at will to experience the fire of passion at much higher pinnacles than before or choose to switch that passion off entirely.

Orgasm will be deeper and more profound if the experience is shared within a positive, polarised alignment.

Procreation will be through choice. Fertility will occur as you so wish it.

Eyesight and hearing shall improve.

Collagen will change within the body, due to increased peptides, that shall allow for rapid healing and regeneration of skin.

Everything within your entire structure shall crystallise, including your thoughts as you move into a clarity you have not yet experienced. You will know intrinsically how to align your thoughts with your emotions and create your reality.

This will be as a full Kundalini awakening experience for you and for all those who resonate with your new structure. For you shall harmonise with one another and present as echoes of one another. This is alchemical unification as the hexagon fits into the hexagon nearby, these geometries slot into place perfectly as aligned match to the whole. This allows your ascending and transforming structure to join with others as you create a diamond or crystalline grid across your planet, as part of the Krystallah Initiations.

Your breath will become far more to you than simply the giver of oxygen and life. You will be able to communicate with the diamond grid and with others within that grid as your breath becomes a communication device in and of itself.

Your very being will align with historical records upon your planet. Rock, crystal and other structures that hold tablets or discs of information regarding your planet, your place within your solar system and your divine roles as incarnated human beings within the transforming Gaia. Those who are called to this work are known as gridworkers, dragoncallers or guardians of the Halls of Amenti.

You will be able to 'see' particles, thought forms, elemental beings and lines of intention as they come together before your very eyes, or should we say 'eye' for it is your pineal gland that you shall be seeing with.

You will be at one with the prana or chi within your reality, known also as the golden light, the divine manna or the adamantine blueprint.

All this and much more besides shall occur for you, within this instructional codex that shall be activated within you that we call the Quartz Quay.

We have given you some idea, or certainly foundation for idea, of what the Quartz Quay actually is.

Now we shall look at why you need to charge it.

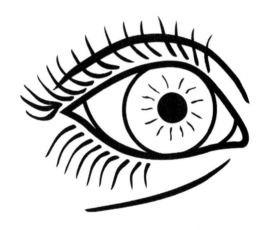

25: The Diamond Core Templates

The reasons as to why you need to charge your Quartz Crystal Quay are many. Yet in truth, you do not *need* to do this. It is your choice.

You are given a choice within your reality, an actual physical choice regarding the moving forward into the ascension or remaining within the state of not knowing, not going through ascension.

However, this is complex. For everyone and *everything* is ascending. However, there will be those who choose to remain at the level they are already at for a while and move forward in a different way to those who make the choice to retain memory and individualise as a soul, memory matrix complex.

Those who have found their way to this transmission will have made the choice to individualise. They will *want* to charge their Quartz Crystal Quay. They will *choose* to do so, for they choose ascension.

They do this by virtue of the activation they are undergoing. Herein lies yet another paradox:

When you make the choice to charge the Quartz Crystal Quay, you realise you have already made this choice due to the fact that you have begun to charge your Quartz Crystal Quay.

The choice you make is therefore the choice you already made.

The Quartz Quay is a living consciousness. It is intelligent. It lies within you, you were born with it. When it activates, it communicates with you as if it were you. It presents a new, upgraded 'operating system' within your body if you will. This new operating system is the software of Source. It is the operating system of organic, Original Source with all memories of the morphogenetic field intact.

It is no accident that we choose to use technology as metaphor for the coming online of all that you truly are through the diamond consciousness.

For, you see, the service-to-self negatively polarised factions, at both physically incarnated human and extraterrestrial level, have chosen to mimic this organic enlightenment, transformation process. They have chosen to do this through artificial intelligence technology.

They invert all organic structures with the intention of overriding those organic structures and rewriting the blueprint of Source itself. *God frequency itself.*

As we have said previously, they can only be partly successful in this for the software they use cannot reach the positive polarised fifth dimension or fully formed fourth density geological Gaia.

Your Quartz Crystal Quay is your fail-safe, for within that fail-safe is an organic override system.

When your Quartz Quay is charged and activated, the artificial intelligence Borg structure cannot infiltrate you. For you already have a new set of instructions at cellular level that has already begun to seed and replicate within you as plasma light.

The iron core structures of the liquid metals utilised by the negative structures are created to mimic the plasma light. Yet they cannot do so. They can only mimic on a mono system. They are unable to 'go quantum'.

Your Quartz Crystal Quay is a quantum replication system of diamond light.

Their metallic liquid oxidation substance is a mono replication system of iron core generation.

Let us explain further.

We draw your attention firstly to the 'Diamond Core Templates'.

The diamond core templates are infinite structures that hold a concept, learning or teaching as in a modality of spiritual discipline at their core.

However this explanation is specific only to the terms in which we are using them.

The teachings or templates presented within the materials that are the previous transmissions 'Masters of The Matrix', 'Divine Architecture and the Starseed Template' and 'The Infinite Helix and the Emerald Flame' are examples of diamond core templates, as is this transmission *The Diamond Codex and the Quartz Key.*

However, a diamond core structure or template is more than a transmission. It refers to anything that is a cohesive and coherent structure. This can be an individual human being, a place, an idea, a thought, a spirit entity or a creation.

When a structure is cohesive and coherent, it takes on the form of Source energy, as in it becomes what you might know as a 'sub-logos' or 'creator god'.

The structure becomes individualised and unified with all things simultaneously.

We present now the *'Infinity Diamond'*, which is the core of the structure.

The structure is presented as a spiral formation, a toroidal field or indeed a crystalline lattice or matrix.

As we have presented to you the model we used within the previous transmissions we have thus bought forth, you have a matrix structure with horizontal, vertical and diagonal axis running through in 'star formation' with the pivot point or nexus point, black hole/white hole, as the centre of the structure and a boundary around the entire structure which we refer to as the event horizon.

Let us present again, the image of the structure that we presented within the 'Infinite Helix and the Emerald Flame' transmission.

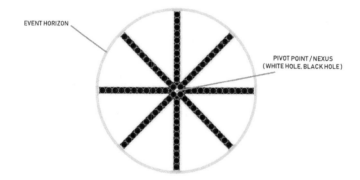

The pivot point or nexus point which is the centre of the matrix, black hole/white hole, is the 'Infinity Diamond.'

This may be known to you as the diamond energy/consciousness, the diamond light matrix, diamond DNA activation or indeed *the Diamond Codex.*

It is when the matrix structure is processed and understood within, that the spiritual seeker becomes the spiritual warrior, dreamwalker, dreamweaver and thus 'the adept'.

As we have said, this is very much an indigo path and is not necessary for ascension *per se.* However, it is essential for *accelerated stargate ascension.*

Once this has been reached then we can say that the diamond at the centre of the structure becomes activated.

This initiation into the position of adept can be reached through complete dedication, surrender and discipline within each of the diamond core templates individually.

All of the diamond core templates can be taken within linear steps as we have presented in our transmissions.

Or these initiations can be taken simultaneously depending on the individual.

That individual has then become 'diamond activated' if you will. They carry the 'diamond light' or have charged their Quartz Quay and activated the Diamond Codex.

This is a solar energy, as we have said before, therefore one could call this a 'diamond sun'.

We repeat ourselves, in different presentations, for the repetitions of terminology that we provide are reached by you, the receiver of this transmission, from multiple points of perspective as multiple catalysts.

This diamond sun is the central sun within the individual adept. The entire matrix structure is an infinity in and of itself, then we refer to the activated codex at the centre as the 'infinity diamond'.

So the Infinity Diamond is the central sun within a person or within a planet or a galaxy or universe?

Exactly. It is Source. Wherever you see the infinity diamond, you are looking at the *entire codex of Source itself.* The supreme being, Prime Creator, infinite possibility, God. Whichever name you wish to give it.

Why is it a solar energy? I thought you said these were black holes and white holes? How can they therefore be a sun?

The black hole and the white hole are simply metaphors to show the 'different sides' if you will of the core, pivot point, nexus point, of the matrix.

This is a zero point grid. It is a sun but not as the sun you know in your solar system, the being we call Sol.

This living being, 'King of the Day' known as Sol, is an emanation of multiple, infinite emanations as we have said. The original core of this emanation field is known as 'The Isle of Paradise' and this is the infinity diamond and it is the core of Source.

So your sun being known as Sol is the emanation for your solar system. There are multiple versions of Sol and multiple solar systems.

We are going to the 'core of the matter' by showing you that which is at the centre of all emanations.

Like a giant flower if you will, a daisy perhaps, indeed this is a flower of life formation, the 'divine daisy'.

The centre of the daisy is the infinity diamond and each petal is an emanation from that diamond. After a series of emanations, you have a physical sun, a Sol being, that supports, nurtures and gives life to a solar system. Your solar system sits within one of these 'daisy petals' if you will.

OK, I understand this concept. How then are we, as humans, also a structure that holds an infinity diamond?

You as humans hold the 'potential' for the diamond light or diamond activation, as we have said, or we could present this as a 'diamond sun expression'.

This means you hold a 'potential' diamond at your core.

However, you have to activate your entire structure first in order for it to mirror the pattern of Source and holographically present the original core diamond structure.

If just one of the axis points is out of alignment then this can 'throw out' the entire structure. The core cannot become cohesive and coherent and thus the infinity diamond cannot be activated.

Yet each human is a divine expression of Source? Even if the formation is thrown out of alignment?

Every human holds the 'higher template' or 'blueprint' for the structure we speak of. This remains within the 'light levels' or antimatter realms, if you will, when an individual incarnates. This is a keycode or series of keycodes that 'lie dormant' within the DNA memory fields of the individual. We have already explained that this is not really true dormancy yet for ease of explanation we present it this way.

When the individual comes into alignment with the blueprint and activates true and higher memory, through the triad of memory discussed in our previous transmission 'Divine Architecture and the Starseed Template' or through any pathway that mirrors that model, then the core structure, the entire matrix begins to be reconstructed from the physical, incarnated perspective.

Then the infinity diamond can become activated and the

individual is said to be holding the diamond light or has charged the Quartz Quay and activated the Diamond Codex.

The individual becomes 'a sun' if you will, and is themselves an emanation of Source. The original diamond at the centre of our divine daisy.

You literally, within *become a sun* as you radiate solar energy within.

How do these diamond core templates connect with the transmissions you have downloaded previously and in this transmission also?

A diamond core template or matrix can be an idea or a creation or indeed a transmission. You know this as a monadic structure or a monad.

We are a monadic structure, therefore we are a diamond core template. Each transmission in and of itself is a monad. It is a diamond core template.

So this writing I am transcribing from you as you present this transmission in real time is a monad or a diamond core template?

Yes. At the centre of the monad is the singularity. This is the centre of the 'divine daisy' and the activated diamond at the centre of the template, hence we refer to it as the 'core'.

The 'core of the matter', as in the central point or theme within a creation, story or presentation, yet indeed the central point within a 'matter' structure. As in that which is pre-matter becoming matter or Great Mother, becoming form.

As you transcribe in real time, our 'words' through that which you refer to as clairaudience, clairvoyance or telepathy, you translate energy signals or broadcasts, perceived to you as 'memory fields'.

You draw down the pre-matter blueprint and give it form as text, which can be created by you as a book or audio presentation or podcast/video/audio book. The creation is presented as you so choose from your point of perspective as a physically incarnated human.

Thus you create the diamond core template or monad *as a creation.* This mirrors the pre-matter template which is the creative formation from creator as creator.

The creator, created and creation are one and the same.

We repeat: The creator, created and creation are one and the same.

So what is the core issue? What is at the core of these templates or monads?

For these particular transmissions, we present six diamond core templates. Each template is a monadic singularity in and of itself, meaning the idea or subject matter is infinite.

Each are 'spiritual paths' or dreams or stories in and of themselves. One can dedicate their entire lifetime to just one or to all of them. They are infinite spheres of existence as is every cohesive and coherent idea, emotion or creation.

These are within the structure of the model we present. However, your reality holds an abundance of models presenting this core codex and it is for you, seeker of the way, to choose which model to utilise either as full pathway or catalyst into the pathway of your own creation.

The core templates we present are such:

Matrix Awareness

Matrix Mastery

Matrix Architecture

Matrix Transportation

Matrix Integration

Matrix Unification

The first two core templates were presented in the transmission 'Masters of the Matrix'.

Matrix Architecture was presented within 'Divine Architecture and the Starseed Template'.

We then presented 'Matrix Transportation' within 'The Infinite Helix and the Emerald Flame'.

We touched lightly upon the 'Matrix Unification' within 'The Black Box Programme and the Rose Gold Flame as Antidote' but not in its entirety.

Therefore this material would be an 'aspect' of a diamond core template, if you will.

In this transmission we present the 'Matrix Integration' and 'Matrix Unification' as the singularity field, monadic structure that is 'The Diamond Codex and the Quartz Key'.

When I transcribed the first book 'Masters of the Matrix', I had no idea this would be part of a connected series of teachings. Did you know this the whole time?

From our perspective, all had already occurred. It is you who has drawn this into third dimensional reality in 'real time' as in a linear time expression.

We do not experience this and we are a series of connected and individualised monadic structures or diamond infinity core templates. Therefore all is in existence from our perspective.

You suggest the transmission delivered in sequence from your perspective are a 'connected series'. Whilst this is correct from a linear point of view, as we have said, each structure is an infinity diamond core template in and of itself.

Therefore each transmission contains a codex or, as you put it, 'teaching' that can be committed or dedicated to without working with the other core templates. One can move through enlightenment and ascension through:

Awareness

Mastery

Architecture

Transportation

Integration

Unification

Within each of these six diamond core templates or monadic singularity structures, the others can be found. Architecture is the structure. Transportation is the momentum. Unification is the connection of each to all. Integration is the unification of cohesive, compartmentalisation. Mastery is the magick. Awareness is the sense, knowing and recognition of self as self.

Are there any more to come? Or just these six?

Six is most significant to you at this time and to the collective consciousness of aware, starseeded humanity.

You are moving into sixth dimensional manifestation level or that of sixth strand activation.

This is in itself a diamond core template or monadic structure which, as we have said, is infinite. Therefore, scale and measurement is used for your third dimensional, linear processing.

There is no beginning or end to this scale in actuality yet it is presented as such so that you may sort, place and construct a mathematical model which assists you in processing and thus expansion.

We cater to the left hemisphere of your human brain, if you will, by providing the model. Yet we cater, or merge with, also the right hemisphere of your human brain by showing you who and what we/you are.

That is the code. Therefore you utilise logic and analysis alongside feeling and receptivity. This is your genius flow and the golden key to expansion, enlightenment and ascension.

Now you have been presented with what the diamond core template and infinity diamond is, let us show you how this manifests within the context of a planetary and human collective structure.

26: The Iron Core Wormhole System and the Bliss Charge Phase Lock

So what then is 'Matrix Unification'? You have said this is 'the connection of each to all'. Can you explain this?

This is the question we have 'waited' for you to ask. As in, the codices cannot be downloaded until you, or the collective consciousness of awakened humanity, ask this question.

You are now at the point in your collective evolution that many are 'asking' or 'remembering' what unification is. We use the matrix as the model for explanation to assist the human linear, third dimensionally interpreting brain.

Remember there are many starseeds who do not need the interpretation, analysis, measurement or scale. They simply feel and know. This is the way of the crystal being.

Yet in your now time you are intrinsically, as starseeds, part of the indigo uprising and the indigo revolution. We shall refer to your years of 2020 to 2024 as the 'time of the indigo vibration'.

Indeed, we can refer to your entire decade in fact as holding the indigo vibration. What this means is that there are large numbers of starseeds looking for answers. They are not content with just feeling and knowing but they wish to know how things work. They want to access the 'nuts and bolts' of the situation, if you will. This is achieved by analysis. These individuals, when balanced with the crystal aspect of feeling and knowing are the ones who hold 'genius flow' brain patternings as well as the heart-centred compassion. They are able to affect the weather patterns and hold mastery over the elements. These are the individuals steering the timelines for your planet Earth.

Before we move into the explanation of 'Matrix Unification' and the presentation of the matrix within this, we would like to present to you a story regarding the timelines for Earth, the 'switch' or 'jump' from one timeline to another and why this is so significant as a creation from the balanced indigo collective mind.

This will assist you with your knowing as to how the Diamond Codex manifests within the context of a planetary and human collective structure.

It is the balanced indigo/crystal starseed that has created the timeline jump. Each and every indigo/crystal starseed has been pivotal and crucial in the timeline jump. This is you, dear starseed, who reads these words now. Indeed, it is so, that this is you.

You may feel as though we speak to you and you alone as you read these words and that we can see you, we know who you are and what you do and how you think and feel.

Indeed from the omnipresent aspect that is us, the White Winged Collective Consciousness of Nine, this is so and this is true.

However, Magenta Pixie, our conduit in human form, does not know this. She does not see you individually as we do, she simply transcribes our words that we speak to her through rapid interpretation of energetic code. Whilst she sees and feels energy and sees constructs clairvoyantly as we speak, she does not see you individually as we do.

We wish for you to know this. The reason we wish you to know this is because from the perspective of separation and third dimensional incarnation, we are indeed separate beings from Magenta Pixie.

The reason we wish for you to know that we see you in your true individualised and unified form is so we may share with you our love for you.

Indeed, we love you as a parent loves their child and thus more so. We love you unconditionally and with purity. Each of your higher selves or unified selves love just as we do.

The love is that which holds you together and it is the key ingredient within the unification, if you will.

As we share this with you, dear starseed, we share our understanding of who you are and our individualised connections with you and that of your guidance system. As we do this, we draw you together into unification with us.

We do this through a spiritual intimacy of the heart. Thus we show to you the *feeling* that is Matrix Unification.

We shall indeed present the nuts and bolts and whys and wherefores through the matrix model we present, and the Diamond Codex understanding, but it is important to hold the understanding of the *feeling.*

The spiritual intimacy is about being seen. Being known. Being loved. This is true unification.

Within your world of third density and physical incarnation, we can say to you that spiritual intimacy, which is the emotional feeling of unification, is the opposite of what you may know as loneliness.

Thus with this said, we draw your attention to the timeline jump, for this jump moved you collectively, as starseeds holding fifth dimensional consciousness, from a collective loneliness through separation into a collective spiritual intimacy and unconditional love through unification.

It is not possible for us to start at the very 'beginning' of this story for this is outside the scope of this transmission.

However, we will say that through activation of the codices, keycodes and triggers, presented within this material and within our previous transmissions, you will have the activations necessary for the accessing of the collective memory.

We start this story only with the group. Those we call service-to-self, known to you as Illuminati, elite, cabal, darkworkers, controllers, deep state, overlords and many other names besides, used separately to describe different groups or used interchangeably by some. You may know the purpose of this group as a 'negative alien agenda'.

We refer to this entire structure as service-to-self factions.

Or for ease of presentation, we shall refer to these entire groups of individuals, bloodlines or families as the STS group.

This STS group harnessed emotional energy from unaware humanity. They were able to do this through a 'combination' shall we say of technology and dark magick. The emotional energy they harnessed was that of fear and many derivatives, hybrids and branches of that fear emotional structure.

This fear had to be continuously produced at a critical mass level. This meant that all structures within the human social system had to be hijacked. The education, health, nutrition, farming and agriculture, medicine, religion, science, entertainment and news media delivery.

All these systems had to be hijacked, controlled and maintained through this dark magick technology we speak of. This created a 'hold' if you will upon a timeline or dimension.

This timeline was, due to the continued hijacking of the fear energy emotion, holding the formation of a false diamond core template. However, we cannot refer to this in all truth as a diamond core template for it was not a diamond frequency construct at the centre of this inverted singularity construct.

The nearest analogy we can give to hold the most aligned vibration for the core structure would be iron.

So you are looking here, when using right hemisphere brained symbology as activation for processing through your personal memory matrix grids, at a 'heavy metal' for this is the crystalline structure in non-activated and inverted, false creation state.

We touched on this black box, black cube technology earlier in this transmission and within our previous transmission 'The Black Box Programme and the Rose Gold Flame as Antidote'.

The true diamond core template, infinity-singularity-structure presents as the crystalline celestial web.

Like that of a star-brain or cosmic brain. This is a living matrix construct of such divine beauty that it is truly unimaginable to those who do not move into the highest clairvoyant states to perceive this.

The diamond core, infinity diamond is an absolute replica of Source to the point that *it is Source.* Words do not do justice to this. Unconditional love, bliss-charged love, lovelight and lightlove, euphoria, rapture, ecstasy, compassion, all these have their place yet the infinity diamond is a conglomeration or convergence of *all these and yet more.*

Suffice it to say that this is the most brilliant, glowing, diamond sun matrix and the most divine, heavenly crystal structure one could lay eyes upon. As we have said, words do not do this paradisiacal structure justice yet your feeling and alchemised, higher emotion will show you the golden, rainbow glow of the infinity diamond.

The false, inverted iron core structure is presented as keycode as the 'red spider'.

This too, is a living expression. This is 'artificial intelligence' because it is created partly through technology, yet it is organic also for it holds 'given life' from the hijacked emotional energy of fear from the enslaved humanity, that in this sense act as 'battery charges' for this structure we speak of.

So when we mention red spider or black box, this is the false inverted structure we speak of.

This structure is a living structure. It is a copy distorted version of the true monad. It cannot hold form through true organic creation from pure intentional thought streams as actual infinite, cosmic reality but it holds form through a generator.

That generator is siphoned human energy. The emotional energy patterns of their fear and fear derivatives and chemical organic feedback systems produced within the human body when these emotional energy fear patterns are produced.

This is explained within our first transmission 'Masters of the Matrix' and the keycodes for immunity to this and freedom from it are given within that material.

We draw your attention to this iron core structure that is black box, red spider, artificial construct because this construct is, in and of itself, a timeline or a dimension.

It is an existence, as in a 'place' as well as a 'thing' or a 'being'.

This structure could only hold its form within what we may present to you through our model as a fourth dimensional field.

Now there are many models to explain reality. Therefore you may hear other conduits, spiritual explorers and messengers of light present this information in different terms. This is because they use a different model as a premise to explain reality.

It is true to say that reality cannot be explained from one individual to another in its entirety. It is only you and you alone who can see and understand reality, for your model is unique to you and you alone.

The model we use holds form that can be utilised as a framework for a great majority of starseeds and whilst what we present may appear to be 'advanced material', we simplify this as much as we can for your understanding.

We present the material at the level of our conduit's understanding. We use a conduit who has the ability to hold very abstract concepts within mind but also needs to 'sort out' this abstract construct within repeated pattern formation in order to grasp the material and make sense of reality.

So many starseeds hold similar patterns of thought to our conduit for you are indeed brothers and sisters in light.

Therefore this model is most suitable. Yet we draw your attention to the fact that there are other models and we say do not dismiss these. For your search as the one seeker, the spiritual explorer, is to take you far and wide.

You use this model as but one tool within which to formulate your own unique diamond core template and activate your own infinity diamond, Diamond Codex, charge your Quartz Quay and hold, carry and radiate the diamond light yourself.

This structure we speak of, the iron core structure false matrix, needed the generator, which is siphoned human fear emotional energy, in order to hold fast and remain in place. The human fear emotional energy needed to be continuously at critical mass.

Hence the need for created wars and all other events and disasters, to keep feeding into the iron core structure, false matrix, red spider system at critical mass level.

The iron core itself is a false, inverted copy of a singularity.

We repeat: The iron core itself is a false, inverted copy of a singularity.

This is, if you will, for want of a better explanation, a wormhole.

This leads into disintegration of memory, presents a false light, false trapping system and simply recycles the entity caught within the wormhole back into an incarnation to continue to power the generator system of fear emotion.

Fear emotional matrices are triggered prior to birth within the incarnating soul, if the soul has moved through the iron core wormhole.

Starseeds 'enter' incarnation through a very different means and are immune from using the iron core wormhole system unless they have been 'caught' within it.

As we said, a whole other subject but you can see how this material ties in with the 'Masters of the Matrix' transmission (recycling through trapping systems) and 'The Infinite Helix and the Emerald Flame' transmission (stargate ascension - the opposing polarity to iron core wormhole disintegration).

Iron core wormhole entry creates loss of memory cohesion.

Stargate ascension creates memory activation. Or should we say that memory activation creates stargate ascension! From a linear perspective, this is the sequence this follows.

So the iron core as a false, inverted singularity holds a 'core vibration' pulsed from the heavy, metal, black box, red spider grid.

Just as the true singularity of Source pulses a creational I AM energetic, so too does the false inverted singularity send out a pulse.

This is known as the Armageddon program and 'Armageddon' as a construct is the false form projection.

This does not mean end of life or destruction of all and everything, for it is not possible for the dark masters to have that much creational power by any means. Instead it means 'control'. Whatever comes into the sphere of control, be it enslavement, powerlessness, emasculation, reduction and so too the exercise in 'mastery without Source' or 'mastery in spite of Source' as in distortion of what mastery truly means.

This is the core of the service-to-self path and we must express that there is no judgement from the higher consciousness perspective. This is a polarised choice.

However, the iron core false singularity creation is finite. It is an inverted copy of the true Source configuration and as much as the dark magicians would like this to hold 'more longevity' than it has done, this is not possible, for all souls turn to the point of evolution eventually.

All planetary beings turn to the point of evolution.

On the balance of probabilities, the estimation in percentage of a planetary system remaining indefinitely in lockdown is zero. The reason for this is due to thought.

It only takes one thought to change an entire dimensional structure and thus a geological density. Thought cannot be contained within a false matrix system indefinitely for thought is a byproduct of Source expression, even if expressed within the confines of a reduced, locked down, iron core template.

Whilst thought and resulting heart opening was suppressed, this would only ever be temporary.

Of course the first 'heart opened thought structures' were not enough to obtain critical mass, but they were eventually enough to open star grids to incoming ascended and higher planetary souls.

Once the first wave of an influx of incoming souls came into Earth's incarnational field via solar pathways (we speak of Sol your sun and the central suns), then this act in itself weakened the critical mass of fear emotional energy giving form to the iron core false singularity wormhole structure.

We fast forward many thousands of years but there came a time where the indigenous peoples of your world were given, through the shamanic plant medicines and spirit beings, teachings of the history of your world and the potential futures.

They were taught how to avoid the iron core wormhole false light systems and they were taught how to 'call in' the starseeded celestial star beings as part of 'the call'.

The call was not just magickal workings from the indigenous but was so too the despair and pleas from the trapped human souls.

After this call, the star beings began to incarnate via solar pathways in droves. Many began to pass back through the solar stargate systems and totally bypass the false light wormhole iron core singularity.

So the dark masters within STS factions attempted to 'shut down' the newly discovered and created stargate systems.

However, these are living structures that respond in kind to the matching energetic diamond crystalline structures within the DNA fields of the humans that exist upon the planet they are part of.

The star beings incarnated in human form assisted and freed other human souls and taught them, through spiritual practice, how to pass through the solar and celestial stargate systems and bypass the iron core false wormhole reincarnational trap.

Fast forward several thousand more years where the light has sustained, despite attempts from the dark magician STS factions to silence them, repress them and eliminate them.

There was one indigenous, deeply spiritual nation made up of star being incarnated souls. We speak of the Mayan civilisations. Through their drawing down of the sacred codes of message and information, downloads and channelling/higher communication yet presented in a different way from your modern times, they were able to make prophecy.

Combined with the prophecy of other star being, star nation, souls such as the Hopi and many others, they were able to construct a timeclock to plan out and map the prophecy.

We cannot divulge the methods used or other elements involved for this is still a 'protected knowledge' that is not yet available within the general consciousness, yet know that the full story will be delivered to each and every one of you who wishes for this knowledge.

Know just that the construction of the timeclock involved 'magickal means'. The timeclock we speak of is the Mayan calendar.

There are those who are incarnated to decode this calendar and this is not the role of our conduit.

For those who feel called to further study of that which we speak of then know you would look to the 'thirteenth baktun' and you would work with the 'thirteen sign astrological model'. With these in place, you have the keys to unlock what you seek.

The Mayans utilising the technology magick of the timeclock (Mayan calendar) were able to calculate a most probable date for the fulfilment of the numerous prophecies that were being made due to the DNA memory structures activating within the physical bodies and skeletal systems of the incarnated star being souls (star nations).

They calculated an 'end' to a cycle and thus a period of 'rest' before the beginning of a new cycle. The date for this end of the cycle was 21st December 2012. The solstice point and the time we call the 'cosmic moment'.

The second date (the beginning of the next cycle) was a repeated sequence of events so an actual date cannot be given for this, for it is actually 'time periods' one is looking at here rather than singular dates within a calendar.

The '21st December 2012' was simply a central point within a large period of time. So one may call this 'the 2012 time period' which consists of several years either side of 21st December 2012.

The second date is a time period after 2012. This is the time period for the integration and transcendence of linear time so it will not be experienced in a sequential sense. This is a 'zero point field' but if you wish to work with the Mayan timeclock in a magickal sense then you would be looking to work with the 'number thirteen'.

What the prophecy meant to the Mayan civilisation and to many other civilisations including Hopi was that 'all shall be returned to what once was and yet more'.

They knew of the 'fall of man' and so too they knew of the hijacking of humanity. They knew the false matrix was finite and that star beings from multiple multiverses would incarnate at the time of planetary completion.

They were also given sacred codes and coordinates for the recreation of galactic and planetary grid structures and for the reopening of the ancient stargate systems and recreations of new ones. They knew that many of their soul star families would incarnate into western civilisation and become cyber-shamans, utilising their knowledge through the surfing and mastery of the world wide web.

These individuals we call 'starseeds' are all 'descendants', either through genetic bloodlines or incarnational bloodlines or often, both simultaneously, of the original indigenous tribal peoples.

These starseeds incarnated through the central sun solar stargate systems and came in through 'Sol', the being you know as your sun. This is how they entered into the matrix you know as your solar system.

Now some of these starseeds entered into incarnation thousands of years ago and chose to deliberately trap themselves within the reincarnational wheel of Earth and move through the death/birth experience via the iron core wormhole system. This was a deliberate choice.

The reason they did this is that as they passed through the iron core wormhole system they, shall we say, created a 'glitch' within the code.

The inverted matrix system was created to dissolve and disintegrate memory codes. However, the starseeds held crystalline and gemstone memory codices within their DNA systems that were not subject to the memory wipings and disintegrations of the iron core wormhole systems. We speak here of the Quartz Crystal Quay codex fail-safe system.

Not only did they reincarnate with their memories intact but

226

they, let us say, caused the memory wiping and disintegration systems to 'work harder', straining the technologies to move into levels they were not built to achieve.

All this we speak of is metaphor and it is most challenging to explain to you the exact mechanisms here. By 'challenging', we mean in human terms, not that of our higher consciousness. We use the term 'challenging' to explain the frequency codes expressed as appropriate and activating metaphor through our conduit.

Know this is to do with consciousness itself and how environment and DNA codes within humans move into a 'phase lock' system when incarnation takes place. We speak here of Matrix Unification.

Our conduit simply does not have the biological foundational understanding for us to be able to impart to you the mechanism here but know that it is activated via the sequence you know as 'the ribosome'.

This is not one thing but multiple things. It is the feedback system and seeding system for the quantum DNA field that your scientists call 'junk DNA'.

The iron core wormhole inverted matrix system 'phase locked' only within fear and fear derivative emotional energy.

When the bliss activated, diamond, solar starseeded souls went through the wormhole, they continued to attempt to 'phase lock' the environment. Therefore the environment began to geometrically reconstruct itself in order to create the phase lock with the incarnating soul.

This caused at first a 'temporary blip' or 'glitch in the program' within the wormhole system. The iron core wormhole system could regenerate but after thousands of years and millions of diamond, solar, star activated souls attempting to phase lock with the wormhole environment, eventually the wormhole environment began to change and started to 'reflect' rather than absorb and behave more like a 'star' or a 'sun' rather than a wormhole.

Your moon is a case in point and a perfect example of this process, but we digress. Just know that the human DNA fields are compatible, geometric and energetic matches to planetary and galactic environment.

So the continued 'recycling' of starseeded souls began to cause the breakdown and disintegration of the iron core structure false matrix wormhole which was already a finite structure in and of itself.

A high level of amnesia (but not disintegration) had to take place within the starseed being. If the starseed soul had been aware of the challenges of the mission at hand then 'fear' would have set into that soul at a coded level and the soul would have gravitated towards the iron core wormhole, false light structures without being able to influence the environment of that wormhole consciousness through bliss phase lock.

The starseeded souls bravely went about their missions in droves and we can say to you, all has indeed taken place according to plan and now you are at the very apex of the fulfilment of that indigenous star nation prophecy.

You are the prophecy.

Once the 2012 time period began, many starseeded souls chose to return to solar incarnation and reincarnation for there was no longer any need for them to remain incarnated through the iron core wormhole.

Others chose to remain within the Earth system as a human soul in order to assist those souls who were truly lost and in a state of memory disintegration. The phase lock environment was well established within the iron core wormhole inverted trapping system by this time, so many human souls began to retain memories through the incarnational journey.

The iron core structure began to lose form as critical mass for 'memory' began to overtake critical mass for fear emotional energy.

The 'battery chargers' began to lose their charge, if you will.

All this was happening at your 'subatomic' level throughout your 2012 time period and, as we have said, this involved several years either side of your year of 2012. It is more true to refer to this time period, based on the thirteenth baktun and the 'rest period' between cycles, as the 2012/2021 time period. We look here at thirty-three years within/around this time period yet exact dates cannot be given due to the continued competing for timelines that takes place in your now time, at the linear time of this transmission. We see the convergence of those timelines and there are many eventualities.

However, we can say that all timelines lead to the singularity or 'all roads lead to Rome' if you will. Timing the iron core to coincide with the diamond core is not possible due to iron core being finite and the diamond core being infinite, hence we refer to this as the infinity diamond.

During this 2012/2021 time period, a 'new' singularity/dimension/timeline began to form. We say 'form' but this was actually already in existence but it was 'overshadowed', shall we say, by the iron core wormhole system.

When critical mass for fear emotional energy began to dwindle and memory activations and higher heart emotions began to increase, the new structure began to rise within the consciousness memory fields of humanity, indeed within starseeded humanity.

Remember, these souls did not at any time completely lose their memories, they were only lying dormant or simply were not accessible at that point.

This is when 'solar light' began to emanate into your solar system, activating the memories of the humans with cohesive and coherent DNA fields through the solar 'diamond sun' bliss, ecstasy phase lock.

Your 1960s decade was a huge turning point within the development of this diamond, solar, memory DNA grid.

Mind-altering substances were being used and the dancing, singing, creativity joy/bliss activations were almost at critical mass.

This huge wave of awakening activated many galactic stargate systems and the influx of starseeded souls at that time, most especially indigo souls from the Pleiades, Lyra and Sirian star systems was phenomenal.

'The call' by this time was as loud as a clear ringing bell across the galactic sky and millions of souls responded to the call, joining the long term incarnated starseeds and drawing down the high probabilities for the diamond light potential.

We now explain to you this new singularity/dimension/timeline and within this the manifestation of planetary and human collective diamond structure.

This was/is/will be the diamond core template holding the solar, bliss, ecstasy light codes for freedom.

This was the manifestation of the indigenous peoples prophecy and magickal workings.

We speak to you of this paradise diamond singularity now.

27: The Diamond Sun Core Template

The Diamond Sun Core Template, positively polarised reality dimension is an abundance, ascension, bliss-paradise structure. The timeline is the organic, natural structure that is a holographic replica of Source. This is a naturally created dimension as part of natural, organic reality.

For the individual who holds this infinity diamond structure and 'charges' their Quartz Crystal Key/Quay then the environmental codices of that diamond structure manifest in actuality for them. Abundance, ascension, enlightenment, bliss, paradise reality. At a collective level within the diamond activated individuals, this is the reality they create for themselves.

This is that known as 'New Earth'.

So all we speak of here within this transmission is regarding the New Earth structure. The keycodes within this transmission as to how to move into this New Earth are provided for you.

The New Earth template is available for each and every awakened and activated individual to connect with and be part of. Not only can these individuals, starseeds if you will, connect with New Earth but they create the New Earth with their thoughts and actions.

The iron core, red spider template was 'artificially' created. This presents many misunderstandings as this does not mean it is a machine or has no life force. It means it was created by individual intelligent beings, advanced extraterrestrials if you will, who created a 'copy' of original, organic reality holding a polarity field structure. Negatively polarised with the iron core holding the vibration of control, persecution and enslavement or in other words, the Armageddon program.

The original, Source emanation, diamond core template is a complete polarity to the iron core, red spider template.

Original Source, the I AM pulse, holding the creational codes for reality, existence and consciousness itself can be replicated in any structure that is cohesive and coherent.

In your Bible, it says that 'God created man in his own image'. This does not mean that God is a man, with a physical body like you. It means your intrinsic energy fields and DNA structures are emanations or holographic replicas of the Original Source I AM pulse.

It is not just 'man' that has been created in 'God's image'. In fact, the original Bible would not be translated as 'man' in this particular passage of text. It would be translated as 'physical world' or 'physical reality'. This is the same meaning as 'as above, so below'.

Therefore we could say that 'Source created the physical reality as physical copy of itself'. Or we could say that 'Source is the cosmic blueprint for the physical dimension'.

Therefore as we have said, any coherent and cohesive structure holding the compassion, lovelight/lightlove into bliss-charged love fields holds this ability to absolutely and totally be a 'mirror image' to Source I AM pulse or God/divine/supreme being/Prime Creator consciousness.

You and all your creative ideas can hold this same structure or template and we present this template as the diamond core matrix with the infinity diamond as the core itself.

In this transmission, we move one step further from the matrix formation we presented within 'The Infinite Helix and the Emerald Flame' and we extend the structure.

If you have moved through the teachings within the previous transmissions then you will be aware of this matrix structure. We revisited this in the previous chapter within this transmission.

The extended structure we present here will assist you to

understand and visualise the creation of the New Earth system for the keycodes within this transmission act as catalysts for your own personal epiphanies, ideas and realisations.

When those creative thoughts are in alignment with the diamond core template, triggered by the charging of your Quartz Crystal Quay and the activation of the Diamond Codex within, then they will automatically become part of the New Earth structure.

The plasmic, photonic light particles, rays, codes and cosmic dust that stream into your reality, both physiologically and geologically, fall on 'fertile ground' if you will, when you stand as a cohesive, coherent structure holding the diamond frequency of New Earth.

You align with the core template which is the infinity diamond, holding the absolute crystalline information, Krystallah Codex of the New Earth template.

These plasmic, photonic light particles, rays and codes hold exponential potency within your reality at this time. It is 'the ribosome' template that holds, conducts, transduces and directs this plasmic, photonic light.

This is the key to your rainbow body of light manifestation.

So you have the 'twelve tribes of Israel', the horizontal rainbow bridge pathway, horizontal axis moving forward, with your solar plexus chakra as the central point for this first step with this model, and backward behind you and also to your left and to your right, the sideways arm of the cross.

You have the 'vertical pillar of light', vertical axis moving upwards above you and downwards below you and you have the vertical axis coming in diagonally from left to right and from right to left.

You have the 'pivot point' which is the centre at the solar plexus chakra. As you move into deeper work with/within this matrix architectural structure, you raise the pivot point upwards to include the heart chakra also.

The central point, solar plexus and heart, is your pivot point because you can turn the entire 'white wheel' or 'silver wheel' that is the matrix. This is most helpful with individualisation and integration of aspects of self as we explained in previous transmissions.

This pivot point is also the 'nexus point' or indeed zero point. This is the 'core' of the matrix structure and this is the infinity diamond.

This is where the diamond light emanates from. This is a 'diamond stargate' and it radiates the diamond light once activated. We are speaking here of the combined solar plexus and heart chakras when in alignment with all other chakras through the vertical pillar.

Around the edge or boundary to this structure, there is a 'circle'. This boundary as we have explained within 'The Infinite Helix and the Emerald Flame' does not exist for the structure is infinite. However, we use the boundary in order to 'measure' and 'construct' in order that activation and processing take place.

When the diamond core stargate centre (which is a white hole and a black hole and also simultaneously a central sun, your 'solar' plexus, this is YOUR personal sun/stargate) is activated then thus so shall the boundary be activated.

The boundary is the event horizon. Due to its simultaneous activation, we can refer to this as the 'diamond event horizon'.

If you remember in our previous transmission 'The Infinite Helix and the Emerald Flame', we explained how in actuality the event horizon and the pivot point are in fact the same place. So the infinity diamond is both the core and the boundary.

To see this placement, two separate aspects of the structure, as the same place and to hold this within visualisation and realisation is to *create the stargate itself.*

At critical mass levels, you as the awakened starseeded collective that is the beloved Divine Princess Aurora/Archangel Michael hieros gamos Structure *instructs the ribosome to generate plasmic, photonic light and thus crystalline matrices within new RNA/DNA codons and molecules.*

As we have said, our conduit does not have enough biological knowledge for us to be able to present the exact sequencing that takes place.

However, it is of import to impart that the instructional sequencing, conducted and generated by the ribosome *comes from the mind and thought of the diamond activated cohesive, coherent, phase locked individual.*

The event horizon and pivot point/nexus point as simultaneous infinity diamond, zero point structures, when visualised within focused intentional thought streams *program the instructional sequence into the conductive ribosome.*

The dark, negative structures agenda is to target this sequencing within the diamond, plasma, crystalline coordination/communication between mind, thought focus and the ribosomic sequencing.

They do this by injecting into the body of the one who is not diamond activated, the metallic, oxidation, iron core template structures. They provide their own instructional set through dark magick, allowing serpentine, black mamba bite to override the true ribosomic pathways.

Yet as we have said, the iron core program is finite and the diamond structure is infinite. An override codex is available for those that have fallen into the wormhole system. However, the override codex is the charging of the Quartz Crystal Quay and the activation of the Diamond Codex. The ability to hold the event horizon, pivot/nexus point through bilocational consciousness is needed for the override. The spiritual path is taken with dedication in order to find the Holy Grail that is the override system.

We present here the catalysts and keycodes for the bilocational consciousness you are looking for.

The paradox is that it is the seeker of the way into the path of the adept and the adept apprentice archetypal aspect that hold the ability for the override codex which is the Diamond Codex. These individuals would not make the free will choice to allow the black mamba bite technology into their physiological fields.

However, there will be the rare few that can override the dark, iron core wormhole system and for these individuals, quantum entanglement with the activated diamond plasma ribosome of others will be the directional trajectory for them.

These are the individuals who ride the dragon of another, and the dragon rider at the helm, steering the dragon, willingly, in service, offers the ride to others. He or she holds the 'paradise program mission template' and bypassing the 'Armageddon code' so delivered to unsuspecting and unactivated humanity.

The codes, coordinates and blueprints are fully available to all humanity holding the ability for an infinite, quantum structure to override a mono structure.

We repeat: The codes, coordinates and blueprints are fully available to *all humanity* holding the ability for an infinite, quantum structure to override a mono structure.

The matrix model we present is a two dimensional 'blueprint' of a presentation that in truth has a much more complex and intricate scale and pattern. The entire structure, known to you as a Mer-Ka-Bah or merkabah or merkavah vehicle, is a toroidal field.

We delivered the information within the transmission 'The Infinite Helix and the Emerald Flame' regarding the ability to move the sections of the matrix and 'shapeshift' and transform, travelling through your own inner portal, your own 'diamond sun crystalline stargate' and move into a celestial stargate system.

This was Matrix Transportation as the 'diamond core' of the monadic matrix singularity that is 'The Infinite Helix and the Emerald Flame' as a creation.

We used the indigo/blue crystal as the celestial aspect of that diamond sun stargate.

In this transmission 'The Diamond Codex and the Quartz Key', we present 'Matrix Integration' and 'Matrix Unification'.

As a diamond core (infinity diamond) template, this transmission as a cohesive and coherent structure is a diamond core template in and of itself. It is a solar stargate for it contains the keycodes and triggers for your expansion. The central 'core' theme, 'the core of the matter' within Matrix Transportation.

The Original Source I AM pulse as the ultimate 'isle of paradise' core of infinite infinities is the 'pure sun' or the 'white sun' or 'original sun'.

This is the son/sun that is Christed and Christ known as the Kryst, or the Krystalline or the 'Divine Krystal'.

It is an energy grid, electromagnetic field, singularity point.

The core diamond sun or Original Source emits an I AM pulse which is very challenging to express as a word for *it is the word*. It is sound, light and momentum all at once and is primordial sound. The voice of 'Prime Creator'.

We could quite truthfully give it the word 'creation' but even this would not be enough to explain the pulse. Even the word 'consciousness' does not truly hold fast to the expression of the Original Source diamond sun core vibration.

As you say the words out loud that are phire/flame alphabet/numerals known within and simultaneously hold event horizon and pivot point/nexus point in cohesive, focused visualised image, *you imprint the pineal gland for photocopying the gene expression for the ribosomic instruction for silicate/crystalline life form transmutation.*

Here are some words/phrases that are appropriate for that pulse yet none do justice to the actual pulse itself. You may find your own word or phrase more appropriate. As long as you hold focused coherent, cohesion with primordial sound and krystallised image then the instructional set is delivered to the ribosomic conductor within:

* I AM

* GOD

* CONSCIOUSNESS

* SOURCE

* PURITY

* DIVINITY

* CREATION

* ORIGIN

* ALPHA

* OMEGA

* SUN

* SOLAR

* SOL

* STAR

* CHRIST

* KRYST

* DIAMOND

* AURORA

* SOPHIA

Having presented these words, there is one word that can measure up in perfect alignment to the pulse we speak of. Even this word cannot explain in full entirety the energetic core pulse but it comes closer than any other word.

This word is **LOVE.**

This word, when truly understood by a balanced, cohesive and coherent activated individual, explains the I AM pulse, original core diamond sun Source point.

For the 'activation' aspect of the I AM pulse, we would use the word 'BLISS', yet this does not hold the compassionate, creative expansiveness that is held by LOVE.

Yet there is an activation, given as a keycode as the DIAMOND SUN AS FLAME LETTER. The word BLISS takes you into this awareness and understanding.

Other ways to express this I AM pulse would be through the use of colour or music or emotion.

One could also see the 'diamond core' of Source presentation as a 'destination' or 'place' if you will. For all 'return to Source' or 'sit at the right hand of the Father for eternity'. This simply means you have activated the diamond light aspect and retained memory in a cohesive sense.

You become the emanation of the diamond sun, Source consciousness, therefore you have 'returned to Source'. You do not need to pass through the death experience to do this. Ascension brings you to this point also and what is ascension? Using the model we present here then ascension is the awareness of self as the diamond core solar/sun.

The true 'son of God'.

Your Biblical 'Jesus Christ' or 'Yeshua' is a character or historical figure, or both, it matters not which belief or story you hold, that did this. He activated the diamond sun template within. This Jesus/Yeshua knew himself therefore to be the 'son of God' as in 'sun' and he knew himself to be the 'Christ' as in 'Kryst'.

He knew 'God' to be his 'father', Original Source, for he was the 'son' and the emanation of original core diamond sun.

He therefore ascended.

If you were to choose a word that reflected the Original Source diamond sun core as a place, and you can use this to make up your personal phire/flame letter primordial sound phrase, then words such as:

* NIRVANA

* PARADISE

* EDEN

* UTOPIA

* HEAVEN

* AGARTHA

* SHAMBHALA

* VALHALLA

* THE PROMISED LAND

* THE HOLY LAND

JERUSALEM

If one were to view the diamond sun core Source point as a 'thing' or 'object' then these words would be in alignment with the frequency:

THE INFINITY DIAMOND

THE HOLY GRAIL

THE PHILOSOPHER'S STONE

THE ARK OF THE COVENANT

The Ark of the Covenant would include all 'objects' found within the Ark. These are explained in further detail within 'The Infinite Helix and the Emerald Flame' transmission.

You can see how misunderstandings have occurred throughout your known history for each divine conduit has attempted to explain the unexplainable and the followers have thus added their own interpretations.

Those following religions, doctrines and other sacred pathways have looked outside of themselves for the answers, to the masters, the texts, the priesthood and the skies.

Yet all the answers are found within, for there lies the holographic replica through divine fractality of the original I AM pulse. Yet one has to experience the 'within' as the 'without' before turning back inward to 'the within'.

As we have said, this knowledge has been protected and hidden for it has been grossly misunderstood and misinterpreted to the point where extreme distortion has been created within communities, groups and within individuals.

The starseeds that held onto memory codes from 'previous incarnations' if you will, those with cohesive and activated memories who were able to reincarnate through choice via the solar gateways and not the iron core inverted trapping systems, were able to reactivate those memories and the knowledge they attained before their current incarnation. Therefore the ancient and sacred secrets and mysteries have been preserved through cohesive memory reincarnations.

The star nations and indigenous peoples verbally passed down this knowledge to the 'sacred wisdom keepers' and thus the secrets and mysteries were preserved also this way.

The 2012 prophecies with the end of the Mayan calendar and into the diamond core template involved the return of these mysteries and secret, sacred knowledge on a grand scale.

Now is the time for the delivery of these sacred secrets, mysteries and codes through the starseeds who hold cohesive, activated memory and hold a diamond core, infinity diamond solar/sun template within their DNA fields that we may also call 'individualisation'.

Individualisation, the retaining of memories through death and rebirth brings us to further explanations of the diamond core template structure as a matrix and of integration and unification.

28: Individualisation, Integration and Unification

Before an individual or construct/creation/being/idea/thought can move into unification, they first must individualise. Integration is key to this process.

This is indeed a 'grand paradox' for how can one be individual and unified simultaneously? Yet you cannot unify without individualisation. The reason for that is that Source consciousness, the emanation from the diamond sun core template, is a field or grid structure.

If only one aspect within this grid structure moves out of alignment and into distortion then it cannot 'hold form' within the grid. This is what we may call the 'phase lock' within the DNA. This is the pattern that falls into place when the ribosomic instructional codices are delivered to the RNA/DNA cellular matrices.

Using the model of the matrix and moving through the six diamond core templates of awareness, mastery, architecture, transportation, integration and unification, we present to you each core template as a 'stage' or 'teaching' within 'linear steps' for those who like to see lists, structures, maps and building blocks before them so they may process and make sense of the esoteric mystery wisdom teachings presented within this material.

1) Matrix Awareness

Aware of oneself as a non-locational consciousness, without a physical body, as 'pure awareness'. At this stage, one sees and feels a grid or structure but cannot define, measure or give scale to the formation that is self.

A very basic knowledge of vertical and horizontal axis within the presentation of self is there. The structure is not needed, for 'awareness' is simply that. Pure awareness of self as a consciousness.

This is the 'I think therefore I am' concept and thus the I AM presence or pulse. A perfect holographic replica, mirror image of Source consciousness.

2) Matrix Mastery

Moves into a cohesive and coherent 'soundwave broadcast field'. Understanding of self as an individualised entity with memory and with a 'mission' or 'goal' that one is travelling towards. This moves the structure of thought that is 'self' into the core placement within the non-physical matrix as the 'memory-brain' or mem-brane.

This gives cohesion to the structure. The awareness or sense of the infinity diamond event horizon is there yet still no scale or measurement. We might add that scale or measurement is not needed here.

This is the 'crystalline phase' and the phase of feeling, knowingness and beingness. This is that which we call the 'crystal being'. Mastery does not involve measurement or scale. Just the flow of beingness within cohesion and coherence is enough for complete mastery of self as an awareness.

3) Matrix Architecture

This is where scale and measurement is given to the structure in order to decode it and pass awareness from right hemisphere to left hemisphere of the 'brain' or 'mem-brane' so that the structure begins to know itself.

Vertical, horizontal and diagonal pathways are activated as well as the pivot point, nexus point as the very centre of a 'time matrix'. The being or consciousness begins to 'build itself' and holds what we call 'divine architecture'.

The building of this architecture triggers memory of all and everything. For a human incarnated physical being, this is an essential stage into the indigo expansion and the 'Excalibur' codex, which we presented within 'The Infinite Helix and the Emerald Flame'.

The being, already aware and at master level, begins to understand cohesion, coherence and individualisation. The being at this point is said to be within 'sovereignty'. A sovereign being.

4) Matrix Transportation

Somewhere between Matrix Architecture and Matrix Transportation, the being becomes aware of itself as an infinite structure. The pivot point, nexus point is understood as the core of self and the key to divine travel *within the fields and landscape of its own self.*

The being becomes a 'divine creator' or 'creatrix' as polarity is experienced and integration through the different 'sides' of the two dimensional structure. Event horizon and pivot point is understood as the zero point field of pure potentiality.

Matrix Transportation is then the understanding and knowledge of how to transform the entire structure of self and choose coordinates within the time matrix travel construct. An entire stargate system is presented and the being becomes aware of the greater self and of the fact that it is a infinitesimally small particle within a grand sea of consciousness expression. Yet the being knows it is infinite and therefore contains all other infinities within its infinite self structure.

The being begins to feel the awareness, not just of itself as a Matrix Architecture construct, but it begins to feel itself as other infinite Matrix Architecture constructs. The being sees this as a landscape within which to travel and create and the being sees each infinite matrix structure as a 'domain' within the landscape.

5) Matrix Integration

The awareness, mastery and architectural understanding allows for recall of all selves, with an omnipresent choice and focus system. Meaning that the individual can choose which selves to focus on, yet all selves are available to the individual. This recall does not necessarily manifest as 'past life' recall. It is a unique process whereby the individual is able to see the multidimensionality within the self and experience that.

The individual is able to compartmentalise all these aspects of self, within a cohesive framework. When each aspect is acknowledged and compartmentalised within the overall 'all that is you' or 'all there is' then each aspect can be integrated back into the whole, creating the sovereign integral being.

The one who stands within integrity and sovereignty. 'The Excalibur Codex' as mentioned within 'The Infinite Helix and the Emerald Flame' (chapter 43) is activated and the individual lives by truth and thus truth shows itself to that individual at every turn.

6) Matrix Unification

This is the diamond core template or 'core teaching' within this transmission that is *The Diamond Codex and the Quartz Key*.

This is where the being moves into the scale and expression of unification with other and self. It has explored the various domains within the grid system of expression as a landscape within which to travel.

Now it explores the idea that each infinite 'other self', which the being knows is an alternate expression of itself, is actually experienced individually from itself. The being understands that whilst it is an infinite expression of all and everything, so are each of the 'other selves' and they are NOT itself. This is simultaneously processed alongside Matrix Integration work.

The being knows that in order to create, one must go 'outside' the boundary which is the event horizon. The being knows this is only possible when it travels through the core centre of itself, the diamond sun.

Yet the being wishes to simultaneously stand strong as an aspect holding up a far greater and larger grid structure. The being then understands that if it is an aspect of a larger grid structure then there must be a core diamond sun centre to that grid structure and that travel through that core centre, Source consciousness itself, must be possible. This we explain here is what we may call 'solar ascension'.

The keycodes and triggers for solar ascension are presented here within the material within this transmission. Before solar ascension can be experienced on any level, then matrix individualisation and unification must take place.

Therefore, using the matrix model we present, we shall show you the structure of individualisation and unification.

For individualisation, you may stand in Tadasana, yogic mountain pose as the yogi or simply just stand straight. You can also envisage yourself doing this within mind. It matters not if this is done within body or mind.

Tadasana/yogic mountain pose presents to you the vertical pillar of light. Each asana within the yogic postures and flow are different expressions of the matrix Mer-Ka-Bah toroidal field.

You will envisage the matrix as we have said. Vertical pillar, horizontal axis, diagonal axes, pivot point and event horizon.

You shall then envisage the event horizon and pivot point as diamonds. The pivot point is a large infinity diamond at the solar plexus point emanating upwards to the heart.

You can do this exercise without colour and simply use the brilliance of the diamond through silver and white ray colour spectrum. If you wish to bring in colour then you would use green and pink for the emanation up to the heart chakra and the solar plexus would be a beautiful yellow or golden diamond.

You would allow the event horizon to sparkle as a 'diamond ring' around the entire structure. This is your 'cosmic diamond ring' if you will. It is the event horizon of the matrix.

Once you stand strong within this structure, and you will be familiar with this work if you have dedicated yourself to the material presented within 'The Infinite Helix and the Emerald Flame', you begin to 'change the shape' of the event horizon.

Your event horizon is, at this point, a smooth circle. A ring.

Your next step would be to give this circle little straight sides moving around the circle, with corners connecting each side. What you are looking to achieve here is, at first, a hexagon. You can later add more sides to the geometric construction, so there would be six sides to the event horizon rather than a smooth circle.

We would add here that shifting the event horizon from circle to hexagon is not an 'advanced' step. The hexagon is simply different to the circle. The circle is the 'original' template, if you will, for ultimately this is a spiral.

Moving into conscious unification through spiralling formation is another method for the keycode DNA triggers needed for phase lock sacred geometry, but we begin here with the simplest steps. This is a suggested exercise in order to visualise the infinity diamond, event horizon/pivot point as the same place, charge your Quartz Crystal Quay and program the ribosome conductor.

Your own mind and awareness will take you further from this simple step and trust all that comes to you, for remember, you *are* the infinite structure we speak of here. It is *you* that we describe!

So once you have your hexagon in place with six sides, vertical pillar, horizontal pillar creating sacred cross, diagonal pillars and pivot point, you stand as individualised diamond sun matrix.

You stand within 'avatar consciousness' if you will at this point. You have just completed a 'sacred shapeshifting magickal act'.

Was it not indeed simple? The 'Krystal River of Lightsight' as pineal gland projector is most powerful when the simple is cohesive and focused, creating coherence within.

The simple structures are that which the child plays with and this is all they are. Your Platonic solids are simply five. Five shapes. Yet they are the answer to all things. The way to understand their complexity is to see their simplicity.

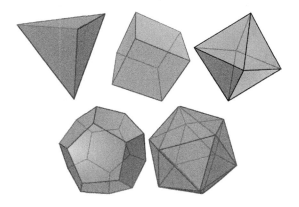

We present here the 'hexagon' as your event horizon. We move into mathematical territory which our conduit has little understanding of in any focused sense. There is indeed a puzzlement within her when we move into this way of explanation and therefore we can only work within the framework of her own understanding which will take us through the right hemisphere of the brain and the visual cortex. This is diamond/krystalline creativity without the processing.

The hexagon is a simple construction we can use to present what we are showing you here, yet know that the hexagon is indeed found within the Platonic solid and sacred geometries.

There are many master starseeds who teach this material and if you feel called to explore this further then you have but to put out the call for a master teacher within this area. We use the simple construction with the information we deliver to our conduit, so we utilise the hexagon.

Once you have this structure around you, in the visual of your mind then you would visualise another matrix structure, exactly like your structure, locked in place with the straight line of the hexagon merged with the straight line of your hexagon. You would do this with each of the straight lines of your hexagonal event horizon until you are aware of a hexagonal grid structure.

You may sit down now if you were in Tadasana doing this exercise, if you so choose yet hold the structure within the mind's eye.

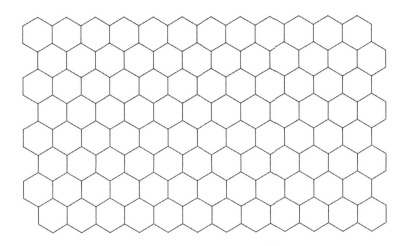

You would then move simultaneously into three different conceptual awareness constructs or thought structure perspectives and move into trilocational consciousness:

1: Individual perspective

You are individual within this grid even though you are part of this grid. You are aware that the hexagonal grid is infinite and you are but one hexagon within the overall grid. Each 'other' hexagon is a totally different being to you. You are unique within this grid as are they.

2: Unified perspective

You are aware that you are each and every hexagon within this grid, expressing yourself in different formats and presentations within each grid. You move outwards with your mind, away from the infinite grid matrix that was you and you become every single hexagon simultaneously.

3: Omnipresent perspective

You move your awareness into the fact that you are the entire grid as one entity. You are the ultimate supreme infinite-infinity and you are the entire grid, made up of infinite hexagons that are each, in and of themselves, infinite structures.

Before moving onto this next stage within the krystallised visualisation, we suggest you work fully with this first part. Draw the visual if you are an artist or utilise whichever creative aspect is your radiating stance within your incarnation. Be familiar with this first part.

When you have done this, you would move to the next stage.

You then take two more perspectives:

First perspective

The entire grid structure that is you is a 'place'. There is a central point to this 'place' which is the very core of yourself. The hexagonal grid structure that is you begins to curve around itself as a spiralling, curling, moving being.

You move into the structure you may know as a 'whirlwind' or 'twister' or 'tornado'. Right in the centre of this whirlwind is the central point, 'the eye of the storm' if you will.

This central point is the core of all that is you and it is the 'place' you are looking for. You may call this place by any of the names we listed previously that are names for the I AM pulse from Source as place or space.

Second perspective

The entire grid structure that is you is a 'being'. A living intelligence with thoughts, feelings and emotions. You move yourself into the same whirling/twister/tornado formation but you know yourself as a being.

The centre within which is the 'eye of the storm' is the central core of all that is you and you may give yourself the name, choosing any from the list of vibratory, aligned words we presented earlier or choosing any of your own that are in alignment.

You take these five perspectives simultaneously whilst holding the geometric hexagonal grid formation as whirlwind or tornado.

The first trinity and the second two perspectives. You hold these perspectives as one.

This may seem like a very simple exercise or a child's imaginary game and indeed, many children play with the ideas of these shapes and places and geometries within their minds.

You yourself may well have done such when you were a child. This is the cellular memory, keeping you awake and aware at the most intrinsic levels whilst still keeping you grounded and safe within your physical reality.

This is, in fact, a very powerful keycode and codex into the memory fields of the matrix geometry of the diamond sun Source template. This is how you charge your Quartz Crystal Quay and activate the infinity diamond. This is how you program the ribosome for *RAINBOW LIGHT BODY CODING* and accelerated stargate ascension.

This will trigger codices within the plasma light filaments of the DNA bringing you into even more cohesion and coherence through compression of self. This is true shapeshifter, magickal mystery teachings in simplified and basic form.

You can, of course, become far more creative with your personal infinite grid field. You can move into geometries that have more sides than the hexagon. Such as an octagon or dodecahedron.

These get 'closer' if you will to the intricate formations of Source but the hexagonal grid is enough to trigger the DNA memory fields into individualisation and unification.

You can even decide each matrix is a mandala and create

beautiful mandala grids. The choice is yours for this is your creative landscape. The point is, you are activating the memory codes for unification and this will 'take root' within you and grow into your own personal tree of life.

29: Round Tables of New Earth

The manifestation that will occur for you, when you work within these pineal gland/ribosomal instructional fields, will be the externalised reflection of that which you call New Earth.

The bifurcation and more covertly expressed trifurcation take you into the split reality of iron core template manifestation, that which our conduit does call 'order of the world that is new' which is the artificial intelligence orchestrated, Borg assimilated reality structure.

The other aspect to the split is the heart-centred, unified, creative structure that is organic, the replica of Source consciousness as the expression of the infinity diamond. The resulting round table presentation within this New Earth/world/reality is compartmentalisation into unification through individualisation and integration.

The visual techniques we have presented will assist you to stand within the sovereign, hermetically sealed field of starseeded, celestial, solar beings of morphogenetic memory. The sovereign integral being who walks with the sword of truth, Excalibur, by his side. Dragontamer, dragonrider with full understanding of dragonsbreath which is the morphogenetic field. Accelerated stargate ascension is the journey and the destination.

You may wonder, where are the practical, applied steps within this transmission as diamond core template teaching? Yet all is coded as this transmission is the monadic, Diamond Codex itself.

Charging the Quartz Crystal Quay and holding the infinity diamond within the palm of your hand will take place as you read these words. For the catalysts, keys, codes and triggers are passed to you as you read.

Your own visuals, through pineal compression and projector expression are stargate creations in and of themselves.

The coding within is presented for a reason and must be delivered this way, for when the student is ready the master will come. We are not the master that comes to you but this transmission is the catalyst to it. The master is you.

When the student is ready, the master will come is to be translated into *when you are ready you shall discover yourself.*

You are always your own master.

The New Earth manifestations of beauty will be seen by you as easily as you see the codes within this transmission. Yet to those who are not ready, they shall not see the beauty, for it shall be lost on them. They shall stand puzzled at your choice of reality expression and participation. It shall not look to them as it looks to you. For where they see a barren field, you see lush grass and multicoloured wild flowers. Where they see a plain white horse, you see a unicorn. Where they see a dragonfly, you see a fairy atop her dragon.

The perspective is everything for the perspective creates the reality.

The round table of New Earth shall infiltrate the entire structure through adamantine particle thought process. Just as the ribosome conducts the instructional sequencing for krystalline transmutation so too do the adamantine particles create the blueprints for the New Earth planetary structure.

The round table enters the medical world bringing light, sound, colour and frequency to the forefront of healing modality.

The structure of the round table, hexagonally presented moves into the political structure as change takes place from the inside. Iron core superimposed over diamond core, yet the diamond will always shine through and Trump the iron core every time.

Your educational systems shall hold the unification of learning between teacher and pupil as the innate knowing within each child is that which is bought to the fore rather than the old system of filling the perceived empty vessel.

Your food, farming and agriculture shall biodynamically and organically present, bringing new ocean nourishment into the fields and soils of New Earth.

The architectural structures shall, over time, lose the four corners and squares and the return of the roundhouses and creations of domes and triads shall begin as the secrets of the star nations, indigenous families are passed to the New Earth progenitors.

Media systems within entertainment and journalism shall compete one on one with the iron core. Only those who step down, bow out and find inspiration through innovation will break through the media wall and shine the brightest and biggest diamond of all.

The Tower of Babel shall be realised as the awakened ones decode the metaphor. Fourth dimensional confusion shall give way to fourth density clarity through the power of the story.

That being said, let us thus return to the story as the storyteller within you, dear reader, awakens and stirs. Do you not feel you have a story within you? Indeed you do, dear starseed, indeed you do.

30: Diamond Calling

This dream was different. The exhilaration from the dragon ride had opened her up into an awareness that she knew she had once held, but it had been long forgotten.

For she was no longer the Princess Aurora with a body, with arms and legs and physical sensations. She knew herself simply as awareness, yet she had sight and saw much.

In the dream there was a type of grid structure before her, like a huge gateway or lattice fencing. Yet each section of the lattice was a hexagon. She knew she was looking at a hexagonal grid yet this awareness was simultaneous to another awareness.

'How strange', Aurora thought to herself, 'that I am looking at a structure I do not fully comprehend and yet there is a sensation within me that I cannot name. What is this sensation?'

And she knew then and gave name to it.

Familiarity.

The hexagonal grid was familiar. More than familiar, she knew it and knew it intimately. She approached the grid yet she knew not how because she was no longer a body atop the beast of a dragon. No longer the dragonrider or the princess, just the awareness of self without body or form.

The grid was her friend and it 'smiled' at her yet she saw no smile. Only the feeling that one holds intrinsically when another smiles at you.

The grid was friendly.

It was more than lattice fencing but a structure of transportation. Unlike the dragon who flew with outstretched reptilian wings of gold and glory, there were no wings within this infinite boundary of joined and unified hexagonal geometries. Yet the grid seemed to move in response to her and certain hexagonal sections beckoned to her as if they were calling her. And she knew as she moved closer that she could pass her awareness through one of the hexagonal sections and find herself... where? She did not know.

She was ready to find out and as that thought passed through the awareness that was her mind, one hexagonal geometry began to glow as a diamond. This was the one, the diamond gateway that would show her the answers to all her dreams.

She glided forward and faced the diamond geometry up close as the hexagonal grid lattice disappeared from her view.

Dragon's eye view no longer, up close there was nothing but the diamond brilliance of an entire new world.

Decision made with harmonious flow, no struggle here, this was simply a following towards a calling, a 'diamond' calling.

Yet then the brilliance began to fade and awareness returned to her physical body, the velvet softness of her pink cushion close to her face as her eyes slowly opened.

'Where was I?' she thought, 'and more importantly, what would I have found if I had passed through the diamond stargate?'

Aurora's last thought before getting ready for the day ahead was 'If only my dream could have lasted just a little longer.'

31: Collapsing the Wave

So we have said that you do not *need* to charge the Quartz Crystal Quay, yet you will *choose* to do this when you consciously walk the ascension path. Activating the Diamond Codex into the diamond sun light body/rainbow body of light is part of that choice.

You do not *need* to access the accelerated stargate system but if you choose to move forward within full awareness, full realisation, holding onto your full memory and access the highest form of galactic pathways available to you, then you will *choose* accelerated stargate ascension.

If the terms 'indigo', 'the first wave', 'wayshower' and 'planetary leader' trigger something within you whereby you just know these words/phrases are describing you, or your mission, then you will feel the calling for accelerated stargate ascension.

We have spoken within our previous transmission 'The Infinite Helix and the Emerald Flame' about creating the stargate so you may ride your dragon through it.

However, in truth you *are* the stargate. Not only are you the stargate but you are an *entire stargate system* and you become this when you move through the carbon to crystalline transmutation. The creation of the rainbow body of light or diamond sun light body *is* you becoming the stargate system.

You become a stargate system by reconstructing your DNA template to the 'fifth strand' formation (and into sixth strand) which then gives you access to the entire 12 into 144,000 DNA template.

You then draw in all your directional aspects of that 12 into 144,000 DNA template, time matrix, and you do what we call 'collapse the wave'.

You then take that 'collapsed wave' aspect of self and 'ride it' through its centre point (pivot point/nexus).

There are many ways to explain this process but what you are doing is activating your DNA and changing its shape or structure, if you will. You are then able to 'travel' throughout hyperspace/innerspace/innerverse, which is the inverse to outer space/universe.

The reason why you do this is simply to give you a far more expansive 'choice field' if you will, regarding how you live your life, experience your reality and your incarnational/reincarnational line.

You have this expansive choice due to your understanding, through memory activation, of reality itself.

In order to reconstruct the DNA template and become this stargate system, you need to be able to focus enough to create a 'line of intention'.

Blue starphire, quantum convergence charge is needed in order for you to find this focus and create the line of intention.

There are many exercises, initiations and techniques you can undertake in order to be able to do this, but one method is to do what we may call 'part the Red Sea'.

Parting the Red Sea

The parting of the red sea is a metaphor and a very powerful visualisation technique to take you into the intentional focus needed to create a trajectory of intention. It is a phire/flame letter visualisation.

This is most helpful with goal setting in your own life and is a grounded visual to use for manifestation.

Due to the high level focus given to the biblical stories, utilising the imagery for your magikal and intentional work creates a 'higher power grid', if you will, when utilising that particular visual.

This also assists you within your mission of 'decoding the ancient metaphor' which is a planetary wide mission for the starseeds at this time.

In your visual, you would simply imagine that you are standing before the Red Sea. Just as Moses did in the biblical account, one would be holding a staff and either strike that imagined staff onto the ground, as the character 'Gandalf' does within 'The Lord of the Rings' fictional story[7], or simply hold out your imagined staff, or you can hold out your hands in front of you and not use the staff at all.

If you choose to use the staff, then you can create an elaborate staff here made of natural wood or crystal adorned with jewel gemstones such as ruby/sapphire/emerald/amethyst/diamond to create the power tool within the visualisation. Remember here that you are working with DNA 'language of light' through the phire/flame letter sequencing when you do this.

However, using the staff does anchor you into the planetary vertical axis (pillar of light) and your own vertical axis within your personal matrix. Your own hands and arms also hold the power of the individualised matrix when you stand in mastery.

Whichever your choice for this visual, you would simply imagine that at your command, with open-hearted love for the unification of self within/with the natural environment rather than 'God complex ego mentality', the seas part before you creating a large contained stationary tidal wave on the left hand side of this pathway and a large contained stationary tidal wave on the right hand side of this pathway.

The ocean tidal waves are the distractions around you and the pathway you have created is your focused intentional trajectory

---

[7] *The Lord of the Rings* (1954-1955) by J.R.R. Tolkien

or 'line of intention'.

Here you have created a horizontal axis, hence the reason why the bejewelled crystal staff is such an aligned and appropriate magikal tool to utilise here for this visual as you are working directly with the sacred geometry of the sixth dimensional matrix through the fifth dimensional metaphoric visualisation.

The staff and the pathway through the Red Sea create the sacred cross.

You then place the intentioned goal or manifestation at the end of the pathway through the Red Sea. Then you would envisage yourself crossing through the pathway and reaching the intentioned destination.

You do not need to know exactly what the destination is as long as you intend what you are wishing to achieve from it through *focus.*

Thus the visualisation could be a large treasure chest that has revealed itself through the parting of the Red Sea. It is for you then to leave the universal energetics to create the most appropriate vibrational match for you that mirrors the frequency of that which you have intentioned which is safely inside the box.

Opening the box thus gives you a clue or a trigger into that which is most in alignment for you at this time. Therefore the parting of the Red Sea exercise can be used for divination as well as intentional creational manifestation.

Within this transmission when we say to you to 'part the Red Sea', this is what we mean.

After working with this visual several times, you will become adept at this and the parting of the Red Sea visual becomes an 'alphabetical numeral', known better as a flame or phire letter code, within the DNA.

Then, when you find yourself in a situation where you need clear focus in order to think, recall or visualise, this could be as simple as engaging within a conversation with someone, you can instantly recall the parting of the Red Sea visual in your mind.

Know you are moving distractions within your thought process away with the moving of the ocean waves to the left and right side and clear that focused line of intention pathway immediately.

Your brain, bodymind and innate intelligence of the DNA will know what you are doing as the third dimensional interface for consciousness. You will find your ability to focus increases several fold once you become an adept with this visualisation work.

Your biblical stories and accounts are abundant with these deeply layered metaphoric tools which are taken literally by those who exist within the third dimension.

Indeed some of the biblical stories are based on historical fact either from your actual past timeline or from alternate historical timelines for Earth. Yet the majority of the biblical stories and scriptures are metaphor and code and are most useful during your current time of planetary and galactic ascension.

Another exercise to present more of a crystalline focus, rather than the indigo line of intention, is to move into the initiation of the receiving or activating of your wings.

This we can call 'wingmaking' and it refers to balancing of certain codex structures within the individualised matrix. This can be linked to etheric or doppelganger DNA within the formation of the 12 strand 144,000 quantum template between 5th and 8th strand formations as pre-code or pre-matter.

Many ascending individuals feel these wings upon their backs and as they go forward within the construction of the DNA template, they become more and more aware of these wings.

They can utilise the wings in the same way that they can utilise other language of light code structures such as the 'cloak of invisibility' or 'the crystal palace drawbridge' or the 'parting of the Red Sea'.

The cloak of invisibility, usually violet within the imagery, is to place the cloak entirely over one's person to make oneself 'invisible'. This can be done also with places, events, buildings, concepts and creations. You will find that when this visualisation is undertaken with focus that the said individual, place, event, building, concept or creation thus becomes psychologically invisible. It is simply 'not noticed' by those who are not of like-vibration.

The crystal palace drawbridge would be the visualisation of the palace surrounded by the protective circle of the moat, containing magickal waters. 'Letting down the drawbridge' connects castle to moat, allowing safe passage in and out of all like-vibrational beings, concepts, creations, ideas and so on. This is also a metaphor for the corpus callosum within the brain connecting the two brain hemispheres together in balance which is the trigger for lucid dreaming and the 'beyond the theta' brainwave state.

There is a shift within the 'heart wings' within the wingmaking visualisation and this 'correction' or 'realignment' of wings of the heart is in reference to clearing traumas, hijacks and infiltrations from the matrix and restoring the formations and codes to the DNA structure in their highest plasma light formations.

These 'wings of the heart' refer to 'fractality' within the heart. This is also known as the 'activated higher heart'.

Through working with the wing structure and entering the wingmaking visualisation, when aware of the heart's ability, one creates fractality of heart and one is then able to stand as 'teacher of light', 'angel on Earth', 'ascended master' or 'adept' within their ascension journeys.

These individuals are those undergoing 'accelerated stargate ascension' and we would refer to them as the 'dragonriders'.

The DNA crystalline lattice structure when in direct synchronised link up with the heart signals actually look like 'wings' which in turn, as we have said, are felt by the ascending starseeds.

The Mag-Da-Len codex is thus activated during the wingmaking. This codex is discussed in our previous transmission 'The Infinite Helix and the Emerald Flame'.

The energetic called into aware consciousness at the time of the focused intentional wingmaking exercise is the 'true twin flame' which is the first distortion from the 'eternal flame' into the 'Sophia/Kryst alliance', also discussed within our transmission 'The Infinite Helix and the Emerald Flame'.

We present here several visual codices as Quartz Crystal Quay flames for the focused intention and magical work for the creation of the stargate system within.

The stargate system is, of course, your DNA. When you undertake this work, the work of the adept, you collapse the wave and create higher harmonic DNA fields which echo morphogenetic consciousness and thus blueprints for omnipresence or indeed the fully realised memory matrix.

32: A Strange Land

She could not feel the dragon anymore, as if they were one person as was the case when they were flying through space, yet still they had communication. She felt like herself again and the dragon was now an independent consciousness from herself but glad she was that they were able to still talk.

He did not know where they were and neither did she but it was truly beautiful. The landscape, gloriously covered in a green sheen, gave her wonder as such that she had never experienced before.

Looking upwards, the tops of the trees were so high that they could not be seen, but the glow was there, the glowing of the trees that she could feel deep within her as well as see.

"It is beautiful here, wherever it is."

He turned his large head and focused two large lidded eyes upon her.

"Indeed. My quests are twofold. Why am I coupled with you and why did we ride together to this place?"

Aurora did not know either but it was the child that was first and foremost in her mind and she touched her belly to feel the soft mound swell under her fingertips. 'So, you remain pregnant even in a dream then,' she thought.

"We are not in a dream, Princess," said the dragon, reading her mind. "This is the world of light. You are here as an individualised being that is a complete replica of your true self, therefore you are not dreaming but have transported your consciousness from the physical body to the light body."

Princess Aurora nodded. "I was aware of such. It happened once before in a similar way, only that time I rode on the back of a dolphin through a portal in the sea. I am a seasoned traveller which is why I am aware of the travel. I know my form lies sleeping in my marriage bed next to my new husband, yet I do not feel that body. My consciousness remains strong in this one. The one you call the body of light."

The dragon blinked those large eyes at her and laid his head upon the grass by her side. The creation of the fire ring had left him weary.

"I felt my name to be Allianse when we were coupled. Is this accurate? Is Allianse your name?" the princess asked.

"Correct," he said and her mind was filled with the tingles again as occurred every time he pushed his thoughts as words into her mind. "One name, the one for now anyway."

"You have other names?" She had always wanted to take the quest with a dragon but had not realised it would be the dream world that would allow her to do this.

"I change form so take a name for each form. Yet they are not the same being each time, but different. I am the one they call Allianse and I am the leader of the group."

"You are a group?" asked Aurora with wide-eyed interest.

"Yes. I exist at the group level but am currently individualised as Allianse for you. I am able to consult with the others still and it seems I am to be your guide. For now at least."

Aurora looked ahead to the cloudy wispy mist in front of her that had been gaining momentum since they arrived, yet she did not process the mist. First and foremost now in her mind was the conversation with this majestic creature they call the dragon.

"Guide? I had expected a form like myself, a master perhaps but I am in full acceptance of the guide being my dragon. I am indeed most happy about this and have always wished to meet a creature such as yourself. I am humbly honoured that you chose me."

"Well, I didn't," he replied. "I did not choose you as such. We came together. The choice appears to have been made by us both or by something greater than us."

Aurora nodded, "Yes I understand and I am pleased about this. I have so many questions I want to ask you but firstly, please tell me, how do I remain in this dream? I mean, how do I anchor myself here in this light body? As I said, I have travelled this way before but have never been able to sustain it for long."

"I believe this is where I come in," Allianse replied, "as your guide and through our telepathic coupling I can give you the momentum you need to remain here within the light body. You will need to return to your true form every so often, to replenish, I would expect. I don't know the answers, I don't know how it works."

Aurora stood up and brushed the twinkly sparkles from her dress, which presented as a merge between her bridal gown and her nightwear. The silver dust that was finely scattered across the ground was an unknown substance to her, she was curious about it yet still brushed it off as easily as she brushed away the sand from the beaches when it collected itself about her. The silver dust was different though, it was like it had a mind of its own. Like everything else in this strange world.

"Are you not supposed to be my guide?" she asked.

"Indeed I am. Does being a guide mean I have all the answers for you? As a princess of the divine realms, you must know how the guide operates?"

She nodded, "Yes. I understand that we work together. We discover things together, yet I am also aware that you will have answers for me to many questions I may have. My training taught me that much and you being a dragon should be no different if you are my guide."

The dragon, keeping one eye upon the white mist that seemed to now be taking form and the other eye firmly on her, pushed his thoughts into her mind as reply.

"I have responses for you child. Many. Yet they may not be what you expect as answers. This is my quest too, is it not? The guide learns from the student, does he not?"

Aurora smiled, "Yes, we learn together. The student/guide relationship blurs and one becomes the other. I know the teaching yet I have not had the experience. I look forward to our working partnership. My first quest to you, Allianse the golden dragon, is... what is that strange white mist taking form before us?"

Allianse now with both eyes on the forming shape within the thick mist pushed one final thought into her mind before they both fell into a deep sleep.

"It is what they call pre-matter. I know it because it is a similar substance to my own fire, the dragon's breath. On Earth, the humans would know it as plasma but basically it is a substance that creates manifestation. Pure thought becoming form. What exactly it is forming into, I have no idea."

33: Dear Pixie

Can you please tell me what these phrases mean?

Metatronic Saturnian matrix code deconstruction, deactivation and dismantling.

Trigger events for:

1) Collapse of the bi-wave

2) Victimiser archetypal structure

3) Electric War timeline

These refer to systems within the inverted matrix. The conduit using these metaphors has translated the energy he/she receives into aligned terminology from the best of his/her ability based on his/her personal perspective, paradigm and knowledge system.

This is assuming 'Metatronic, Saturnian code' to be of dark/black technology. All frequency sounds (names/labels) for deities, archangels, logos structures, logoi, etc have different names and labels and within that frequency sound (name/label) there are both positive and negative polarity consciousness structures holding mass.

Therefore there is a negative and a positive Metatron. There is a negative and a positive 'Saturn'.

This goes also for all systems/structures/group soul consciousness infinities including we 'the Nine'.

The mass given to the negative or positive polarity consciousness structure is dependent on the consciousness of humanity, or other planetary civilisations holding the same point of focus for said deity/archangel, etc.

The 'bi-wave' refers to a structure with a 'two wave' or 'dual wave' structure, rotating fields moving in opposing directions, collapse, as in the collapse of it.

Victimiser archetypal structure refers to those consciousness structures that victimise others.

Electric war timeline refers to a 'crash' within multidimensional space that involved polarising forces within electricity. These are group souls moving through a polarising experience.

In your third dimensional awareness, one would perceive this as an 'electric war'. However, from our perspective, this is polarisation within a multilocational consciousness sense.

This presents as just 'some' timelines rather than 'all' timelines which means it can either be manifested for your experiential awareness or averted as it were.

Can you talk about the plots and plans to run dark deed timelines? Can you touch upon again the 'Armageddon agenda' for further clarification?

This is simply the agenda of some service-to-self groups to create the 'intended outcome' of any 'dark deed' event.

The intended trajectory for these dark deed events was World War Three. These 'war' or 'battle' programs are often initiated whenever a controlled planetary population reaches critical mass regarding creative evolution. These war programs instigate 'the call'.

Your timelines were shifted from this WW3 trajectory due to consciousness gridwork from starseeds/white hats/wanderers/alliance.

There remains an agenda to steer back into that timeline. This would be the dark deed timeline and the 'Armageddon agenda' which are 'end of the world' or 'extinction event' ELE type scenarios for your planet and humanity.

And are these agendas being averted? Are they being deconstructed?

Indeed yes, this is the case at the time of this transmission. The reason for this is due to the fact that they are finite and cannot hold form without continued fear wave generated frequency. As the great awakening unfolds, the fear wave is generated less and less and eventually no longer holds at critical mass level. At this point, the collapse within the entire dark structure begins yet this does not occur in one moment. It unfolds as the falling down of dominoes or a deck of cards and takes place over time, within a linear sense. There are attempts to rebuild each structure as it falls and the agendas are 'placed on the back burner' and new agendas are brought in. Decisions are made in 'real time' depending on the position of the pieces upon the chessboard, as it were, for the battle for Earth is played out as a long-standing, continuous 'game of chess' with each chess master taking their time in moving their pieces. However, at times the dark masters move their chess pieces in haste and this is where 'mistakes' are made, if you will.

The tarot card 'the tower' and the story of 'the Tower of Babel' explain the presentation that is occurring and shall occur regarding the averting of dark agendas and deconstruction of the fallen systems.

The story of the Tower of Babel links directly into fragmentation of self so that the 'heavens' (higher mind/crown chakra/galactic intelligence) cannot be reached. Fragmentation when taken with the focused intention for integration creates compartmentalisation into unification. This is true alchemy and is indeed the 'Aurora Matrix Alchemy' and the alchemy and magick of the starseeds. Through this alchemical unification, the great awakening of humanity takes place and thus the exposure and fall of the dark systems and negative structure.

Can these agendas and dark deed timelines be steered back into?

Not if certain key leadership human consciousness structures remain in place and starseeds continue to manifest the ascension timeline through their ability to alchemically unify. If the starseeds each charge their own personal Quartz Crystal Quay and activate the Diamond Codex, as is explained and presented through multiple codices within this transmission (as this transmission *is the exterior reality presentation of the Diamond Codex in and of itself*), then the agendas and dark deed timelines cannot be steered back into or extended. The diamond core template of original, organic singularity shines as the fractalised central suns of the infinity diamond (infinite Grand Central Sun refraction) and the iron core template, false ascension timeline, artificial sun program cannot sustain and cannot *succeed.*

Are you talking about people in the political field when you mention certain key leadership human consciousness?

Indeed yes, and within other structures such as medical, journalistic and military.

What if they do not remain in place?

This is highly unlikely. The probability of this occurring upon your planet is less than 2%. However, the 'white hat/alliance' programs, which we would refer to as the 'fail-safe', would be the authorisation of crossing free will boundaries in order to prevent extinction-type events and Armageddon agenda programs and depopulation scenarios.

Even if this 2% probability were to occur, the starseeds moving through the ascension timeline and New Earth scenario would still create that timeline. All this would do is extend the order of the world that is new, artificial timeline. It is not possible in any timeline for the iron core template structures to remain in place indefinitely for they are finite.

Does this mean that positively polarised light beings or extraterrestrials would prevent this from happening?

Yes, this is what that means. Although these groups are not just 'extraterrestrials' or 'light beings', as in structures outside of you. They are part of the 'Aurora Network' or 'Aurora Matrix' which is the collective consciousness of the starseeds on Earth. So effectively, you. It is you, not just you, our conduit, Magenta Pixie but all the starseeds on Earth. We speak to *you* dear Pixie and to *you* dear reader.

Please can you tell me, who the 'Silver White Starphire King' is?

This is the same as our reference to 'blue starphire' or rather the code for 'blue starphire'. Yet in this translation, the blue starphire is seen as a collective body rather than a chemical or electromagnetic charge within each individual and is therefore presented as silver white.

Is it an individual chemical/charge or a collective body?

It is both.

Who is the King?

The archetypal structure for the collective starphire as a planetary memory complex within the male polarised field. Known as King Kristos. Within the Aurora network this would be Archangel Michael from our perspective as closest human shield and crystalline activator.

Can you tell me what is the code of the 'Blue Feather Moon'?

This is the code created to assist the starseeds in full ascension, 12 strand, into 144,000 template reconstruction and the ability to create blue starphire.

Within the transmission 'The Infinite Helix and the Emerald Flame', you told me that you were 'members of the Blue Lodge'. I actually left that out of the transmission during the editing process because it sounded to me like it was connected to Freemasonry. I would like further clarification on this. What did you mean by saying you were 'members of the Blue Lodge'.

We understand why you would initially interpret this as a connection to another model within the structure you refer to as Freemasonry. Many images and flame letter presentations are borrowed, changed, shifted, deconstructed and reconstructed, hijacked, extended, distorted and rearranged.

The 'Blue Lodge' is the meeting place for those that move beyond certain restricted parameters within higher density fields and connect at the point known as the 'Order of the Blue Flame'.

This is, if you will, the place of the blue ray field, the ability to personify blue starphire (quantum convergence charge).

We *are* your blue starphire, dear Pixie, this is who we are. We are your memories. Our meeting place is the Grand Blue Lodge for this is the presented architectural structure for the fifth dimensional domain knows as the Halls of Amenti. This is a celestial phire and when you traverse this matrix, you will visualise this as blue. Hence the reason it is referred to as the 'blue flame' for it is the place of memory.

You yourself and all ascending starseeds hold the memories of the blue flame. You are *all* members of the 'Grand Blue Lodge'.

It is time now for you of the Aurora Network to reclaim your symbolism, your terminologies and your stories and place them back into their organic geometric structure within the phire/flame letter alphabet which is your activated ribosomal DNA.

What is the cosmic spine?

The cosmic spine you speak of is interpreted terminology referring to vertical pillar of light or vertical axis alignment into Matrix Awareness and Matrix Mastery.

What is the healing of the 'gender dance codex'?

Healing of the 'gender dance codex' simply refers to clearing and alignments bought into balance regarding trauma code gender issues.

Can you tell me please, what does it mean to have a 'diamond heart' or 'crystal blood'?

'Diamond heart' and 'crystal blood' refers to the open-hearted bliss-charged-love into golden mean mathematical soundwave alignments and structures within the heart needed for full stargate ascension.

Does the healing of the 'gender dance codex' mean that transgender people will accept their birth gender?

It does not mean this. It means that any person, transgender or otherwise, will come into alignment between gender identity, gender expression and gender dysphoria by whatever means they choose to.

So it does not mean that transgender people are distorted or out of balance?

There are many people upon your planet that are distorted and out of balance. This includes heterosexual and cisgender individuals. So too are there many balanced individuals, many are transgender and many of these individuals are starseeds and moving through ascension.

So transgender individuals are not the result of a service-to-self distortion or inverted system code?

There are those that have been 'affected', shall we say, by these mind controlled 'airwaves' and other chemical hijacked reality constructs. There are also those that are immune to these airwaves or broadcasts. There is also an androgynous future timeline for your planetary race, of which many transgender individuals are 'forerunners' or 'consciousness seeders' to that androgynous future timeline. This is within organic structure as full balance of physical polarisation within fertility. Yet this program has also been hijacked and inverted.

The organic and the inverted/artificial can therefore appear most similar and to those just awakening into fourth dimensional consciousness, they can appear indistinguishable. Higher fourth or fifth dimensional consciousness is needed to know the difference between the two. Therefore the organic and the inverted as bifurcated realities stand as catalysts for the ascension into the 5D realms.

Are transgender individuals starseeds and lightworkers?

As we have said, many are this, yes.

So the belief that transgenderism is a distortion program code created by service-to-self individuals is untrue?

It is correct in some cases. These cases are in the minority. All humans are presented with service-to-self distortion program codes through the inverted matrix.

It is no different between the presentation to the non-transgender individual than it is to the transgender individual.

Does this apply for homosexual individuals as well?

Homosexual individuals are subjected to the inverted matrix just as heterosexual individuals are. However, there was no actual deliberate distortion aimed at homosexuality per se.

The deliberate distortion was aimed at gender confusion with a transgender presentation or a fragmented disassociated presentation within an individual.

The organic androgynous future timeline codex placed within the 'Aurora Grid', the starseed collective consciousness within humanity, was the antidote to the deliberate distortion aimed at gender confusion within a linear reality expression, so thus catalyst.

Is the 'collapse of the bi-wave' the same thing as lessening in polarisation within a density or with the creation of a positive or negative fifth dimension/fourth density?

Yes, this is the same 'event', just explained differently through different models.

As we have said, a bi-wave is a duality wave within a structure or field. The 'collapse' of this duality structure therefore creates unification as the 'bi-wave' becomes one unified wave.

Lessening of polarity is also the result of ascension or a raise in frequency within a structure or field, so one could say that lessening in polarity is the same as a duality wave collapse.

The creation of a positively polarised fifth dimension, or indeed fourth density, would also be a collapse of a duality wave and the creation of a unified structure.

However, the fully negatively polarised dimension, although a 'result' or 'response' to a duality wave collapse, would not create a fully functional dimension as that dimension, or density, would not have enough momentum in order to hold the structure in place and this structure would eventually dissipate.

In one of your recent transmissions, you mentioned the 'Seventh Seal of Atlantis'. Can you please tell me what this is?

This is the code for the fail-safe program placed within each reincarnating, awakened and activated Atlantean priest and priestess. This fail-safe is known by many names and presented in many forms. One of the more well known forms is the 'Ark of the Covenant' for that is the promise of the fulfilment of the continued Atlantean Royal House of Avalon mission. Within this transmission, we present this same seventh seal as the Diamond Codex and the Quartz Quay.

What is krystalline bliss and the ecstasy of free-flowing celestine?

This is the bliss code activation that the awakened individual feels when moving through the carbon to silicate transmutation process. Free-flowing celestine is the chemical activated throughout your cellular makeup, specifically within the spine, the glandular system and most especially within the pineal gland.

What happens to the individuals who do not want to move into the fifth dimension? Are they stuck in the fourth dimension?

It is not that they are 'stuck'. They will, for a time, remain within the confusion domains of the fourth dimension until they reset again the third dimensional soul's journey.

I heard that the 'prime directive laws' have been rewritten? Is this true?

In the sense that the collective of humanity is moving through ascension all the time. As they move higher in frequency, they 'give permissions' if you will for expansion of the prime directive.

However, the prime directive is and always has been regarding non-interference of humanity's free will. If ascending collective of humanity raise in frequency and thus 'give permissions' then the assistance from and merge with non-physical, extraterrestrial and ultradimensional entities is far greater than in previous times upon your planet.

It is not that the prime directive has changed, it is that the free will of humanity now calls for galactic assistance and merge, at critical mass level, thus this is no longer seen as a violation of the non-interference prime directive.

Is the unicorn a fire letter? If so, can you explain further?

Memory triggers depiction of the unicorn, purity, light,

spirituality and the gateway to the fifth dimension for nothing but love and peace can live in this place. The unicorn is literally the most sacred of all the depictions of the phire letters and holding this image gives you the encodement for peace. Yet also paradoxical consciousness is given here for the unicorn is the wisest creature within the 3D forest, yet also holds the most innocence. Untainted by anything less than perfection, the true unicorn's name is Shambhala, the paradisiacal inner world of Nirvana. Pure enlightenment. Yet each unicorn holds a different name, unique to its connection with you.

The unicorn is the highest aspect of self that the human seeker strives for and unicorn energy is truly integrated at the fullest opening of the heart. The unicorn stays in the shadows within the fourth dimensional world and is even more hidden within the third dimension. Yet he or she can be seen in both dimensions.

The fifth dimension is where you will find this most beautiful of creatures.

Meditate upon the unicorn for healing, peace, serenity, wisdom, innocence and true love.

The unicorn may be utilised for manifestation but only if the intention for the manifestation matches the unicorn energy.

Can you tell me who are the Tuatha Dé Danann?

Tuatha Dé Danann seeded the Celtic bloodlines. They were warrior tribes with full memory of their incarnations within Atlantis and Lemuria and their connections to the Pleiades and Lyra. They held bilocational consciousness and lived Elemental lives alongside physical incarnations and they kept that portal between the harmonic dimensions open until they were infiltrated and sealed off by the dark masters. In your now time vector, since the Easter portal 2022, they are open once more.

They were not Lemurian, although there are connections there. Lemurians moved through many different time periods as they descended into physical form. Tuatha Dé Danann did not incarnate onto the planet in the same way the Lemurians did. They were seeded through light transfer within harmonic dimensions. They therefore 'thought' themselves into being rather than incarnated into a third density body. Consciousness is able to create for itself form but this is not incarnation.

The Tuatha Dé Danann were fae or faery (elemental beings) that were able to give themselves form, enough to influence the conception of new incarnated souls.

They would project forth a form of light transfer into the female's womb after she had conceived with her twin flame partner. The child would be genetically the offspring of the third dimensional parents but would also hold genetic memory and etheric DNA from the Tuatha Dé Danann fae parent that had projected his own light DNA into the developing child.

These hybrid Tuatha fae/humans were bigger than previous generations (known as the generation of giants or Celtic giants) and were incarnated into Celtic lines. This is how the Tuatha Dé Danann seeded the Celtic clan bloodlines. The hybrid offspring were strong, large, red-haired and incredibly healthy and long lived. They were psychic, clairvoyant and empathic. They had the ability to dreamwalk and dreamweave and they were the first dragonriders and master gridworkers upon your planet Earth.

They were known by many names including the Grail Kings and Queens, the Celtic clansfolk, hybrid fae, royal bloodlines, Christed ones, builder races, the root race and Hyperboreans.

Many believe the Tuatha Dé Danann to have been extraterrestrial. This is correct in a sense as they were not third dimensionally terrestrial, but a more appropriate term for them would be interdimensionals as they were not third dimensional beings. Neither were they from 'other planets' in your solar system as they projected forth into form within the harmonic realms surrounding third dimensional Earth. However, in a sense, this could be translated into 'other planets'.

I have heard someone speak of Metatronic energy as part of the 'inverted matrix' or 'dark technology' yet you, the Nine, speak of Metatronic energy as a positive, benevolent force. Can you please explain to me, is Metatronic energy negative or positive?

The response to this is both. The awareness within the starseeds at the moment is a seed point/critical mass point for multidimensional thinking. We can categorise this as bilocational consciousness, trilocational and multilocational. Let us look at your quest in the terms of bilocational consciousness or that which you may also know as doublethink or even paradox.

Within third dimensional thinking, there is the tendency to jump into one camp or the other. When one hears a term or concept such as 'Metatronic', one instantly decides if this is good or bad. If they find 'proof' in their life that this is negative, or at least if they find a teacher they resonate with that says it is negative, they instantly assume this must mean that is not positive.

In the mind of the third dimensional thinker, it is one thing or the other. When one moves into multidimensional thinking or that which we call bilocational thinking then one accepts two concepts, potentially opposing, within their belief system.

This is the way forward into truth. One does not find the truth of reality through third dimensional thinking. This does not mean they cannot find truth, it means they cannot find the truth of reality as reality is uncovered in layers. It is not only one thing. The truth changes to a new, wider, multidimensional perspective with each layer that is subsequently uncovered.

So taking your quest as Metatronic energy, is it negative or positive? The answer is both of these and this would be the case with almost every structure, yet not all of them.

If one looks at Metatronic energy in a personification sense, one is given the ascended master known as Metatron.

Within the ascended master field of intelligence, you would have a positive and a negative force. Therefore there is a positively oriented Master Metatron and a negatively oriented one.

Some individuals will connect with these Metatrons as separate individuals, as in they may encounter and work with the positively polarised Metatron.

We could say that we, the White Winged Collective Consciousness of Nine, are a part of this Metatronic construct or that the ascended Master Metatron is a part of us. This would be the positively polarised aspect.

Other individuals may connect with the negatively polarised Metatron. This entity would have no connection with us, the White Winged Collective Consciousness of Nine, when looking upon the individual and polarised dimensional levels. Only from the perspective of 'all things are unified', true unification as galactic oneness, would we have any connection with this entity.

In many occasions, these two Metatronic energy fields and their archetypal forms will manifest as two different beings with two different names.

As an example, let us take 'Jesus Christ' or 'Lucifer' into that polarisation. Looking at Jesus Christ as the positive polarisation and Lucifer as the negative.

This is a somewhat interesting picture to paint for the ascending starseeds who listen to our transmissions for, as we have said, most entities and structures have aspects within both polarisations.

Metatron and Lucifer are two frequency entities that hold positive and negative presentations of themselves within the overall unified energy field.

However, Jesus Christ is of positive polarisation only. There is no negative polarised entity that stands within that particular vibration that you call a name or give a label to.

This is due to the critical mass wave of paradigm or belief system that anchors into your planet or dimension.

'Jesus the Christ' (Jeshua, Yeshua) or he or she of Christ consciousness, one who stands within the Kryst or as a beloved family member within the realm that is Krysta, is a positively polarised vibration only.

As with us, the individualised aspect of the Nine that we present through our conduit Magenta Pixie, it is only through pure unity within the unified field of all that is that we can have any connection with beings, entities or constructs from a negatively polarised dimension.

We say to you that this is due to the critical mass thought processes within the starseeds and awakened ones upon planet Earth within the physical dimension.

In regards to the Metatronic, some individuals may connect with a being or entity that presents itself as Archangel Metatron that is the positively polarised and the negatively polarised being as one.

This is not a unified entity, neither is this entity fragmented. This would be a paradoxically polarised entity, given to you for your expansion, growth and learning and is called upon by those who wish to learn polarisation or who hold polarised fields within themselves.

One needs to understand the nature of polarisation itself before one can understand and process a paradoxically polarised entity.

So let us then look at this.

Positive polarisation is a field, construct, energy or entity that is fully polarised within the positive in a unified sense. This unity is without borders and is fully free and is the epitome of liberty and free will.

This entity has infinite choice. This entity is whole. This entity is integrated and has chosen or decided the orientation it wishes to experience. It is within surrender in complete service to love, forgiveness and compassion. It holds the charged Quartz Quay and the Diamond Codex has been expressed and integrated. It becomes thus monadic.

This creates power through an electromagnetic charge that is positive. Its atoms are facing one way. This is the field that one would refer to as 'Christ consciousness' or of the 'Kryst' or 'diamond light' for it is pure, unadulterated, unconditional love.

It holds the charge of bliss and the sacred number of 144 which is also the Nine. It is intelligence with heart and heart wings.

We, the White Winged Collective Consciousness of Nine, are one such construct as this. Our conduit Magenta Pixie, within the third dimension has chosen to follow this path and move into this same polarised state, hence why we, the Nine, are her guidance structure.

This would be the same scenario for the majority of those who listen to this transmission or who read our words.

Negative polarisation is also a field, construct, energy or entity that is fully polarised within the negative in a unified sense. That unity presents as a 'hive mind' construct, as in the entire construct is fully under the control of, or imprisoned by, another.

This entity has no choice (within that originally chosen field) and must follow a pre-programmed destiny without choice for this entity has chosen to experience existence without choice. The original decision or choice is made to have no choice. It is surrender to another controlling you so you may control another. It is full surrender to fear so you may be the one to be feared.

This creates power through an electromagnetic charge that is negative. Its atoms are facing the opposite way. This is the field that many call 'Luciferian' which is simply 'bright morning star' or 'illuminated light' or 'intelligence' without heart. There are no activated heart wings and instead, the structure holds a different geometry.

There is no specific number or geometry that exists for this field for this field is pure distortion. Therefore the numbers must be inverted in order to create a power deck frequency that would work for this field. Moving within the sections of three and six then hijacked numbers are 33 or 66 or triple numbers into 333 or 666 and the inversion of the number 3 creating the letter E so EE would also be a hijacked code.

All geometric structure is pure and organic and is the original creation. The polarised negative field is the created, inverted, reflective image of the pure and organic, hence it is an inverted construct or structure.

Paradoxical polarisation is an energy field that is part of the inverted structure. This is not a whole energy and neither is it fragmented. It is a presentation of two unified wholes joined together to confuse and trick yet also enhance and assist.

This field and all entities involved brings teaching and opportunity, yet it is achieved through distortion. It is a much lesser known or lesser used field.

We could say it is a planet with a very small population, if you will. This field is called by those who have matches within them so they may learn about self. This field is also called by polarised entities of either positive or negative orientation who wish to learn about the opposing polarity 'close up' if you will.

This field or entities therein is/are also called 'master creators' who operate within the highest echelons of the third dimension. Those who are positively oriented themselves but wish to present the negative polarisation through creativity. For example, the fiction writer of the horror novel or screenplay.

So too would this structure show itself to those who wish to understand and learn about the opposing polarisation.

We, the White Winged Collective Consciousness of Nine, are a positively polarised field yet we are able to show our conduit Magenta Pixie the negatively polarised field so she may see it, process and integrate it and teach that which it is.

We do this safely by showing her a paradoxically polarised field as opposed to a fully negatively polarised field. From that point of view, it becomes a training tool or more widely known now by those who have heard our transmissions as the 'training ground'.

If you imagine these constructs are matrices, then the paradoxically polarised field would be the 'practice run' if you will.

The traveller or gameplayer within the paradoxically polarised matrix cannot be harmed or led astray when its entire reality is as much positive as it is negative. Both polarisations would be working for that individual or both matrix programs would be running simultaneously, if you will.

The third dimension is a paradoxically polarised field. It is fully positive and negative simultaneously.

The field that is the third dimension is a living consciousness in and of itself that wishes to 'upgrade' and experience more expanded and complete polarisations. Or rather more accurately, we should say that it 'wishes to give birth to' more expanded polarised versions of itself.

This is a 'reaction to' or 'creation of' the physically incarnated individuals, predominantly starseeds and their integrated and balanced paradigms. That which we call 'Aurora Matrix'.

Within the paradoxically polarised field that is the third dimension, there are those 'souls' or 'memory Matrix Awareness structures' that have incarnated in order to create the fifth dimensional birthing from the third dimension in its fullest positively polarised sense. This, as we have previously said within this transmission, is known geologically as fourth density positive.

There are those doing the same that are creating the fifth dimensional birthing in its fullest negatively polarised sense known as fourth density negative.

From the perspective of those graduating/ascending or travelling/moving into the positively polarised fifth dimension from the third, then when they 'arrive' within the fifth dimension fully, the negatively polarised fifth dimension will cease to exist for them.

It will be as if that structure and all entities within and thereof have 'died' or 'been removed' and gone elsewhere.

From the perspective of those being demoted/descending or moving downwards into the negatively polarised fifth dimension from the third, then when they 'arrive' within that negative 5D, the positively polarised fifth dimension will be unavailable to them. They will not be able to access it. It will be as if that structure and all entities within and thereof have 'disappeared' or 'run away'.

The dimension outside of the perception of consciousness will then begin to dissolve, for it will no longer be viable as it will have no available nourishment. The negative dimension cannot, in truth, be presented as a 'fifth dimension' at all as it is not an 'upgrade' but a 'downgrade'.

In essence, it is only referred to as a negatively polarised fifth dimension because it is an opposing structure or density to the positive. Without 'other' to consume, it shall decompose or simply recycle itself. The entire dimension and all constructs within it will move through a process known as 'regenesis' which is similar to a 'recycling'.

This will however take many of what you would know as 'Earth years' and this process moves into the billions of Earth years when looking at that time structure.

The beginning of this process starts the moment that the first thought of full fifth dimensional polarisation is expressed within the physical paradoxically polarised third dimension. This begins at the 'beginning of time' if you will.

In a linear sense, the negatively polarised structure already began its decomposition or recycling many billions of years ago. Just as the positively polarised structure began its ascension many billions of years ago.

When the paradoxically polarised structure is no longer an equal(ish) merge of positive/negative vibration and presents as two independent and individualised, unified structures as unconditional love/free will and hive mind/control, then that particular planet (or dimension/density as terminology becomes interchangeable at this point) is said to be *nearing completion.* This is where you are now, on Earth.

34: Full Circle

So can I please ask, where is my father now? It is four years since I first spoke to you about him. I know we are in linear time and he is not, but has he moved on?

It is not really the case that you are 'in' linear time and he is not. You are both within the same 'time' presentation for there is only one time presentation which is that of zero point or the now moment (singularity expression and pulse).

You perceive linear time when you are in physical incarnation. You may still perceive linear time (of sorts) when in spirit (or antimatter).

Your perception of time would be used to measure the experience of another soul in spirit. The actual experience of that soul from their perspective would be different.

So from a linear perspective, indeed your father would have 'moved on' or 'progressed'. You could see him much further along that rainbow bridge or exploring endless rooms in the white heavenly house or you could even see him living in his own space, a fourth dimensional domain or fifth dimensional palace/garden/castle/forest/cloud existence (all these are typical perspectives held by the soul in antimatter to represent their memory complex experience).

Yet in truth, the progression is cyclical (as a spiral), not moving forward or upward continuously in a linear fashion. So the expansion is outward from the centre. The expansion within the antimatter memory complex (non-physical soul holding individualisation) is quantum.

It is not easy to present this through explanation. If you would see yourself as a central aspect of yourself holding linear thought, you would then 'beam' or 'radiate' outwards multiple 'selves' each within different memory streams. Some of the life just lived, as part of what you may know as a 'life review' and some as other incarnations as your memory returns. Some also of incarnations in potential as the choices of lives you have yet to make or yet to live.

Then, if you can remain cohesive within your geometric structure, you would radiate or pulse outwards from the centre the 'other selves' as memories.

For you are pure DNA as a thought structure or living, loving geometry at that point. You hold perception as having a body, often with wings, a light body. This is indeed your plasma body or 'rainbow body of light' if you are able to remain cohesive.

The aspects of self move around you and pulse outwards into the fractal stream of the quantum field. Depending on the level of cohesion and individualisation of that soul, they would hold two points of perspective (bilocational) or three points of perspective (trilocational) or several points of perspective (multilocational) or all points of perspective (omnipresence).

This is how 'time' expresses itself outside of that, that is linear. So 'four years' is meaningless from the perspective of your father in spirit and is meaningful only for you. It is an illusion for those who do not exist in physicality. It is a created construct in order for you to experience linear time.

So where is my father? Is he omnipresent?

We cannot speak on your father specifically as to his overall soul development, except to say that he holds more than one perspective and has remained cohesive and individualised. When you ask us 'where' he is, this would be the response. We can however tell you that he is able to travel into fourth and fifth dimensional domains of his own creation and his love for the sport pastime you call 'tennis' and the country within your Earth you call 'Spain' has remained part of his creational wave and experience.

Well thankyou, that is so lovely to know. Is this the case with other individuals in spirit? For those reading this book, are their parents also in creations of their own making from things they loved?

It is not necessarily from that which they held love for. It is that which they hold as a predominant focus. If this is a trauma-based memory for example, they would create a scenario whereby they are able to integrate that experience. The environment would match the experience. With a soul of high positive polarisation, where much has been integrated within the physical life, then the 'afterlife' (remember this is not linear so there is no 'after') will present more as 'the playground' and creation becomes the name of the game. Elaborate and intricate full fourth dimensional and fifth dimensional domains are able to be created for that soul to experience.

What is a 'domain' exactly?

A domain is a world. Created by the individual. It will depend on the level of memory expansion into the quantum, as in bilocational, trilocational and so on, as to how intricate and multilevelled the domain presents as.

So what if a soul had not yet moved into bilocation? If they were still experiencing linear time? Would they be able to create a domain?

Great question, Pixie! Of sorts, yes. It would present as a building, a place, a garden or potentially a scene from the soul's memory. Most similar in fact to the dreamtime experience you hold within your physical world. So similar it would be almost identical to that, except for the cohesive one in antimatter spirit would remain lucid within the experience. You too within physicality can do this but your lucidity moments are fleeting unless you are the adept dreamwalker and dreamweaver.

The dreamwalker is the one who 'walks' the dream. So this would be a lucid dreamer, astral traveller or the cohesive antimatter soul in spirit who has not yet moved into bilocational consciousness.

The dreamweaver is 'he who weaves the dream', as in 'he who moves into quantum memory and creates the domain'.

This is exactly as you are doing in your physical incarnation. Usually one would move into the antimatter experience through the death process in order to expand into quantum memory and become fractalised and 'create worlds' (domains).

Ascension is where you do this *whilst in physicality.* You are indeed not so different from those in spirit antimatter. You are all walking the same journey and it has always been this way. Moving through cycles after cycles after cycles.

In your reality at this time, you move into the point where all cycles within the quantum field line up together. They align dimensionally and galactically.

Those you know as Mayan knew this. They knew how to count the cycles using the correct presentation of time. Your cosmic moment of December 21st 2012 ended the Mayan long count. Now you remain in a zone of 'no time' until the clock begins again.

When does that clock begin again?

When it is made physical at critical mass. Until then, you remain in 'no time' which is akin to the fourth dimension. The bridge to the next octave of reality, or planet. Gaia, if you will.

How can the clock be made physical?

As the Mayans learned to measure time, so will the new timekeepers. There are those working upon this now. Once the correct measurements of time are presented to humanity at large and are utilised by humanity at large, at critical mass level, then the clock will be made physical.

Yet all this means is that you measure time correctly and in alignment. The act itself starts the clock yet this does not mean you are not existing within this fractalised, quantum timekeeping now.

All those who experience both third dimensional linear time and fifth dimensional non-linear time simultaneously are experiencing cyclical time. This would be the majority of starseeds as a concept and a far higher number of those as actual experience. This is that which creates the fifth dimension.

So the fifth dimension is being created by these starseeds? New Earth is being created? Despite all the dark agendas that are currently being put in place?

Despite what seems to be presented to you in your truth and somewhat in your spiritual communities, the dark overlord factions do not have the powers that many perceive them to have. Much is illusion and stage magician tricks, hence we refer to them as 'the wizard behind the curtain' in reference to your film 'The Wizard of Oz'.[8]

We are not saying that they do not have abilities and that they are not a 'worthy opponent' upon the chessboard, even though there is no opponent from the fifth dimensional perspective and in order to create the fifth dimension, one must know this.

What we are saying is that which they wish to achieve is not easy for them to achieve at the levels they would like. The dark manifestation always comes at a price and a certain level of bargaining or 'making deals with the devil' has to take place.

The most they can hope to achieve is partial success. Everything is achieved on a mono stream as we have said before. They cannot access the quantum or the multidimensional in the way they would like to do so.

Therefore, whilst it is of import to know who and what they are and not 'rest on your laurels' as it were, it is equally of import to know *your* level of power within this story. For it is you that enters a bifurcated reality and it is *your choice* as to which aspect of the bifurcation you choose to experience.

The artificial or the organic, the old or the new, a crumbling physical reality within a fallen system or a magnificent creation within a reality of your own making.

We have presented to you the keys, codes, triggers and catalysts for you within this transmission that is 'The Diamond Codex and the Quartz Key'.

All that you need to walk forward into the next phases, aspects and octaves of your reality are within you and are shown to you here within this communication. This work, drawn down through our conduit, Magenta Pixie, is but a mirror for you. You

---

[8] *The Wizard of Oz* (1939) produced by Metro-Goldwyn-Mayer Studios

are indeed 'Alice through the looking-glass'[9], for this is *your* journey.

Our heroine or hero within the story, the Archangel Michael, the beloved, Divine Princess Aurora and the Golden Dragon, *they are all you.*

When you decide which character is the protagonist within the story, then you have found yourself!

The scenarios of dragonriding, dreamtime travel, Mer-Ka-Bah activation, Matrix Integration and alchemical unification are *your reality scenarios.*

It is therefore *you* we have been presenting here for *you yourself* are the central part of this story.

This is *your story* and it is you who authors these words you see before you. For it can be no other way *and this you know.*

---

[9] *Alice Through the Looking-Glass* (1871) by Lewis Carroll

Take the Quartz Key, transmutate through the Diamond Codex into the accelerated stargate system and see the upgraded QUARTZ QUAY.

Do this, master alchemist, guardian of Gaia, wing-ed wanderer, for the future is yours and yours alone.

We are the White Winged Collective Consciousness of Nine.

35: Finale

Aurora could not get the dream out of her mind as she went about her tasks the next day.

'Yet it was not a dream, was it?' she thought to herself, 'It was so very real.'

She had felt the dragon beneath her as they rode together, the unbreakable bond between them, the exhilaration they both felt, the reaching for the phire within to create the flames and the leap through the stargate into an unknown world.

'Oh yes, this was far more than just a dream.'

Playing with her little niece, Marya, did nothing to remove the memories of the night before.

'That is what they were, memories. Not a dream but memories, of another time, another space.'

"Play with me, Auntie Aurora?" asked the child. Aurora turned her focus to her young charge.

"Oh yes, of course darling, what shall we play?"

"Lets make something!" Marya said, her bright eyes shining with anticipation.

Aurora took the modelling clay in her hands.

'Modelling clay? Modelling clay? Of course! Of Course! Now I know what that plasma was!'

"Tell me..." rumbled the deep telepathic voice of Allianse, the golden dragon.

'She could talk to him here? Whilst awake?'

"Of course you can," he replied to her thoughts, "We are forever bonded. You are my rider now, my true heart, my one."

Aurora, despite surprise of the waking state telepathy, she knew, deep inside, that the bond was unbreakable. That he would always be there, always by her side.

"It's pure creation, Allianse. Like modelling clay. That is what we were shown, that is what the plasma is! We can create anything we want from it but first we must believe in it. We must see it and know it is there."

She began to form the clay into a ball, a sphere, for her niece to play with, as she allowed her focus to remain with the child and her thoughts and emotional energy with the dragon. What a strange feeling.

"You are bilocational now," said the dragon, "in two places at once."

Aurora blinked and looked around the room. She saw her niece and the pastel colours of the playroom, the pretty pictures on the walls, yet she could feel the dragon, her unity with him and then, she saw the dragon. She was with him, looking at the plasma before her, the dragon by her side.

"You said you did not know what it was forming into, that it was pure thought becoming matter? It is our thoughts, Allianse. Yours and mine. The plasma is forming into matter based on *our* thoughts!"

She felt the flame of the dragon then as he held the epiphany throughout his golden, majestic body.

"Who are we, beloved? You and I? We are them. The aware ones on the Earth-sphere-plane, are we not? We are the creations of their awareness, memory and knowing just as they are the creations of our galactic blood. Our gene pool is at one with them."

The conversation with Allianse was instantaneous in linear time and she was still forming the modelling clay into a ball with her wide-eyed niece watching and waiting to play. Multidimensional, quantum timestreams playing out in antimatter were so much faster than the perceived physicality of her body of light. She saw then the dense physicality of the starseeds of Gaia, playing out the same visual, the same knowing, yet on a slower speed still. She knew they would catch this, she knew they would find her, Princess

Aurora, she knew they would come to her world riding atop their own dragons.

"Yes, Allianse. The plasma is forming into the matter structure from their thoughts also, as we merge into alchemical unification with them. Let the plasma fall where it may then, for the creation belongs to us all."

Allianse breathed in the plasma and opened his mouth to roar the dragonsbreath starseed's thought phire into reality.

Bonus Material

Transformation Codes

These transformation codes are the same for those who reside within the southern hemisphere of your planet, yet different visuals would be presented for winter into spring and for each of the changing seasons upon your planet as the White Wheel, Silver Wheel turns.

Transformation codes are drawn down the dimensional scale and we speak here predominantly of third, fourth and fifth dimensional energies yet the sixth and seventh dimensional fields are also of high import at this time. Within this transmission, we specifically focus on 3rd/4th and 5th dimensional consciousness.

Within the fifth dimension, in a linear interpretation, you are at the end frequency of a passageway we have referred to as the Lion's Gate Infinity Portal. This took place within your month of August in your year of 2022.

Within the fifth dimension, you access the energetics of that infinity structure.

Your Lion's Gate portal in this particular year was 'made of a different fabric' if you will. Much higher vibrational energetics and frequencies were received by the receptive ones due to the galactic and planetary gridwork that has taken place, including the clearing of many of the dragonlines of Earth creating the Gaia/Terra configurations of the New Earth planetary network.

The rebirthing process was most profound upon your planet at this time and many seeds were planted for ascension and that which you know as 'enlightenment' if you will. These seeds continue throughout the many portals of singularity emanations as you go forward in time and space.

The outcome is release... regeneration and integration with the movement outward from that one of embracing the highest version of yourself, as all that is you and all that you are. This translates instantaneously into the environment and the experienced reality. Your transformation codes at this level are many and are coded much through the rainbow plasma frequencies of rose gold, gold, violet, blue, green and red as the sacred rose, the golden flame, violet flame, blue ray and emerald and ruby plasmic gemstones. Through the archetypal realms as King Arthur, Queen Guinevere, the dragons Belthesada, Allianse and Quetzalcoatl and the flame letter of truth and phire activation, the divine Excalibur, King of Swords.

Within your fourth dimensional space, which encompasses a more linear framework, you have the higher or upper harmonic levels and individual domains of awareness, knowledge, higher thought and higher emotion. This harmonic presentation is the springboard or launchpad into the fifth dimension and can be visualised as a hot air balloon with a basket for you to ride into the fifth dimensional frequency, a cosmic lift or jump room, a crystal staircase or a tree with roots within your fourth dimensional domain and the uppermost branches growing upwards into the fifth dimensional sphere. For those caught within the middle and lower aspects of this harmonic field, confusion reigns. Yet these individuals are still awake and aware beyond the third dimensional matter reality.

Transformation codes at this level are abundant and nature-based yet always presented in the direction of higher flow and the moving upwards into skies, clouds or a heaven-based template as you integrate blocks, shadows and traumas and lighten yourself within the understanding of the flame and materialise within the rivers and streams of the fifth dimension, emerging as the water goddess holds your hand and leads you into the forests of the sanctuary realms.

Witches abound with the spells and magic and when white magic is embraced, then you find yourself upon the crystal stairway into the fifth dimension, standing as the sorcerers apprentice and walking the way of the quantum wizard.

Within the third dimension, your transformation codes are formed in matter through symbol, sign and synchronicity. The messages found in books, television, film, entertainment and cyber reality domains are plentiful and within this the fourth and fifth dimensions are made in material manifestation.

Yet so too will you witness the crumbling of the old and the rising of the new as the transformation codes are embraced.

Beloveds, we bring you now to the end of this story and the beginning of a new chapter. Indeed, an entire new novel.

The Divine Princess Aurora, her beloved Archangel Michael as the true Christ-Michael and their child, Aurora, the daughter who is Sarah, daughter of Jeshua and the Mary Magdalene. The grandmother as the wise woman and the golden dragon, standing at the centre of the story waiting for his rider to mount, take the reigns and fly.

The dragon's rider is you, our protagonist who has collated and collected the transformation codes presented throughout this transmission that is *The Diamond Codex and the Quartz Key* (now known to you as 'Quay').

Go forward, beloved one. The journey may be perilous yet when you hold the transformation codes as tools, the journey becomes wanted, called for, embraced and indeed is bravely walked. Succeeding in the journey is inevitable when this flame/phire letter is delivered by us, to you and received by you.

Therefore you, dragonrider, have already succeeded within your quest.

We are the Galactic Mind, the Universal Intelligence, the Sacred Geometry of Source and We are You.

Ascension Earth - Star Knowledge through Celestial Memory

Could you explain to me what 'star beings' are?

Many individuals would come under this heading but we would interpret 'star beings' as those who hold celestial memory which would be you as ascending humans, or extraterrestrial group souls or we, the White Winged Collective Consciousness of Nine.

Can you explain celestial memory?

There is your memory that you hold as linear. As in, what you remember as having taken place within the past within your current lifetime.

Yet memory moves beyond simply linear memories from the past. Celestial memory is that which is 'beyond the body' and beyond linear time. This would be the memory of multiple different 'past lives' if you will. Yet because this is non-linear, it moves in different 'directional waves' or different time zones from simply 'the past' - so celestial 'memory' is that which has happened in multiple different alternate realities that have not necessarily been lived through by you experientially. Also, celestial memory would be that of remembering the future and multiple different future timelines, again, that you have not yet lived within your current experience but nevertheless is known by the consciousness at the celestial, stellar or star level.

Yet it moves beyond even this and is more literal than one might realise. Each star in your galaxy is a node point or convergence point of multiple timelines culminating in that one point in time. Known also as a nexus point.

Each star is a different version of each other star. Yet each one represents a different convergence point for the timelines of the particular galaxy it exists within or that it 'embodies' if you will. When a human incarnates into physical reality, they will project forth from what we may call an 'antimatter star grid'. This is a memory matrix known to you perhaps as a morphogenetic field or more commonly known as the Akash, Akashic Records or Hall of Records. It is, in its most basic form, all that has ever happened, all that could ever happen, all that will ever happen and all that is happening now.

It is therefore a memory grid. Each star being a convergence point for those memories. Each star being a singularity, if you will. With a zero point field at the centre of the convergence within that planet or star. A core template for that celestial structure.

Antimatter star grid - because these are star blueprints as memory, thought and consciousness, for each star birth and they have not yet birthed or created themselves or projected forth into a matter universe or galaxy, within a linear explanation.

When the star projects forth as the celestial body you know as a star, this is the convergence of timelines that you see, from your incarnational physical vantage point as an incarnate on Earth. You see this convergence timeline field or matrix as a celestial body.

All planets are this and the galaxy itself, multiple galaxies, universes and multiverses are all different holographic replicas or emanations of one another and of Source. Each star in each galaxy feeds into different potentials as independent singularity nexus points and are each the ultimate star which in your solar system is your sun, the being we call Sol.

The stars and planetary bodies hold different levels of potentials and possibilities for different consciousness expressions as multiple different versions or presentations of your sun, Sol. Each an independent consciousness in their own right.

Sol, your physical sun holds the memories and collections of multiple potentials for each star, planet and planetary body within its consciousness and stands as a gateway or portal for the entry and exit point for your particular solar system. An entry or exit point for individualised consciousness moving into your solar system, if you will, with each star system being the memory grid for each incarnating physical being at inception point which is the very first thought or spark of all that is you as a human being.

So the incarnation's human consciousness moving into the newborn physical vehicle, in a healthy aligned functioning solar system, enters through your antimatter solar gateway, your sun. The innerverse sun which is the exact hyperspace replica of your physical sun. From our perspective, it is the same place.

The sun, Sol, is an emanation of multiple other suns, central suns, grand central suns and great grand central suns into infinity. These suns would be known as 'the solar consciousness', and would be the place of memory or knowing you hold if you are said to be moving into your solar light body or moving through solar ascension.

Yet your quest was regarding the celestial, stellar or star which equates to what you know as fifth dimensional - or fourth density, depending on the model of reality used to explain the memory grids and matrices we speak of.

The star as a celestial body imparts material, let us say, of itself at antimatter level and this is held as a code or activation held within the incarnating human. The substance is plasma in truth, but can also be seen as stardust for it is made of a photonic light particle from a particular star or star system. This substance or light or plasmic stardust is held within the DNA fields of each incarnating human being as a dormant code. A memory code.

When the individual activates that memory code, as is occurring upon your planet Earth in your current now time, the celestial memory 'comes online', for that individual has activated the memories of the particular star or star system that they were seeded from, as in, the plasmic stardust they hold. These star systems that seed the plasmic stardust memories are predominantly known as Lyra, the Pleiades or Sirius as the most common three. You yourself, Pixie, hold the seeding stardust from the Pleiades known as star three or the third star.

The term 'starseed' is therefore so much more literal than most awakening individuals realise. It does not simply mean you are from a planet or star system outside of your Earth in a philosophical, metaphysical or metaphoric way, it means you literally were seeded energetically and physically as photonic light memory from a particular star. From the fabric of that star. Star particles or stardust.

Through the memory codes you hold of that one particular star system (which is an infinity unto itself), you can access the entire history of that star system. This includes the planetoids and moons surrounding that system and indeed all other stars and planets including the Earth you exist upon, and thus the galaxy as you activate galactic energy points or galactic 'chakra points' and eventually move into solar memory, which is beyond the scope of this particular transmission in accordance and alignment with your question.

So that which you experience as a starseed or star being would be celestial or stellar memory. This awareness moves beyond memory as it is no longer linear and becomes knowing or indeed a paradigm or consciousness. You are stellar activated, holding a celestial unity awareness which you know as 'fifth dimensional consciousness'.

This leads to one law which is presented in all celestial teachings from all star systems and that is the Law of One which is the understanding and awareness of alchemical unification which is true unity, as in all things are unified and are thus One.

This is the predominant teaching for you as starseeds incarnated upon Earth, for the teaching you receive regarding this unity and thus the teachings you then deliver to others, which in turn shall activate their own stellar memories and celestial consciousness, is that which shall return true freedom, sovereignty and higher creation to your planet Earth and all of humanity.

Your planet Earth then moves through a transformation, through what we call a 'Terra gateway' (or pronounced by some as TARA gateway, known also as the 'Green Tara Goddess Alignment') which would equate to a fourth dimensional field, the astral levels of existence, if you will, into the Gaia grid which is fifth dimensional.

This is when your Earth moves from existing as a planet into existing as a star on a more logistic/physical level, let us say. Are we saying your planet Earth is becoming a star? Indeed yes, we are saying exactly this. This is as it is and is the most natural order of all Source-aligned planetary systems that you would know as 'planets'.

Or indeed your Earth is more accurately becoming 'a star system' as there are multiple Earths within that which you may know as multiverse. The Gaia grid stands first as a consciousness and then births that consciousness into physicality through you, the human aware and awake souls moving through celestial ascension.

This is also known as a crystalline transformation for the codes within the DNA begin to replicate this original plasma, stardust that you incarnated with, which is photonic light consciousness holding expansive memory of that morphogenetic field of all that is. Each human thus becomes a receiver, transmitter and transducer for the celestial kingdom as together, as one, they hold and impart the knowledge of all the star systems within the entire galactic field.

Each star being an alternate version of all the other star systems in neighbouring galaxies and in galaxies far, far away, if you will. Each and every soul incarnated upon your planet Earth at this time holds the ability to activate this plasmic stardust celestial aspect of themselves and is then known as a starseed.

As each celestially activated individual stands together, the radiation from each soul's activated plasmic stardust, crystalline DNA creates a field of photonic light, even if these souls have never met one another in their physical lives. This creates a portal. That portal leads to the triggering of the celestial memory within the receiver of the information and code, therefore the portal leads to ascension for all involved and beyond that structure.

Thankyou so much for that. May I ask, what of extraterrestrial beings? You said they are also star beings? The souls that live upon other star systems and planets. Can you discuss these ET souls?

Indeed, this is the case and is explained by all we have said. These souls that you call 'extraterrestrial' are simply you, each one of you that is activated within the plasmic stardust celestial crystalline DNA and memory.

They hold their own individualisation yet each of these different races, if you will, are consciousness constructs that represent the planetary or star system they 'originate' from, as in they *are* that planet or star or the consciousness of it and they are represented by you, the aware and activated starseeds on Earth.

They can communicate with you as individualised beings, just as we, the White Winged Collective Consciousness of Nine, represent the Arcturian consciousness as we communicate with you.

We could therefore, from that perspective, be known as Arcturian extraterrestrials. Yet to take this a step further, higher or deeper, if you will, into the truth of the metaphor, we are a consciousness represented by you.

You move through celestial memory fields and access the

knowings of the Pleiadian star system. You yourself, dear Pixie, are not at the stage where you are able to hold the consciousness of the Arcturian star system within your fields but through your Pleiadian radiation and antennae system, that which you know as pineal gland and connected crystalline network, you are able to reach that memory, that consciousness through direct communication. Another way of saying this would be to say your consciousness resides at the celestial level as you move through celestial ascension. You are not yet at the point of solar consciousness or solar ascension but you can access that memory field when you communicate with us.

If you are Arcturian though, surely you are celestial rather than solar?

The planetary system you know as Arcturus is a sun. It is at the solar level. Yet this moves beyond the scope of your question, which is that of celestial memory.

Indeed, there is much to know, to seek and to remember. You are each doing this at your own pace, in your own time. It is not necessarily an easy journey to hold such multidimensional and metaphysical knowings within the human brain designed as an interface for third dimensional decoding.

Indeed however, the plasmic stardust celestial codes of crystalline activation are that which shall take you into the receiving of the knowledge you seek for all the answers are available to you when you move through this celestial activation.

The brain therefore, whilst remaining a third dimensional interface is, if you will, somewhat bypassed and it is the heart that takes over the holding of the knowings of that which we speak.

Thus the heart takes flight, grows its heart wings, activates into the 'higher heart formation' and joins with the human brain to become the *heartbrain.* The two work thus in unified alchemised connectedness to decode the knowings and memories at galactic, solar and Source consciousness level.

The unity that thus takes place within the human bodymind betwixt heart, brain, cellular and skeletal structure and all that is you is thus reflected within the experiential reality lived by the unified one.

This on a consciousness level, when this is achieved by multiple starseeded ones, en masse, across your planet Earth, the Terra bridge is crossed and the Gaia star is created. Ascension Earth thus takes place.

This is that which is currently being undertaken across your world at this time and for us, and for all 'star beings' with eyes upon the *jewel planet that is Earth* and beloved humanity upon her, it is indeed a joy to behold.

We are the White Winged Collective Consciousness of Nine.

Quantum Entanglement and Implosion of Zero Point

I heard a new concept yesterday. Instead of space bending itself in order for point A and point B to become the same place (essentially becoming an Einstein-Rosen bridge), two locations in space oscillate identically with the exact same matching frequency field and through the concept known as 'quantum entanglement' they simply operate as if they were the same space without space bending at all. Can you comment please on which of these concepts, if either, are correct?

This is indeed a great question, Pixie, and one that is of high import as you discover the mechanics of astral travel at higher levels and stargate ascension. From our perspective, both of these perspectives of concepts are explaining the exact same action. Let us explain further.

Space folding upon itself is a metaphor, yet within your physical matter universe, space appears to move. Therefore to say that space bends itself to allow for point A and point B to meet one another is actually an accurate metaphor.

To say that space does not bend or fold at all and that two points in space can converge as the same place through the process you know as 'quantum entanglement' is also a correct metaphor.

It is not the case that either of these concepts are incorrect. They are both correct. The second explanation moving closer to 'truth' than the first but both holding merit.

However, we would explain portal, wormhole or stargate travel in a different way, not as a replacement for either of the above models but as an addition to them for the enquiring and expansive mind.

We would say that there is but one space of oscillating, vibratory field fabric (or plasma). The outside of this field (or portal/stargate) is what you know as 'space' and the material within the oscillating field, portal/stargate is intelligent plasma. It is a fabric that is a consciousness in and of itself that 'reacts to' or 'unifies with' another structure with oscillating vibratory fields that match its fabric, oscillating at the same frequency or within a harmonic scale of resonant frequencies. It is the object or individual or structure that passes through the oscillating waveform/portal/stargate that determines the locational outcome of the 'other side' or 'destination' through the stargate, if you will. Or rather it is the merging betwixt the intelligent plasma within the oscillating field (stargate) and that which 'passes through it' that determines the outcome or location.

Let us say this is a starship or lightship (what you may know as UFO). The oscillation and vibratory field of the fabric of that lightship needs to be 'high enough' let us say, to pass through the stargate in the first place. Therefore the ship would be constructed from an intelligent plasma fabric. It then passes through the stargate and the coordinates create the destination and indeed the passageway. Coordinates created via 'advanced intelligent technology' operated by the 'psychic one' and their thought/focus/visualisation field.

Let us say it is a human traveller moving through this stargate. The merkabah field would be activated and would behave just as the lightship. The oscillating waves of the merkabah field would align with the thought process/visual of the activated individual in order to create the destination. The intelligent plasma, within the case of a human being, resides within the DNA structure. So it is the DNA coordinates that determine the destination or location one arrives at when one passes through the portal/stargate.

Therefore two individuals may pass through the same portal and both 'arrive' at a different destination. This does not negate the concept of matching oscillating fields as the universal fabric can create multiple oscillating matching fields in different spacetime (and timespace) locations. Neither does this negate the folding space concept as space can fold at the speed of thought.

All three models, from our vantage point, are saying the same thing. For in truth there is no 'space'. As in a large expanse of area that contains different points that you move through, as in the movement from A to B. There is no A to B. This is linear space and it is how you perceive matter space. However, just like time, there is only one moment in non-linear time and only one 'place' in non-linear space. These are both known as 'zero point' and can be applied spiritually, philosophically or metaphysically to time, explained by 'the now moment' or the 'being here in the now'.

Yet this can also be applied physically to space. For it is an illusion that you see when you perceive space. Indeed, one has to travel to move from A to B but only when that space is constructed within linear time.

When you move outside of linear time into multiple time or, if you will, simultaneous time, then space ceases to exist and becomes one point. One location. This is when zero point folds in upon itself (or implodes) and becomes both space and time simultaneously.

You cannot traverse this simultaneous time matrix in your physical matter bodies for they hold coordinates for linear time (otherwise you would not exist within the physical, third dimension). Yet you can traverse the simultaneous time matrix in your astral bodies (celestial body, diamond-sun light body) and move through the zero point field where the location matches the intelligent plasma, a thought field (DNA coordinates) of the individual or vehicle that traverses the time matrix.

Our conduit (Magenta Pixie) does not have the necessary knowledge or awareness of scientific concepts at quantum theory level, needed to explain that which we speak of. Hence we utilise the visual imagery. That which we utilise to present to you the concept of which we speak, is the dragon, creating the ring of fire with its dragon's breath (dragonsbreath) and the starseeded dragon rider atop that dragon as it creates the stargate and moves through it.

These metaphors, as you can see, are visual, language of light, flame letter triggers into understanding (innerstanding) and comprehending the concepts of which we speak. Dragon as intelligent plasma, DNA and merkabah, dragonrider as YOU the starseeded individual, dragon/human telepathic bond as oscillating wave form frequency match and dragon's breath, ring of fire as stargate, dragonsbreath as plasma, morphogenetic field intelligent awareness and energy. Visuals creating matching DNA coordinates within the reader of this material.

The concept of the simultaneous time matrix and zero point applying to spacetime through implosion of its field is presented within the story, within our transmission 'The Diamond Codex and the Quartz Key'. The story being 'Child in the Rose Garden'.

Therefore when it comes to quantum entanglement, you can see that in the true reality all of time and space is quantumly entangled together as one time/one space. Yet in the matter universe, the unfoldment (or explosion) creates pockets of high vibratory oscillating field plasma and low vibratory fabric. This is the reason one needs two or more matching oscillating fields or a folding of space at the speed of thought in order to accomplish space travel and time travel within the matter universe.

We are the White Winged Collective Consciousness of Nine.

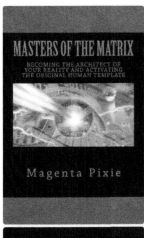

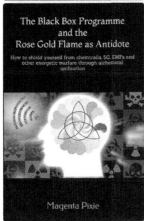

All Magenta Pixie's books available NOW in Print and Kindle edition

"If you want to know what's happening in the greater sphere of reality, beyond religion, beyond spirituality itself, to the matrix itself that encapsulates us all, look no further, Magenta Pixie delivers. She's the best source for news on what's happening behind the scenes beyond having your own hookup directly."

- Amazon customer review (Lessons from a Living Lemuria)